ELY CALLAWAY'S GOLF SWING, C. 1936

THE UNCONQUERABLE GAME

Ely Callaway's first golf swing, age 3,
New York City, 1922.

Ely Callaway by Yousuf Karsh, New York, 1959

THE UNCONQUERABLE GAME

My Life in Golf & Business

ELY CALLAWAY

Edited by NICHOLAS CALLAWAY and ANDREW MOORHEAD

NEW YORK 2025

Ely Reeves Callaway III,
Sports Car Club of America, Formula Vee Runoffs,
Road Atlanta, Georgia, 1973

DEDICATION

To the memory of my late brother, Ely Reeves Callaway III (1947–2023), designer, engineer, builder, and pilot of fine automotive and aeronautical machines, who so admirably carried on Ely's name and his entrepreneurial spirit.

To my children, Nikeyu and Issey; and Reeves's children, Peter, Augusta, Sebastian, and Walker, so that they will have their grandfather's legacy in book form and will carry it with them always.

And to my wife, Rhea Nair Callaway, without whom this book would not have seen the light of day and whose beautiful golf swing Ely would have loved.

— *Nicholas Callaway, East Hampton, New York, November 18, 2024*

CONTENTS

INTRODUCTION

By Nicholas Callaway

It was the twinkle in his eyes that captivated everyone – men, women, and children of all ages and from all classes and walks of life. It was knowing, slightly conspiratorial, questioning, and a little bit naughty.

My father was smarter than most, but had the everyman touch. He always seemed one step ahead in the conversation, knowing something you didn't that he very much wanted to share with you. He delighted in engaging you in the exploring of ideas and experience, and teaching you a little – or a big – something.

As he spoke in the Georgia drawl of the Southern gentleman that he was, Ely (pronounced EE-lee) would lock your gaze with his – and you were hooked. He was a drop-dead charmer. He was not handsome in a conventional way, but a palpable charisma, born of his combination of intelligence, insight, conviction, wit, and vital energy, made him irresistibly attractive. His oldest friend once recommended that in order to understand the effect he had on all listeners, "Watch the look on anyone's face as they listened to Ely talk – talk about anything." No one who ever met him forgot him, and everyone had an Ely story.

In endless conversations, often over dinner, he would regale guests with a question, a theory, a quiz, and a story – one that usually made you laugh, but also required that you reconsider your assumptions. He used to say about gaining customers that it was much more powerful to overturn people's cherished preconceptions and opinions than it was to reconfirm their conventional expectations. He was a legendary marketer and salesman, but what he really liked to do was to convert skeptics and unbelievers. After all, he did come from a line of 39 Southern Baptist preachers.

Most people slow down as they age, and their sphere of influence narrows. Ely was just the opposite: his circle continued to widen until it became worldwide by the end of his life, with millions of devoted admirers and customers.

Twenty-three years after his passing in 2001 at the age of 82, the memory of the man is fading. He has become a name on a golf club. Few realize that Ely started Callaway Golf Company in 1982 at the age of 63, when he invested in a fledgling golf club maker he discovered in a garage in Temecula, California. He had become the quintessential California start-up entrepreneur, after a 40-year career in two other industries: textiles and wine. Fewer still know that it was the culmination of his lifelong passion and impossible pursuit of perfection in the unconquerable game of golf. If there was anything that gave a thread of continuity to Ely Callaway's multiple lives, it was golf – as avocation, as enterprise, and as metaphor.

In the last six years of his life, when Callaway Golf had gone public and became the biggest golf club equipment manufacturer in the world, I encouraged him to write a memoir. He passed away before finishing it, but leaving behind hundreds of pages of manuscripts and interviews with several distinguished interlocutors and co-writers, including Larry Dorman, John Huey, John Rothchild, and Bud Shrake, without whom we would not have this legacy.

It seems to me that my father's life story traces the arc of so many defining trends of the 20th and 21st centuries, mirroring and heralding macrotrends of culture, lifestyle, entrepreneurship, global commerce, politics, civil rights, and personal ethics. He's even been called the Zelig of the American century, his path intersecting with eight U.S. presidents, potentates, entertainers, and countless other luminaries. He negotiated deals with titans of industry like Akio Morita and Jack Welch, served wine to the Queen of England, and had a relationship with nearly every great golfer of the 20th century, from Bobby Jones to Arnold Palmer to Annika Sörenstam.

Ely had an uncanny ability to see far ahead – often by a generation and more – to some of the challenges, trends, and critical issues that define our world today. Over the past year, as I delved into the raw material of the book with my co-editor Andrew Moorhead, I have been amazed to find that the things Ely cared about are often even more relevant and valuable now than they were during his lifetime. And so, with the help of my late brother Reeves Callaway and Diana Duvall, chief of The Callaway Family Office, Andrew and I compiled and completed this manuscript in the hopes that Ely's unique perspective and prophetic insight might provide guidance to readers today, just as it did for me when he was alive. We hope that the book is both timely and relevant, and its messages inspirational and perennial.

Before I began work on the project, I thought that I knew his life story. But one night, as I was completing research for the book, in his archives I stumbled upon a packet on which he had written by hand, "Private Paper To Be Opened Only in Case of Mr. Callaway's Death."

The dossier contained about 175 meticulously compiled pages that revealed a tale he never shared with his family, friends, or the public during his lifetime. His story began in 1968, the year when so much of America seemed to be coming apart at the seams. He had discovered a saga of corporate malfeasance, personal corruption, and conspiratorial cover-up at one of the world's largest companies, where he had just been appointed president. The discovery prompted a profound crisis in his life – professional, personal, ethical, moral, financial, and legal.

It was an existential dilemma, a defining moment that compelled him to leave New York, his home for more than 30 years, and to start all over again in the desert of Southern California. It was exactly at the same moment and in the same place where three other industries were being revolutionized: in Hollywood, with the New American Cinema directors; in the Bay Area, with the food and wine revolution; and in Silicon Valley, with Intel, Fairchild Semiconductor, and Hewlett-Packard (and Apple a few years later). In my view, Ely belongs in the company of these great latter 20th century innovators and entrepreneurs.

If he had not made this leap, he would not have become an entrepreneur at the age of 53. There would have been no Callaway Vineyards and no Callaway Golf Company, and he would not have fulfilled his potential or his destiny. And how different the game of golf would have been! This book tells the story of facing utter failure and personal ruin, trying to do the right thing, and the lessons Ely learned from it. This may be the real source of the twinkle in his eyes.

I hope that Ely will inspire and amuse you as he did me over a lifetime of dinner conversations. As you read, imagine yourself across the table from Ely, being regaled with his greatest stories.

I treasure many private memories of this public man. He read aloud to me as a little boy: *Horton Hears a Who* by Dr. Seuss ("Don't give up! I believe in you all. A person's a person, no matter how small") and "The Jumblies" by Edward Lear ("Far and few, far and few, are the lands where the Jumblies live. Their heads are green and their hands are blue, And they went to sea in a Sieve"). He sang "Red Light, Green Light" by Peter, Paul & Mary and his favorite hymn, "Amazing Grace," on his Martin ukulele. He loved to play with names and language. He spent years building a magnificent Japanese water garden in his backyard. He was a devoted gardener all of his life, growing old roses and heirloom tomatoes. He loved playing with his beloved dogs and cats, and feeding nectar to the hummingbirds from his hand. He was the most elegantly dressed man I ever met, and he cut a fine figure on the dance floor.

Ely was a lifelong passionate amateur photographer and filmmaker, and the gallery section in this book includes a small selection of his previously unpublished portraits. They include some of the last images of President John F. Kennedy, Jr., made two weeks before his assassination and The Beatles's final performance on August 14, 1965, on *The Ed Sullivan Show*, of which his company Burlington Industries was the corporate sponsor.

He was insatiably ambitious, but he wore it lightly, like a cashmere blazer thrown around his shoulders. If there is one word that describes how he conducted himself in golf, business, and life, it is the Italian word *sprezzatura* – the art of making difficult things seem effortless, with grace.

He was hopelessly romantic . . . and I mean *hopeless*.

When I was young, before he became a California entrepreneur in the 1970s, he seemed to epitomize the buttoned-down New York corporate master of the universe – always in control and in command. But after working on this book, I see more of a restless, creative soul, a maverick willing to risk everything, like a dancing Shiva, or a cool Southern California surfer dude cavorting on the edge of oblivion, seemingly about to wipe out but somehow keeping his balance against the odds.

His balance was so good, in fact, that he usually played golf in loafers – he didn't need spikes. My brother Reeves, my sister Lisa, and I had the pleasure of a lifetime of playing golf with him; I learned how to walk, holding my parents' hands, at the age of two on the 18th fairway at Wee Burn Country Club in Darien, Connecticut, where they were the Couples Club Champions.

Ely was a scratch golfer with an elegant, balletic swing, which he modeled after his hero, Bobby Jones. I never saw him get angry or frustrated with a shot or with his game. When I would play with him he would always say, "Now, don't try and hit the ball hard; just swing! And don't worry about the score — if you hit a bad shot, drop another ball, then try again — just hit 'til you're happy."

For me, Ely Callaway *was* golf. I have never met anyone who loved or understood golf more deeply than Ely — its history, traditions, practice, and spirit. In this book he shares his knowledge and insight about the game that he called a legal addiction. At the end of his life, Callaway Golf issued a new line of balls called Rule 35, which he said was his improvement of the official 34 Rules of Golf. It sums up everything about him and his outlook on life: Enjoy the Game!

Ely at Augusta National Golf Club, April 11, 1994

A NOTE TO THE READER

Ely made his final written contribution to this book in June 2001, a few weeks before he died on July 5. For that reason, the Editors have decided to set the book at that precise moment in time. When he references "now," "the present," "today," etc., he is speaking from his perspective in June 2001.

The Editors have taken care to preserve Ely's language, voice, and phrasing as he shares stories that span almost a hundred years.

CHAPTER 1

DEMONSTRABLY SUPERIOR AND PLEASINGLY DIFFERENT

How a Chance Discovery of a Hickory Stick Led to the Creation of Callaway Golf

The Power of a Good Story

As long as you've got a good story, you can convince anybody of almost anything. I've been around quite a while, and I have told an awful lot of stories. Sixty years ago, in 1941, one of my stories convinced the New York Mafia to help me, a 21-year-old skinny kid from LaGrange, Georgia, procure $350 million worth of uniforms ($4.2 billion in 2001 dollars) for the U.S. Army during the Second World

War. Over 25 years ago, in 1974, I persuaded the Bank of America to loan me a million dollars on the basis of a few sips of wine. And 10 years ago, in 1991, I prophesied to the golfers of the world that if they tried a strange-looking driver with a funny name and a funnier sound, made by an itty-bitty company that they had never even heard of, it would change their lives and the game of golf forever.

I'm 82, and I've lived at least four lives: each one had a different career, a different home, a different wife, lots of golf throughout, and a few bits of hard-earned wisdom I carried from one life into the next. When we look back on our lives, we have a tendency to rewrite history – not to change the past but to justify the outcome and make ourselves look better. I will do my best in telling my story to be as forthcoming and accurate as I can, because the most important lesson I've learned in business and life is that there is only one story worth telling: the honest and true one. I will go to my maker saying that to anyone who will listen.

Speaking of the hereafter, I recently decided what I'm going to have engraved on my tombstone – but I better not give away the ending just yet. A few years back, a lady friend asked me, "Ely, you're always going out to dinner, so how do you stay so slim?" And I told her, "Because I never shut up long enough to take a bite of my food."

The story of Callaway Golf began nearly two decades ago, in the summer of 1982, and my chance encounter with a most peculiar golf club. That morning was pretty hot, as I recall, about as hot as it gets in Palm Springs, California. I was at the brand new Vintage Club in Indian Wells, walking through a trailer that served as the temporary pro shop. I was getting ready to go out and play some golf by myself. A few months before this, I had sold my winery, Callaway Vineyard & Winery, to whiskey giant Hiram Walker. Here I was, without a job, feeling too young to be retired, and looking for something new. I had no idea what I wanted to do, but I was about to find out.

Strolling through the shop, an unusual wedge on display caught my eye. It had a beautiful hickory shaft that looked at least as old as I did – and I was old enough to have cheered for Bobby Jones when he'd won the Grand Slam 52 years earlier in 1930. I remember thinking, "What in the world is that?" The clerk behind the makeshift counter assured me this "Hickory Stick" was new merchandise and not the bygone variety. Intrigued, I paid the $100 price, about double the going rate for a normal wedge, and headed out toward my golf cart.

I was wearing my usual straw hat, polyester slacks, knit shirt, and white golf shoes – the uniform of the corporate retiree. My cart was number three in the queue, the one with the bag full of MacGregor Muirfield irons strapped to the back. Muirfields were designed and promoted by Jack Nicklaus. The Golden Bear himself owned 20 percent of MacGregor, and the 80 percent owner, Clark Johnson, was a pioneer resident at The Vintage and a golfing buddy of mine. Johnson had gotten Nicklaus to send me the Muirfields as a gift. They were good enough to use, but not good enough to rave about, so I never did.

I slid the Hickory Stick into the middle of the Muirfields with their shiny steel shafts and metal heads. It stuck out like a blowgun in a reunion of rifle barrels. Other golfers were available for twosomes, threesomes, or foursomes, but since testing a new club can drive other players nuts, I decided to play the round solo. The starter gave me the thumbs up, and I headed for the first tee on these lush 18 holes that had sprouted in the California desert. It was a magnificent layout. The sand traps were indigenous, while the grass, palm trees, and color-coordinated flower beds were imported. A second golf course was under construction, along with several clusters of expensive houses and condos. My fourth wife, Cindy, and I had moved into one of the condos on the edge of a manufactured lake along the tenth hole of Course 1.

I had been coming to Palm Springs to golf since the 1950s, when it was already a playground for the rich and famous, though not nearly the golf resort mecca we might think of today. The Vintage was only five minutes from Eldorado Country Club, where I'd been an early member since it opened in '57, playing with former presidents Dwight Eisenhower and Gerald Ford and assorted captains of industry (with a few lieutenants thrown in). The Vintage was trying to attract a similar clientele, but not so exclusive that they'd exclude me. I was attracted to its two golf courses and the fact that Cindy and I could split time between our condo here and the one we'd bought at Bear Creek, another golf community 75 miles to the northwest.

Bear Creek was our summer home, and The Vintage was our winter home, the way some people have a winter home in Florida and a summer home on Cape Cod. After one career in the textile business and another in the wine business, I had arrived at age 62 with money in the bank and a Rolls-Royce in the garage, and plenty of time to improve on my game.

With the Eisenhower Mountains in front of me and the sprinkler heads popping up like groundhogs all around the 6042-yard par 72 course, I started to play my round without warming up on the range. On the first hole, a 346-yard par 4, I hit my five iron twice – first off the tee and again for my approach shot – and reached the green in regulation. On the 348-yard second hole, I pulled out a wood for the first time – a 3-wood – and then hit my 7-iron from the fairway, reaching the green in two again. But on the 400-yard, par 4, number-one-stroke third hole, my approach shot landed 50 yards from the flag in the fairway to the right – the perfect chance for the Hickory Stick to show what it could do.

I removed it from among the Muirfields, addressed the ball, and took a whack. It was heavier than the normal wedge and easy to control – at least, I thought so after the ball landed a foot from the cup. There was something clunky and reassuring about it, like an old toaster or a radio with tubes. When was the last time I had gotten this same feeling from a golf club? It must have been in the 1920s, when I was in grade school.

I shot two over par, an average score for me, but throughout the round, the Hickory Stick kept me close to the flag. I decided to discard the Muirfield wedge in favor of this one. By noon I was leaving The Vintage, passing through the receiving line of royal palms, waving at the guard at the security checkpoint that rivaled the CIA's. With the Hickory Stick in my bag and my bag in the trunk of the Rolls-Royce, I drove back to our summer home, where Cindy had finished a chipping lesson. "You've got to try this new club," I said.

A week later, the phone rang. It was Paula Longstreet, a real estate agent at The Vintage.

"I hear you're playing with a Hickory Stick," she said after we exchanged pleasantries. "Do you like it?"

"Who'd you hear that from?" I asked her.

"Kyle Burton." Burton was the pro at The Vintage.

"I bought it last week and used it once. It's a nice club. Has a solid feel. Is this a consumer survey?"

"Not really," said Paula. "But would you like to meet the guys who make it?"

"Why should I?"

"They sure want to meet you."

"What for?"

"They're looking for investors."

It turned out Burton had spied me with the club and told Paula. Paula had passed the news along to the manufacturers, who were friends of hers. This sighting of the ex-winery owner with cash to burn swinging a Hickory Stick aroused their interest.

"Richard Parente will be getting in touch with you," Paula said. "Is that okay? He's the head of the company."

"Okay," I said, but not very enthusiastically.

Before the receiver had cooled, I got another call. Parente was on the line. He talked in a gravelly voice, at a fast pace. He invited me to visit "the headquarters of Hickory Stick, USA in Temecula."

Temecula, of all places. The winery I had just sold was located there, only 66 miles away. The Bear Creek complex where I had just bought a condo was on the outskirts of Temecula. I'd lived and worked in this remote California cow town for 11 years. When I first got there, it had a population of 275. The shopping district had five stores and one traffic light. Up to now, I was sure I knew everybody in the business, from the barber to the horseshoer. That Parente was in Temecula and I'd never heard of him or Hickory Stick, USA was not the kind of news a prospective investor wants to hear. But I was curious.

Hickory Stick, USA

I found the building in the tiny industrial park section a few blocks from Main Street, stuck between an air conditioning repair shop and a self-storage warehouse. It was made of corrugated aluminum, with a garage door for an entrance. The door was open when I approached, and I could see three people scurrying around. The one with the beard came out to the edge of the concrete floor.

This was Parente. The combination of the beard, the plaid shirt, and the blue jeans made him look more like a hippie than the golf pro he said he was. He introduced me to the other two: Tony Manzoni, another golf pro, and Dick De La Cruz, a golf club "consultant."

Behind them around the edges of the room I could see a small refrigerator, two bar stools, several folding chairs, a file cabinet, an aluminum ladder, a desk on which sat an old electric typewriter and a black telephone, and a hide-a-bed sofa. In the middle of the room was a cardboard box filled with clubheads, a pile of wooden dowels, a bunch of steel shafts, a couple of metal workbenches with vice grips attached, and a funny-looking machine.

"What's that?" I asked Parente.

"A gun drill," said Parente. "It's designed to hollow out rifle barrels. We converted it to peacetime use. Let me give you a demonstration."

I stood on the sidelines and watched as Parente grabbed a 40″ dowel from the heap on the floor. He clamped it down in the path of the drill and pulled the trigger. With a loud *wham*, the drill blew a hole through the entire length of the dowel.

"Never in history has anybody done this," Parente said. I believed it.

He removed the dowel from the gun drill and carried it to a workbench, along with a steel shaft he picked up from the group of shafts. He slathered the shaft with glue and shoved it into the hole in the dowel, the way a doctor inserts a pin into a leg bone.

"This hybrid shaft steel on the inside and wood on the outside is the key to the Hickory Stick concept," Parente explained. "We make putters and wedges like the one you bought the same way. Once we attach a clubhead on one end and a grip on the other and do a bit of sanding and polishing, the club is ready for the sales and marketing department."

"Get the man a brochure," Parente said to Manzoni, who turned out to be the sales and marketing department. Manzoni ambled over to his desk and returned with their only advertising piece, printed so it looked like a handwritten note on a Hallmark card: "The harsh feel of the standard wedge can be greatly reduced by the Hickory Stick. The natural wood absorbs harsh vibrations, producing a soft feel golfers raved about before the advent of steel shafts."

"You can keep it," Manzoni said after I finished reading. His job was to man the desk and work the phone, trying to convince pros at various golf courses to carry the Hickory Stick in their pro shops. I sensed he wasn't having much luck, so I said:

"Are you guys about to go busted?"

"As a matter of fact," said Parente, "we are."

Parente described how they had run up a tab with various suppliers, including Tru-Test for the shafts and another manufacturer for the clubheads. After having made several rescue loans, their bankroller, an airline pilot named Paul Sanders, was cutting off the credit line. Without a cash transfusion, Hickory Stick wedges and putters were on their way to the graveyard of golf equipment.

"Where is Sanders?" I asked Parente.

"He doesn't come around much. He's a silent partner."

I looked around at the dust and the piles of dowels and the sense of impending doom, trying to contain my enthusiasm.

"I'll get back to you," I said.

I Realized I Was Hooked

On the way home from Hickory Stick, USA to Bear Creek, I drove up a hill on a long, familiar dirt road in Temecula, past the rows of red and white grapes, and into the parking lot of Callaway Vineyard & Winery, where I had started my first entrepreneurial venture 14 years earlier, in 1968. I had sold the business to Hiram Walker the previous year in 1981, and was pleased to see the fall harvest in full swing, with the pickers in the fields, tossing grapes into metal gondolas that carried them to the processing center a few yards away. Next to the processing center, tourists lined up at the gift shop to sign up for the tour.

The vineyard manager, John Moramarco, emerged from the gift shop. He was a tall man with a droll sense of humor, a long gait, and a face that was weathered from a lifetime of tending grapes – in recent years, Callaway grapes. When I'd hired Moramarco in 1968, the winery was nothing more than an empty field with an aluminum shed for an office, smaller even than the headquarters of Hickory Stick, USA. As the ex-owner returned to the scene, I didn't feel the slightest twinge of remorse for having sold the business that Moramarco and I had built from scratch.

"What are you up to these days?" Moramarco wanted to know.

"I'm going into the golf business," I said. It was the moment I realized I was hooked.

Over the next few days, I canceled my golf dates to spend time with Don Dye. Dye was my lawyer from the vineyard: an ex–Air Force pilot and UCLA grad with a sense of humor straight out of Vonnegut. He never hesitated to speak his mind, which was unusually sharp. Beyond being a legal advisor, he was a sounding board for my occasional great idea. This one didn't sound too great.

"What do you want to do that for?" was his first reaction.

We were in his office in Escondido, where he and three partners had opened a new law firm.

"These guys have a unique product. And they're about to go bust."

Never invest before you investigate, they say. Dye guided me through the due diligence phase, asking Parente and Manzoni for the usual résumés and references. On Parente's list of references was a dentist, a golf pro in San Jose, and an investment advisor at Cape Star Financial in San Clemente. Neither Don nor I had ever heard of Cape Star. Manzoni's résumé contained the following roundup: assistant pro at a couple of golf courses, manager of the pro shop at Mission Hills, and golf director at Cathedral Canyon in Palm Springs. In 1978, he had designed a series of new putters, which he'd sent to Wilson for possible manufacture. Wilson hadn't gotten back to him.

The more we investigated the financial side, the worse it looked. Production was about to be halted for lack of funds. The company owed $17,515.72 to the National Brass Works for clubheads, and the founding fathers were delinquent on their payroll taxes and in hock to their accountants (never a healthy strategy). The airline pilot had opened his wallet four times and was holding personal notes totaling more than $30,000, a substantial amount of debt for a company that reported sales of $60,000 for the prior year. There was also the $15,000 loan from the Security Pacific Bank, which was about to go into default, collateralized by the pilot's house.

Dye wasn't much of a golfer, but I gave him a Hickory Stick to try for himself. He could understand why I might want to play with one, but owning the company was another matter. I imagine he wondered why Ely Callaway, the ex-president of Burlington Industries, once the largest textile manufacturer and merchandiser in the world, and the ex-winemaker who had sold his vineyard and his label to Hiram Walker, would want to bother with three dreamers, a gun drill, and a telephone?

What I saw was that this Hickory Stick had the fundamental qualities I always look for in any product: it was demonstrably superior and pleasingly different, or as I would say, diffrunt and bettuh. This is the first and most important rule of business. For a product to be successful, it has to be different and better than anything else on the market. Though you never want to be *un*pleasingly different. "Better" is easy to define: it means more satisfying. The consumer really doesn't know what they want, except they know they want a more satisfying product than the one they've currently got. And I knew that if I brought it to them, they'd buy it.

From my post-war boom years working for Roger Milliken and Spencer Love, two of the geniuses of the American textile industry, to my start-up California days growing grapes in the desert fit for the Queen of England, I believed in creating the new, radically different, and significantly improved. If I did that, I was willing to gamble, I'd sell my product at a profit – and so far my gambles had a pretty healthy rate of return. In golf speak, a radical design change meant creating a club that would improve the average player's chances of hitting a good shot with his generally not-too-good swing. I saw the opportunity to do just that with Hickory Stick, USA.

I fell in love. I invested. And the game of golf would never be the same.

"The consumer really doesn't know what they want, except they know they want a more satisfying product than the one they've currently got."

CHAPTER 2

AN IMPOSSIBLE GAME, A LEGAL ADDICTION

Early Lessons in Golf and Business from My Father, the Army, and Bobby Jones

Self-Reliance and Self-Destruction

Some fathers encourage their sons to weed lawns, work construction jobs, or play football to toughen them up. Ely Callaway, Sr. (1880–1956) wasn't like that. He urged me to play golf. It wasn't because he wanted me to learn a discipline or hand-eye coordination. Instead, my father saw it as my best chance to compete against adults at a young age, and beat 'em.

My father played left-handed and was what you might call a regular hacker, and that was about the only regular thing about him. He was a man with no shortage of folksy wisdom. "Ely, be slow to sign and quick to pay" and "Late to bed, early to rise, work like hell and economize" were two of his favorite mottos. I remember when I was five or six, he told me, "Golf is the one game where if you work at it, and you try really hard, you can compete with adults and win." I didn't listen to him at the time, or I would've started playing sooner.

My father's father, Abner Reeves Callaway, was a Southern Baptist preacher descended from a long line of 31 Southern Baptist preachers. Abner and his first wife, Sarah Jane Howard, had nine children, and after Sarah died in 1878, Abner married Mary Wilbourne Ely a year later. Abner and Mary had three more sons, including my father, Ely Sr. Fuller Earle Callaway, Sr. (1870–1928), my father's older half-brother by 10 years but the youngest of Abner and Sarah's children, was only eight when his mother died, and he had to learn quickly how to raise himself. By the age of 18, Fuller had acquired his own store. In 1895, at the age of 25, Fuller opened Callaway Mills, the first modern textile mill in his hometown of LaGrange, Georgia, 60 miles southwest of Atlanta where I spent the first 17 years of my life. My father adored Fuller, and followed him into the family business.

Uncle Fuller believed a successful businessman went against the grain of conventional thinking, and he was a visionary with relentless drive. He was also a fair and compassionate industrialist who took exceptional care of his workers. Whenever Fuller built a new textile mill, he surrounded it with new parks, a new school, a new church, and other facilities. But he never built a company store, because it would have unfairly competed against the local businesses that were already there. Fuller believed in improving communities, not conquering or monopolizing them, and was guided by a simple creed: "I make

American citizens and run cotton mills to pay the expense." By the time I was born in 1919, Fuller was one of the most influential industrialists in America, and the Callaways were one of the most prominent families in Georgia.

About the time I finally picked up my first golf club, when I was 11, I also undertook my first business venture: growing peaches. There was a very palatable variety called J. H. Hale, which my father thought would be the easiest peach to raise successfully. I made a little bit of money growing and selling those sweet Georgia peaches, and with my father's encouragement, I used my profits to take out a $5,000 life insurance policy. I'm not sure how many other 11-year-olds had life insurance policies, but I did.

My father wanted me to become self-reliant at a very early age. Perhaps he had been inspired by his prosperous half-brother Fuller, who grew up a motherless son with nothing but a nickel and a few spools of thread to his name. By age 40 Fuller had become a major textile industrialist, railroad magnate, banker, and trusted advisor to Woodrow Wilson as a member of the Industrial Relations Committee.

And what better way to teach self-reliance than golf? Golf is the most difficult game on Earth. And what makes the game so damn difficult is it's a one-man show. You're fundamentally fighting only yourself. You're also dealing with moving an object a long way. I don't believe human beings move any other object under their own power as far as a golf ball. Besides that, there are all these variables like wind, rain, sand, and bad bounces that can ruin even the most flush shot.

It also happens to be the only major sport where the ball sits still before it is hit, so the golfer's mind has ample opportunity to send a secret message to any one of the 250 muscles involved in the swing, ordering it to screw up the shot. In other words, the golfer has a lot of time to commit suicide. By the time a player checks the lie, gauges the wind, chooses the club, takes a practice swing, and addresses the ball, the demons have already had several minutes to crawl out of the golfer's subconscious. Compare this to tennis, where the ball travels at high speed over the net. Other than the serve, the tennis player has to react so quickly that the mind has no time to sabotage the body. There's no misery quite like the golfer's as he leisurely self-destructs.

Golf is impossible and irresistible. It's a legal addiction. I call it the unconquerable game. For years, everybody thought Callaway made golf clubs to lower people's scores, and we don't. We don't know what the score is going to be because no matter how good your club is, too many things go on in the mind and body before and after you tee off. And therefore you can't find one Callaway Golf ad (and I would know because I've written or helped write or checked the copy on all of them) where we've said that if you use our clubs, it'll improve your score, lower your handicap, or increase your distance off the tee.

Besides, the thing that really brings people back to this addictive, impossible game of golf is not the score or a lower handicap: it is the amazing human experience, both physical and emotional, of a well-struck shot. And nothing more so than a well-struck drive. No matter how poorly you play, all you need is one good shot a day to bring you back.

There's no other game like it. There's no other pursuit like it. And when I was a kid, there was no other player like Bobby Jones.

It's funny how events can align in a person's life. I don't know if it's providence or luck or a bit of both that causes things to work out the way they do, but I do know that I couldn't have picked a better year to start golfing. I had barely swung my first iron when in the summer of 1930 Bobby Jones won his fabled Grand Slam – the first man to ever win all four major tournaments in a single year. And I sat enraptured by the radio for every minute of it. Everybody described Bobby Jones's swing as the most beautiful they'd ever seen – effortless and fluid. It was low and slow on the backswing, with an absolutely free turn of the body on the downswing and follow-through. Even on the radio, I swear the sound of the ball coming off Bobby's club just sounded different than it did for everybody else.

My affection for Bobby actually went back to when I was eight years old. My mother, Loula Walker Callaway, was Bobby's first cousin once removed, and became a big fan of his. She told me what a great man he was, and I believed her. He became my childhood hero, as he was for a majority of the population in the late 1920s and early 1930s. After he won the Grand Slam, he got a ticker-tape parade in New York City and a banner headline across the top of the front page of *The New York Times*, about the same size Lindbergh got when he landed in France with the *Spirit of St. Louis.* There wasn't a bigger star in the entire country, and perhaps in the world.

There was so much I admired about Bobby. I finally saw his fabled swing at a movie theater in a series of instructional short films called *How I Play Golf,* released by Warner Brothers beginning in 1931. In plain, simple terms, Bobby showed a group of kids and Hollywood celebrities the essentials of how to hold a club, address the ball, and swing with perfect form and balance.

Before or since, no one has distilled more precisely or eloquently the keys to the golf swing than Bobby did in those films (and in the columns he wrote for Bell Syndicate two times a week for eight years – later compiled into his sacred text, *Bobby Jones on Golf*). The master had a lot to say about how to swing a golf club, so I better let the master speak for himself:

> *At the top of the swing the shaft of the club, which for the long shots is in a position approximately in a horizontal plane, should at the same time be pointing to a spot slightly to the right of the object at which the player is aiming. This will be found to be a uniform practice among the best professional golfers. It is the result of swinging the club back to the top, rather than lifting it up as so many beginners do.*
>
> *Now, from this position it is important in what manner the club is started downward. The necessary elevation of the hands at the top of the swing draws the right elbow away from the ribs, where it should have remained until the last possible moment. The elbow is not, however, lifted into the air aimlessly; the right forearm should point obliquely, almost vertically, toward the ground, and be drawn away from the side only by what is necessary to accommodate a full swing of the club.*
>
> *Many players advance this far with fair success; but the next step usually trips them. The almost irresistible impulse now, when all is in readiness to wallop the ball, is to allow the right hand too much freedom. They allow that ubiquitous member, which has to be watched continually, to whip the club over their right shoulder towards the front of the player whence it must approach the ball from outside the line of flight. Whether a smothered hook or a bad slice results, depends only upon whether the club face is shut or open when it reaches the ball. If anything like a decent shot results from such a procedure it may be ascribed to accident.*

The proper start down from the position I have described is in the direction in which the grip end of the shaft is pointing. Since the head-end of the club is pointing slightly to the right of the objective aimed at, the grip end will be directed away from the vertical plane in which the ball rests. In other words, instead of immediately beginning to approach the line of flight as the downward stroke commences, the club head should first be made to drop away from that line.

The importance of this movement cannot be overestimated. The right elbow quickly drops back into place close to the side of the body, and the player is in a compact position ready to deliver a blow squarely at the back of the ball. There is no possibility of cutting across the shot.

I modeled my swing after what he taught me in those films and became a pretty well-known junior golfer in my hometown. I won my first junior tournament only a year after I started golfing. To quote a local newspaper, "Remember this name – Ely Callaway. Though he's only 12 years old he has a fine swing, which they say is the most important thing in golf." A few years later, I won the Highland Country Club Championship four years running from 1936 to 1939. Some people noted that my swing reminded them of Bobby's, which pleased me no end. I briefly flirted with the idea of turning pro. Perhaps the reason I never did was that Bobby didn't either.

Bobby remained an amateur his entire competitive career. Millions of people admired him for never turning pro and winning all those tournaments as an amateur. He preferred to make his livelihood as a lawyer, and not to take money for playing his favorite game.

Golf fans also remembered the highly publicized incident when Jones hit the ball into the woods during a big tournament.

He emerged from the woods and gave himself a one-stroke penalty for accidentally tapping the ball with his foot. That stroke cost him the tournament. Nobody saw him move the ball, but Jones saw himself do it and turned himself in. The reporters on the scene congratulated him for this unusual display of honor, but Jones was insulted that they made a big deal out of it. In his words, "You might as well congratulate me for not robbing a bank."

The Military, My First Industry

When I graduated from LaGrange High School in 1936, I really had no idea what I wanted to do with my life, other than that I was pretty certain I did not want to follow my father into textiles. More to the point, I did not want to work for the family business. Fuller Callaway Sr. employed my father and his two sons, Cason and Fuller Jr., at Callaway Mills in LaGrange. There was a lot of sibling rivalry and family troubles as a result. My father was hardworking, industrious, and witty, but lived in the shadow of his half-brother, Fuller. I learned early on that family business can lead to nasty business.

I left LaGrange and enrolled at Emory University in Atlanta. I chose Emory because it had the best academic reputation in Georgia; it was a place where people could work hard, have a good time, and not have their lives dominated by football teams. They had a golf team, as well as an attractive and respectable fraternity life, and I got involved in both immediately. I wasn't one of those bookworm studious types. I was a B student in an institution where academic excellence was the standard.

Still, I worked hard and did a lot on campus, and eventually became president of the senior class. I was the business manager of the yearbook like I was in high school, and the chief financial officer of my fraternity, where I lived. I was even elected to the senior honor society called Omicron Delta Kappa, ODK. And of course, I golfed . . . a lot. But compared to my closest friends, academically I was rather mediocre. For instance, my two closest friends and fraternity brothers, James Wilson and Covington Hardee (aka Cuz), went on to become number one and two in their class at Harvard Law School. I would call on Cuz's legal expertise to come to my personal and professional rescue when I most needed it three decades later. But I'm getting ahead of myself.

Many of the people I've admired most in my life – Bobby Jones, Cuz Hardee, Jimmy Wilson, Mark McCormack, Vernon Jordan, Morris B. Abram, Sr., Don Dye, and Steve McCracken (don't worry, we'll meet all of them later) – were lawyers. For me, the law is a noble profession and lays the best possible foundation for anything you might want to do in life. Whenever I've started a new business venture, I've always wanted a first-rate legal mind at my side.

I attended Emory from 1936 to 1940, and by far the biggest news of the world during my college career was the rise of Nazi Germany. My friends and I were very concerned about what Hitler was doing long before he invaded Poland on September 1, 1939. If you read anything, you knew he was already a menace to mankind. And yet most of the United States was isolationist – apparently, it didn't matter that our ships were being sunk by the hundreds of millions of tons right off our coast, and all over the North Sea trying to get supplies to Russia and Great Britain. Though America wasn't at war yet, anybody that was 20 years old like me and didn't think about how all this was going to affect them was unconscious.

Around that time, I began seeing advertisements in my college publication: "Become an Army Officer by Mail." The correspondence course would train you in a specialized area in the Army Reserve Corps. You would only be required to serve a year of active duty, after which you could retire as a second lieutenant. In the event of a national emergency, of course, you would be called upon to serve without notice. But that was true no matter who you were. I had no idea when or if a national emergency would ever occur, so this seemed like a way to serve my country, fulfill my duty to the military, and then begin my working life.

I took the correspondence course and received my commission in June of 1940. I was assigned to the Philadelphia Quartermaster Depot, the procurement agency for the ordering, purchasing, and manufacturing of all military clothing. *Textiles.* I couldn't believe it – I had gone to Emory to get away from the family business, only for the army to pull me right back in. To this day I'm not sure whether it was a mere coincidence or if they knew of my family. Whatever the case, this commission would define my time during the war, as well as the next 33 years of my professional life.

My father and mother and two sisters escorted me to the Atlanta train station on, I believe, October 11, 1940. When you think of a young soldier going off to war, you probably imagine flags flying, his mother, sisters, and girlfriend crying while he's led away toward a parade or something. Well, my departure was not that notable or dramatic. There was no troop ship or line of marching doughboys with flags flying. There was lots of crying (I know I cried), but my actual departure was very uneventful and non-military. I just walked up the steps of the Pullman car, the train pulled out, and I waved goodbye. That was it. While my friends Cuz Hardee and Jimmy Wilson were off to Harvard, I was off to war. We had no idea what the destiny of the world would be. I was 21 years old, and Pearl Harbor was a little more than a year away.

The Philadelphia Quartermaster Depot was one of the oldest continuous installations in the United States Army, purchasing and manufacturing all military clothing since 1799. Very few operations had remained in one area with one function since the Revolutionary War. At the time, most U.S. military offices were temporary buildings built in World War I, even those in D.C. The Philadelphia Quartermaster was different. There wasn't anything temporary there. It had been rebuilt from scratch a couple of years before with all-new brick buildings and a factory. When I arrived, roughly 5,000 people were working there. I think I came in with a dozen other second lieutenants who had just gotten their commissions. There might have already been 50 other officers there, counting the general and the department heads.

Still, ours was not a military institution in the normal sense. When I arrived, rather than an army jeep shuttling me to my barracks, I was driven by cab to a private residence in South Philadelphia. Nobody lived on campus, we just worked there. Most of the people who worked at the Depot were civilians, and we all wore civilian clothing, even our commanding officer, Brigadier General "Wild Bill" McCain (grandfather of Senator

John McCain). There was not a uniform in sight; this was the pacifist influence.

In the United States, there wasn't supposed to be a military. Heck, at the time the entire armed forces were less than 350,000 people. This was a peacetime army, and there wasn't supposed to be any glory in the military. After all, we thought we had fought the last war for democracy in 1917. So what in God's name would we be wearing uniforms for? That was the atmosphere. It was no big deal. It was just accepted.

In the first year, I was assigned to Procurement Officer Colonel Thomas W. Jones. I was still a lowly second lieutenant, a trainee who hadn't been given any responsibility yet, but all I had between me and the Quartermaster General was Colonel Jones, General McCain, and Bob Stevens, the future Secretary of the Army who later became a target of Senator Joseph McCarthy and his cronies. My point is that the function was very unusual; you didn't have 400 people between any single person and the top man in the unit. The Philadelphia Quartermaster was still a relatively small operation, and the military was looking to expand exponentially, so my age, rank, or experience didn't matter. They just needed people who could get the job done.

After about four months, Colonel Jones told me to go up to New York to work with our private contractors, so that I might learn something about the apparel industry. Once again, I was accidentally following in my father's footsteps. In 1921, when I was two years old, my ambitious Uncle Fuller sent my father up to New York to open a Callaway Mills sales office there, and my family lived on Riverside Drive for a few years. Callaway Mills was already a regional success, but like many southern industrialists, Uncle Fuller wanted to break out of their southern roots. However, my uncle's gambit didn't succeed, and my father moved the family back to LaGrange as soon as his brother would allow.

I had a car by the time I received my New York commission, so I drove north and lived in a dumpy little apartment on 86th and York Avenue with a couple of Navy officers, one of whom I knew very well from Atlanta. In those days, almost all of the New York garment industry was Mafia-dominated. That's where Murder, Inc. was active. Study your history of crime in New York, and you'll find Lepke Buchalter, the alias of Louis Buchalter, also known to his mother as "Little Louis." By the time I got to the garment district of Manhattan, Lepke was already in prison for smuggling heroin (and was executed in Sing Sing for first-degree murder a few years later), but his gang of hitmen and labor racketeers still controlled the entire apparel industry in New York City, as well as trucking, garbage, and liquor, in the New York metropolitan area – and maybe still do.

Since organized crime appeared to have a monopoly on garments, I had no other choice but to go to the Mafia's plants and convince them to teach me what they were doing. The army needed to know what kind of equipment to buy, whether they could convert women's apparel manufacturers to make men's uniforms – those kinds of questions. They were all very open with me about what went on in their plants, at least the legal side of it. Everybody loved the government contracts, and the workers thought it was special to work on army uniforms. In a few short months, the New York Mafia taught me everything I wanted to know about the apparel industry. They were killers and crooks, but they helped us win the war.

By the time I got back to Philadelphia, my year was nearly up. I could leave the Army Reserve Corps and return to Georgia at the government's expense. It was September 1941, and Colonel Jones came to me and said, "I hope you stay. Because if you do, I'm going to make you the youngest procurement officer in the history of the Quartermaster Corps."

And I said, "Fine."

It was a no-brainer. Not only was I beginning to learn something useful, but I was damn sure we were going to have a war by then. I remember Colonel Jones told me, "Ely, I think you've made the right decision. I can't say when it's going to happen, but we're going to fight that son-of-a-bitch Hitler. If we don't do this, we're all going to die. Everybody in the free world will die. After he takes England and everybody in Europe, he'll come over here and occupy the United States, and we'll all be his slaves."

And I said, "You're right, thank you."

My life wasn't all boots and raincoats and pants in those days. On one of my days off, my childhood friend, Hal Thompson, introduced me to my first wife, Jeanne Delaplaine Wiler, a *Philadelphia Story* girl from the Main Line with a Donna Reed-esque glamor. She was a fine golfer to boot and flattered me no end by complimenting me on my golf swing. She told me that's what made her fall in love with me, as well as how I moved on the dance floor. There was only one tiny little problem: when we met, Jeanne was engaged to a doctor and had already chosen her wedding date. But I didn't let that stop me.

I was not what most people would call a handsome young man. As a kid I was beanpole-thin, and a terrible case of acne plagued me from adolescence, which caused me to struggle with my confidence and self-esteem, particularly where the ladies were concerned. My senior year at Emory, I took a date to see the world premiere of *Gone with the Wind* in Atlanta on December 15, 1939. Vivien Leigh and Clark Gable were in attendance, as well as 18,000 ecstatic fans. The date didn't end well, however. We were necking in the back seat of my car after the show, when she accidentally set her skirt on fire with a cigarette. The curtain came down on the Old South and on our relationship.

I have already described how I was no Einstein in the classroom either, which meant the only skills I could rely on when it came to business or courting the opposite sex were golf and talking. Fortunately, I did both pretty well. And as Jeanne often said, I simply would not take no for an answer. I convinced Jeanne to break her wedding engagement and marry me instead.

Shortly into our engagement, we saw the great pianist Arthur Rubinstein at Carnegie Hall on December 7, 1941. In the middle of the Brahms Piano Concerto No. 2, the house manager walked out on stage and tapped Rubinstein on the shoulder. The maestro stopped playing, and the manager turned to the audience. "Ladies and gentlemen," he declared, "I have an important announcement to make. The President of the United States has just reported on the radio that the Japanese have bombed Pearl Harbor."

The audience was in complete shock, and many burst into tears. Without missing a beat, Rubinstein began to play "The Star-Spangled Banner," and everyone sang along. Afterward, Jeanne and I and the rest of the emotional audience spilled out of Carnegie Hall into the Manhattan night. We looked at each other and said, "Well, we'd better get married now."

A Salesman for Uncle Sam

The moment Colonel Jones had predicted three months earlier had arrived. Suddenly we were at war, and the Quartermaster Depot started accelerating promotions. I was made a first lieutenant in early 1942, a little over a year after joining the army, when the usual trajectory for a *second* lieutenant was five to seven years. I moved back to New York to the Army-Navy Purchasing Office, located at 111 East 16th Street. I was head of my office, with about 200 people working under me. As a contracting officer, I was authorized to negotiate and award contracts to private companies and spend money authorized by Congress to procure supplies for the army. I was 22 years old and, just like my father had intended 10 years earlier when he gave me my first hickory shaft club, I was a kid competing against adults.

My job was essentially to get the best manufacturers in America to give us all of the products we needed whenever we needed them. Once we awarded contracts, I had to see that they were delivered on time and with the right quality. I had unlimited budgets, and I had power. Under the law, I could give out mandatory orders and even shut down businesses if they didn't comply. I never had to do that. In fact, I believe I was the only contracting officer who never had to give out one mandatory order. In part that was because the apparel industry had a large capacity and could deliver what we needed. In part that was because many in the industry had a lot of compassion for the war effort. But it was also because of my ability to talk them into it.

I was a salesman for Uncle Sam, trying to help our boys overseas win the war one contract at a time. While in peacetime we would have fielded bids for, say, 100,000 shirts, now we were soliciting quantities of 50 million. That meant we needed the best, like Arrow Shirts, Levi Strauss Jeans, and Blue Ridge Overalls, who could deliver at that scale. I went after them and I made them bid, by God! They'd only offer 19 million units, for instance, even though if they wanted they could make 50 million. I wanted to have the cream of American industry working as much as I wanted them to work on government contracts, so I had to go in and get them to give us more than they wanted to. I lived on the telephone for the next three years.

That's how I learned to be persuasive. All you've got to do is have a good story, and my reasonable argument was, "For God's sake, what do you mean you don't want to make more than a million and a half denim shirts? You've got the capacity to make four million. We need them. What else is of greater interest to you than winning this war?"

I was 23 or 24, dealing directly with people like Carroll Rosenbloom, the president of Blue Ridge Overalls Company and a visionary who later helped turn the NFL into the biggest business in American sports history. Rosenbloom and his counterparts would complain that I never let them off the phone, to the point where eventually they had to comply. These were pretty tough customers, to be sure, but after wooing Jeanne, schmoozing the chief executives of the largest garment manufacturers in the world was a cakewalk. Despite or perhaps because of all the grief I gave him, Rosenbloom offered me a job after the war. I turned him down, though if I hadn't, maybe today I'd be the owner of the Atlanta Falcons.

I learned an awful lot about what to do and what not to do in those years: don't cut corners, and do the right thing. I saw so many people doing wrong. Our contractors tried to get away with cutting corners, not delivering to specifications, trying to save a little money, and trying to bribe me and the inspectors. I remember one of my top administrative assistants was charged with taking a payoff from some of the bidders. I looked up one day and saw him being escorted out by the Secret Service.

After Jeanne and I got married on October 7, 1942, I got hundreds of gifts. I'm talking whiskey and cigars and clothing and everything that you can imagine, all from potential bidders. We sent every one of them back. As a result, my reputation got around right away: "Ely won't even take a Christmas gift or anything." I never made a big deal of it, though. Just like Bobby Jones said, they might as well praise me for not robbing a bank.

By 1943, we were dealing with literally thousands of garment manufacturers, and the opportunities for malfeasance were there. Most of the officers didn't touch this stuff, but a few did, and they got in trouble. The big lesson that I learned was that neither cutting corners nor taking bribes would improve the quality of your business. On the contrary, good ethics is good business.

Though Jeanne and I got married right after Pearl Harbor, we were separated for much of the war. She started her training as an officer cadet candidate on August 16, 1942, at Fort Des Moines, and was commissioned as a third officer in September, only a month before she got married. She became a poster girl for the army, stationed in Iowa at the recruiting office for the Women's Auxiliary Army Corps, or WAACs. The following year, 1943, Jeanne gave birth to our first child, a daughter who only survived a few hours. She had a birth defect called spina bifida. This was devastating to us as young parents, and thus began Jeanne's lifelong battles with illness, both mental and physical.

I made major in late 1943 or early 1944. The rank had an interesting effect on me. In wartime, the most important thing in the world outside of family was rank, because every man and woman was either in the military or had someone in the military. It was the only power you had. In today's world, power is money, or esteem, or achievement, but what good was money during the war? You couldn't buy anything, not even a new car. The main thing you wanted, besides staying alive, was to have a rank, and I learned how to respect my rank, not misuse or abuse it, and it brought me a nice little sense of pride. That's about all it brought, but that was important to me.

I was younger than most majors, certainly younger than any major in the Quartermaster Corps. Compared to the rest of the army, though, my situation was not unique. On the frontline, men my age or younger were frequently elevated to officer, since officers were being killed so often. Air Force pilots were famous for having the youngest men with the highest rank, and with that they carried the greatest recognition of achievement. The Greatest Generation of young men and women, as General Van Fleet aptly termed us, was called upon to save civilization and freedom itself from the forces of evil, under the leadership of great men like Churchill and FDR. You can never overestimate the importance of the individual to change the world, both for good and evil.

By the time my military service ended in the fall of 1945, I'd accomplished quite a lot in the textile industry. A month before I got out of the army, Colonel Thomas Jones recommended me for the Legion of Merit. In his letter to the Quartermaster General, he stated that as a matter of practice, I had procured approximately 65 percent of all clothing purchased for enlisted personnel of the army during the war; made over 6,000 contracts calling for a total of more than 500 million units of cotton clothing and related items; dealt with 700 different garment manufacturers located throughout the United States; and authorized the expenditure of approximately $350 million in government funds. I had made decisions and taken risks and gotten things done on a massive scale, and this gave me a sense of self and self-esteem at a very early age. It was the end of the war, but I'd already lived an experience that almost no one else in the history of business ever had, and certainly not in textiles.

Six days after he wrote my recommendation, Colonel Jones received a letter – not from the Quartermaster General, but from Roger Milliken of Deering Milliken Inc. Milliken needed a chief salesman for his work clothing fabrics department, and asked Colonel Jones to release me early from my service so that I might work for him at the new office he was opening in Atlanta. He told Colonel Jones that he was "extremely anxious" to secure my employment as soon as possible and that given the nature of the work I would be doing – filling the country's barren work clothes shelves for the mass of citizens who were now leaving the army and returning to the labor force – it was in the national interest of the army to release me right away. I took the job, moved to Atlanta, and began my adult life. Jeanne and I bought a house right down the street from the family of my childhood hero, Bobby Jones.

"No matter how poorly you play, all you need is one good shot a day to bring you back."

CHAPTER 3

GOOD ETHICS IS GOOD BUSINESS

My Career in Textiles from the Post-war Boom Through the Sixties

The Blended Revolution Begins

After five years and two months of service, I got out of the army in November 1945 and went to work for Roger Milliken on January 3, 1946, opening up the Atlanta sales office for Deering Milliken & Company. This was the elite of the textile industry. I sold cotton fabrics made by Milliken to the same garment manufacturers I'd been dealing with in the army, who would find I was just as relentless a salesman in peacetime.

In the entire history of the American textile industry, there were probably only three real geniuses, and I might be the only person to have worked for all three. Roger Milliken was the first.

Deering Milliken & Company was a good old-fashioned family corporation. Roger's grandfather, Seth Milliken, had co-founded it as a small woolen fabrics company in Portland, Maine, in 1865. The Deering half of the partnership left a few years later, but Seth kept the name and moved the company to New York. Milliken drew up its first southern contract in 1884, with Pacolet Manufacturing Company in Spartanburg, South Carolina, run by a former Confederate captain. This began the company's long and prosperous relationship developing the textile industry in the post-antebellum South (a tradition my grandfather brought to LaGrange about 10 years later). After Seth died in 1920, his son, Gerrish Milliken, took over. Gerrish had a shrewd business sense, which allowed them to survive, even thrive, during the Great Depression.

Gerrish's shrewdest practice was investing in the development of man-made fibers, such as rayon. Rayon was the world's first artificial semi-synthetic fiber, accidentally invented by a French chemist looking for new ways to make things explode. Rayon exploded in a different sense in the 1920s as a popular fashion fiber, particularly for women, beginning with socks, lingerie, and clothing. The variety of fabrics and finishes meant that any woman could now wear garment types once available only to those who could afford silk. You might even say rayon was as much a part of the flapper milieu as the bob haircut. It was Milliken's commitment to innovative, durable textiles that caught the attention of the War Production Board, who in 1944 commissioned Deering Milliken to build a state-of-the-art factory to produce all kinds of fabric and yarns, most notably man-made fiber for military tire cords.

When Gerrish died in 1947, Roger inherited the throne. A new generation brought new ambition: Roger wanted to continue the company's shift away from commission selling toward manufacturing, which had begun during the war. He wanted to build an empire. His first step toward global domination was founding the Milliken Research Institute, which, in addition to inventing new textiles, manufactured chemicals that made firefighter gear flame-resistant and gave Jello its smooth, creamy quality. If you wanted to be on the cutting edge of the textile or chemicals industry, Milliken is where you went. When I started, I was only 26 years old. Roger was only 29.

Roger called me one day in December 1948 and said, "Ely, you're doing a great job, but I need you up in New York. I want to get into woolen and worsted menswear, and you're the guy to do it. So come on and move back north." Suddenly, I was to become a merchant – deciding what to make, when to make it, how much to make, what price to sell it at, and who to sell it to, and then collecting the money. In other words, I became a product creator. My promotion made headlines in the apparel trade journal *The Daily News Record.*

Despite Roger's confidence, I couldn't shake the feeling he had the wrong man. Menswear was a totally different industry than the one I had dealt with in the war. The equipment itself was totally different. I had no experience with it at all – in fact, nobody at Milliken did. What I did have was experience converting machines from making one type of fabric to another, as the New York mob had taught me to do during the war. Besides, Milliken wasn't looking to make men's suits the way everybody else did. He wanted to experiment with all kinds of new man-made fabrics and make men's suits out of them. I was surely the wrong person to be making men's suits, but perhaps the exact right person for this job.

Roger began with men's clothing because he figured men were more likely to appreciate the pluses his new fabrics would theoretically bring. At the time, wool was the standard fabric for fine men's suits. Styles changed, but wool remained. However, wool had incredible disadvantages; it got too hot in the summer, it wrinkled too easily, and you couldn't wear it in the rain. If I was wearing a suit in New York in 1949, got caught in a shower, and got a little damp, I'd be done! I'd look like hell, wouldn't I? It was a fabric for no seasons. The top men's clothing manufacturers wouldn't touch existing alternatives, like rayon, because they considered them too cheap for finely tailored suits. If Roger and I could just find a high-end man-made fabric that improved upon wool, we'd really have something.

A few years later, we found it.

In 1953, DuPont came up with an experimental fiber called Fiber V (V as in victory). DuPont didn't manufacture fabrics or sell clothes; they were a chemical company, and by far the largest in the world. They got rich making products that were truly better than their competition – better rubber, better polymer, better plutonium. Their goal in their own words was to "beat nature" – they literally said that. DuPont's decades-long battle against Mother Earth included making what became known as "blended fabrics" – a blend of man-made and natural fibers.

Their résumé already included inventing nylon hosiery back in 1939.

Nylon was DuPont's first experience in taking a natural fiber, in this case silk, and improving it with man-made brain power and machinery. Nylon made women's hosiery sheerer, prettier, more robust, lighter, and more comfortable. Furthermore, the nylon fiber was more consistent – produced out of a spinneret under perfect control, which made it easier to handle in a mill. Everything about nylon was an advantage compared to silk, so everyone shifted to it. They converted the entire world to a superior product.

Dacron polyester, as Fiber V would soon be known, was DuPont's opportunity to improve wool and cotton. They knew if they did that, they could sell pretty much all the fabric in the world, which was their objective: total domination. Dacron was far stronger than natural fibers, which meant it could spin a finer yarn. It also had great wrinkle recovery. When it comes to wrinkle recovery, nature did a pretty bad job. Wool has a little bit of memory, but cotton has none. Cotton's comfortable and absorbent, but if you took a clean, freshly pressed cotton handkerchief and wrinkled it up just a little bit, those wrinkles would never come out. On the other hand, if that handkerchief were made of 100 percent Dacron, even in the earliest days of Dacron, the wrinkles would come out within 10 minutes. The handkerchief would be flat because the fibers would be in recovery, thanks to their built-in memory. It's all a question of chemistry.

DuPont may have had the science, but they couldn't do it on their own. The modern clothing industry was really a combination of three industries: the chemical, like DuPont, who made the fibers; the textile, like Deering Milliken, who took that fiber and made fabric out of it; and the apparel manufacturer, like Blue Ridge or Arrow, who bought fabrics from us.

The problem for DuPont was that most textile mills wouldn't touch Dacron. They thought it was too expensive. The price of DuPont's experimental new fiber was $5 a pound. Compare that to rayon, which was 32 cents a pound; or cotton, no more than 35 cents a pound; or even the finest wool, which ran only $2 a pound. DuPont charged over twice as much for a man-made fiber that nobody had ever heard of and, well, everybody thought it was silly. But Roger, always inclined to experiment, took one look at Dacron and said, "God almighty, we have an opportunity to do something nobody else will do." He didn't care about the cost because he figured if he made a product that was truly superior, he could price it any way he wanted. It was that simple.

Less simple was converting our entire operation from manufacturing wool to Dacron, which of course became my job. Nobody knew how to process Dacron; we had to make it up as we went along. We had to relearn how to spin and how to dye. Every piece of equipment had to be converted. This caused everything to slow down, sending costs sky-high on top of the $5 a pound we were already spending just to get in the game. It took us 18 months to get the first samples. Fortunately, I had middle management below me that was inquisitive and ingenious.

Finally, we produced a single 100 percent polyester suit, and by God, it had advantages. The suit was lightweight and extremely wrinkle-resistant. A person could stand in a rainstorm for an hour and get soaking wet, wear it until it got dry, and by the time the damn thing dried out, it still looked good. We also learned that polyester had one big negative: it's hot as hell. The nature of the fiber was such that when it touched skin it didn't absorb any sweat, making it impossibly uncomfortable in the summer. DuPont never told us this, because they hadn't learned it yet. We learned and said, "Thank you, but no, we're not going to sell a 100 percent polyester suit." You never want your new product to have any negatives against the standard product. You want nothing but pluses.

DuPont came back and said, "Okay, try blending it with wool, because wool will give it enough absorbance to make it comfortable on the skin." We spent another eight months working on it, and we came up with a fabulous tropical suit that was 55 percent Dacron and 45 percent wool. I even gave it a name: Viracle, because it was truly a miracle fabric. This was my first time naming and branding a product, and I discovered I had a real knack for it. Viracle had so many advantages that we decided paying $5 a pound was worth it, because we could price our fabric accordingly.

This was one of the greatest lessons I ever learned from Roger. He constantly told me, "For God's sake, don't make standard products the easy way; anybody can do that." Instead, he encouraged me to make something that genuinely contributed to the satisfaction of the user. If I did that, it wouldn't make any difference what it cost. After two or three years, DuPont lowered the cost of its fiber and we became more efficient at processing it, which significantly reduced our production costs. Still, we did not reduce the price of our fabric. This might sound like an anomaly, but to this day I've never priced on cost. Companies make the most money if they price on intuition and the merit of the product, and then successfully communicate to the buyer why the increased price is worth it.

Now visualize this: for the past five thousand years or so, the standard fine fabric in the world had been 100 percent wool, and now I had to convince the apparel industry to switch to something else. My office was at 261 Fifth Avenue, which is at 29th Street and Fifth. 200 Fifth Avenue was the Men's Clothing Center, located directly across from the Flatiron Building. All the top clothing companies in the United States had offices at 200 Fifth Avenue. My salesman and I marched down the street with our samples, and we attacked that building. I showed off my fabric to men's ready-to-wear suit manufacturers like Hart Schaffner Marx. They immediately saw that Viracle had real merit. They agreed that it was demonstrably superior and pleasingly different. We got a lot of the manufacturers to convert, and they each put out a special line of suits made from Milliken's 55/45 Viracle blend.

Of course, not all manufacturers were so enlightened. We faced stiff opposition from the New England–based American Woolen Company, which at the time was the biggest woolen and worsted company in the world. Like most people or companies at the top of the food chain, the heads of American Woolen were terrified of change. They went to all their top customers and got them to sign a pledge promising that they wouldn't use any blended fabrics – the textile equivalent of a horse and buggy company asking their customers not to drive cars. Then they ran the pledge as a double-page ad in the *Daily News Record*, a direct attack on Roger and me.

American Woolen's resistance proved to be something less than futile. Within a few months, many of the people featured in the ad reneged on their pledge and apologized to Roger and me. Our Viracle suits went on the market in 1954, and within two years the whole industry had converted. It was simply a better suit.

Bad Bidness, or: Nepotism, Greed, Chilling, and De-worsification

In those days, textile men like Roger were the big swingin's of American business, with their roots in the Old South. I grew up in that environment, then grew out of it, but Roger stayed entrenched. We're talking about one of the real, rock-ribbed Republican right-wingers in the country. He has been called the godfather of the American Conservative movement. He was a card-carrying member of the John Birch Society, a chief financial backer of Barry Goldwater, Pat Buchanan, Strom Thurmond, and a supporter of Richard Nixon's Southern Strategy.

I believe that Roger Milliken would've closed any and every plant he had if he felt threatened by the unions. This is illegal. You can't do that. In fact, we used to have a word for it: chilling. I know for a fact that's what happened at Darlington Manufacturing Company, a prominent South Carolina mill he owned until he closed it in 1956. The workers at the mill successfully campaigned to organize themselves under the Textile Workers Union, and the National Labor Relations Board found that Roger closed the mill six days later out of anti-union animus, which was illegal according to the National Labor Relations Act. He chilled that union.

But the story didn't end there – not even close. In 1965, Roger's legal battle with the NLRB reached all the way to the U.S. Supreme Court. Roger had an extremely skillful lawyer defending him named Stuart N. Updike. I believe Updike was general counsel for Milliken at the time. Updike argued that Roger had every legal right to close Darlington Manufacturing Company for any reason he liked because that mill constituted a single business entity. The Supreme Court didn't buy that argument, concluding that Darlington was not its own business but merely a small part of the larger Deering Milliken enterprise, and therefore discrimination against a union in one Milliken mill could threaten unionization efforts in all of them (this was during a time when lots of southern textile mills were unionizing). The court asked the NLRB to prove Roger had closed Darlington because he wanted to chill unions across Deering Milliken, but Roger stuck to his made-up reason why he closed the mill and the NLRB never got any documentation or anyone on record contradicting him, so he won the case. He got away with it.

Did I know of any evidence? Maybe I heard a few things from folks in his inner circle, but Roger never brought up this stuff with me directly, because he knew I disagreed with him. Short of Bobby Jones and my father, Roger was one of the single greatest influences on my life, but when it came to politics we did not see eye to eye. We argued about it all the time. He used to send me books that espoused his cause, and I sent him books that made him mad as hell.

Our relationship actually reminded me a lot of my cousin Cason's friendship with FDR. They became close when President Roosevelt began visiting Warm Springs, Georgia, in the 1920s to recover from polio. Cason took over Callaway Mills after his father, Fuller Sr., died, and was very active in Georgia politics – but the exact opposite politics as his good friend, Franklin. During the Great Depression, Cason led a successful union-busting campaign at Callaway Mills. Still, I know Cason thought of FDR as a great man and leader.

As for me, I never got into a fight about Darlington with Roger. I knew he was going to do whatever he wanted anyway. Maybe I could've gone public with what I thought I knew about Milliken's anti-union strategy, but it's too late now – the statute of limitations has passed. Anyway, it happened so long ago, and I really did consider Roger a friend. He was no crook – except in this one way.

My relationship with the rest of the Millikens, however, was not so congenial. I don't think anybody, particularly at my age, which at that point was 34, ever really knows all the reasons why they get fired. What I knew was that I had been very independent. The army had pushed me into positions that were far ahead of where I would have gotten if I'd gone into the business through civilian channels. I was out of sync with my contemporaries, holding down jobs that men with gray hair and capped teeth normally would have held.

The year was 1954, and I was running the woolen and worsted division from New York, with the plants in the South. I was an entrepreneur within the company. I would go off and do things without asking anybody's permission – pricing the product how I liked, deciding who to sell it to, who to deny it to, and who to hire. Roger liked that, but Roger's brother-in-law, Dick Stroud, who I reported to directly, did not. It ran him nuts! Stroud objected to my opinions about everything, but I didn't pay much attention to his misgivings because I didn't think he was very smart. He was about to prove me right.

Dick called me in one day and said, "Ely, you're the best promoter I've ever seen in my life, but we're just not getting along because you don't follow my instructions, and you don't believe in me, or in my leadership." So far, all true statements. He told me, "I think we ought to part." I guess he'd gotten sick of listening to me. And I said, "Okay, do Roger and Minot approve?" Minot was Roger's cousin, another product of the rampant nepotism throughout Deering Milliken. Dick informed me that yes, Roger and Minot approved of letting me go. So I was gone. That's about the way it happened. I recommend that everybody be fired at least once in their career. It's like falling off a horse. If you do it once, you're no longer afraid of it. Then you have an easier time handling the next horse.

I've always believed nepotism was a very bad way to do business. There are some good exceptions, like Henry Ford, but there are more failures than successes. The reason is very simple: you cannot mix objective business judgment and love. I don't mean you can't love the people you're in business with, but when you get the family into it, sometimes your objective judgment of the person goes out the window. Because it's emotional.

I've always had a policy against getting into business with my kids, which I think I absorbed from my family and witnessing all the disputes they had running Callaway Mills. I was quite close with my father's half-brother's grandson, Fuller Callaway III. My wonderful cousin was 10 years younger than me, so I became a kind of adoptive father for him. He was handsome as hell and a brilliant young fellow who graduated at the top of his class at Harvard Business School, before joining the Air Force during the early Korean War. But Fuller Jr. and his son Fuller III had a bad relationship, so when the youngest Fuller got out of the service, he did not want to work for Callaway

Mills. By then, Cason had resigned, Fuller Jr. was running the family business and Fuller III just couldn't stomach the idea of working for his father. Instead, he moved to San Francisco and became a world-class sailor, early venture capital investor in Silicon Valley and jetsetter. Every now and then, he'd call me and say, "Do you think I should work for the family company?" Generally, I would say no.

Seeing my family succeed, and squabble with each other, I made up my mind early on about a few things. I wanted to expand my horizons beyond the South, but I also knew that I didn't want to work for my father or his brother to do it. I desired to expand my scope beyond Callaway Mills, beyond textiles, beyond what my family had accomplished – achievements in business that, while renowned in the South, were stuck in the South. Years later, when I had kids of my own, I decided I wasn't going to encourage them to get in business with me either. I hoped they would strike out on their own and build something for themselves, as I had. Fortunately, it happens that they were all interested in something else anyway.

The other problem with nepotism is even if the child accomplishes a lot, they will always be in the shadow of the parent. They'll suffer by comparison. It's sort of like the Gary Nicklaus syndrome in golf (there have been very few sons of great golfers who could match their fathers, and the Golden Bear's cub was no exception). People generally won't give the son a chance unless they are super-exceptional. Roger Milliken was, but he had the habit of giving jobs to some unexceptional in-laws. This habit would come back to bite him, but more on that in a bit.

The day that Milliken fired me, I went home to Darien, Connecticut, and played with my kids. My eldest son Reeves, who was seven and a planes, trains, and automobiles kind of boy, had an elaborate Lionel O gauge model electric train set. I was so distraught that I throttled that locomotive until it jumped clear the rails, rattling Reeves and embarrassing myself. Well, I felt pretty lousy after losing the only job I'd had in my adult life.

A week later the job offers started rolling in, and I didn't feel so lousy anymore. I guess I'd built a bit of a reputation for myself at Milliken, inventing Viracle and some other things. I got offers from old companies and new companies, but one, in particular, caught my eye: a whole new kind of corporation being formed by Roy Little, the CEO of Textron and the second genius of the textile industry.

Originally from Providence, Rhode Island, Roy Little had founded the predecessor to Textron, Special Yarns Corporation, in 1923. Much as Roger Milliken had done, Little expanded Textron Inc. into the manufacturing of fiber, cloth, and finished garments after World War II, but the post-war industrial boom had not been as kind to Little's rate of return as it had been to Milliken's. By 1952, Textron was losing $6 million per year despite over $99 million in annual sales. Little decided that the best way to save his textile company was to get them out of textiles and into, well, everything else. He began a process of unrelated diversification, acquiring companies in upholstery filling, ball bearings, helicopter parts, gas meters, radar antennas, and more, and folding them all under the Textron umbrella. This new kind of company was called a conglomerate.

It's important to remember just how revolutionary this was. Until Roy Little came along, Coca-Cola made soft drinks and General Motors made cars. Everybody stuck to their specialty and produced one kind of thing. Little reversed this equation. By conglomerating, he found Textron could increase its market capitalization and make its shareholders a lot of money very quickly without necessarily having to increase its profit margin. So long as Textron kept eating more and more companies (or, in some cases, smaller conglomerates), it didn't seem to matter how much debt he had to take on to do it. None of this happened by accident; low-interest rates and the Celler-Kefauver Act, which curtailed companies from growing through the acquisition of their competitors or suppliers, created the perfect conditions for Little to indulge his addiction to leveraged buyouts.

The practice of conglomeration Little began in the early 1950s came to dominate the U.S. economy in the '60s. Though the great conglomerators of this era – I'm thinking of James J. Ling of LTV and Harold S. Geneen of ITT – have mostly been forgotten, they changed American business forever. Whenever a CEO or economist talks about the need to diversify, they should be sure to thank Roy Little for the idea. I actually came up with a different word for it: de-worsification. In general, I think these conglomerates got worse and worse at making more and more.

When I joined Textron in 1954, I didn't care about de-worsification, I just wanted to make textiles, and Roy Little was willing to pay me a hell of a lot more than Roger Milliken to do it: $55,000 a year plus stocks and bonuses.

Roy had just merged Textron with Robbins Mills and my old rival, American Woolen Company, and I got the idea to convert one of the plants Textron acquired – Raeford Mill in North Carolina – from wool to blended fabrics. But when I looked around the company, we realized nobody at Textron knew anything about worsteds, except me. All the people in the American Woolen Company were still living in the past (remember, these were the naysayers who had tried to stop my Viracle). They didn't know anything about making blends, and they didn't want to. Which meant I had to find people who did.

Where did I go? I went back to the team I'd built for Milliken. I convinced Red Hines, the head of manufacturing, to come with me. Hines persuaded four of his top people to come with him. Then I poached Greg Staff, my number one sales associate. In six months, I stole six people away from the company that had just fired me.

Perhaps the single biggest reason I was able to lure the fellows away from Milliken was that Textron could offer stock. Roger never wanted anybody to own Deering Milliken stock outside of his own family. This was another consequence of being such an insulated family company: they never went public. I did own some stock at one time, but it was a rare case and I had to beg him for it. I made him sell me some of his personal stock. That's why I knew that as soon as I got my own business, I would share.

The fallout of my mini-exodus was dire for Deering Milliken and the entire Milliken family. Roger was so incensed that Dick Stroud had fired me and then lost half a dozen of his top guys that he fired Dick. Apparently he kept telling everyone, "Dick lost the only people I ever loved." Perhaps Roger hadn't been so keen on letting me go after all. None of this sat well with Roger's sister and Dick's wife, Joan. She and Dick became estranged from the Milliken family, and Dick and Roger didn't speak again for 30 years. See what the seeds of his nepotism wrought?

The feud between the Strouds and Millikens lasted for decades, reaching its apogee in 1987 when Dick's seven children tried to cash in their chips on the 17 percent stake they owned in Milliken & Company (as it was now called), which they had inherited from Joan. The story goes that the Strouds tried to sell their stock directly to Roger, but he wouldn't pay them enough for it (and knowing Roger, that was probably true). The kids got mad and tried to sell their stake to a buyer outside of the family – a competitor of Roger's, no less – so Roger sued them.

Suddenly, Roger had to face one of only two things in the world he was scared to death of: the first, of course, was a union; the second was to have anybody inquire about how he was doing financially. But I'll tell you how he was doing – he was filthy, stinkin' rich! Years later, in 1968, Deering Milliken bought Callaway Mills from Fuller Jr. When he made the sale, he took a check out of his pocketbook and filled it out for $65 million – didn't need to go to the bank.

Roger was notoriously secretive about his business, which you can be when you own everything. He never filed a report or anything. But now all kinds of litigation was filed and depositions taken. The Milliken civil war dragged on for five years, reaching all the way to the Delaware Supreme Court. In the end, Roger won outright, but not before his finances were put under a microscope. Roger claimed the conflict wasn't nearly as acrimonious as it appeared, which doesn't make a whole lot of sense to me: if I wanted to show my family I love them, I wouldn't take them to court!

All this was a direct result of Dick Stroud firing me. There's no question about it. I had embarrassed Roger. He had all the money in the world, and a Fortune 500 company that made great products, and yet I had come along and convinced his top people to jump ship for a second-rate operation. But Roger brought it on himself – he was greedy. Perhaps he didn't know that old philosophy, as simple as any other thing my mother and father taught me: it's better to give than to receive.

My Discreet Mistress

With the Raeford divisions of Textron now employing some of the top minds in textiles, we were dying to make something better than anything we'd done at Milliken. We looked at the Milliken fabrics, which we knew intimately, and thought about how they could be improved on a technical level. After two weeks, Red Hines, now the boss, said, "Hell, let's make it two 80's. It'll be a sensation. It's never been done before."

So we said, "Okay!"

"Two 80's" refers to the weight of the fabric (in grams per square meter). Milliken's fabric was two 45's, meaning if you made two 90's it would be twice as fine, because there would be twice as many units of yarn per yard. Though 80 wasn't quite 90, it was pretty darn close. This new fabric, which we named appropriately Raeford 280, would be more tightly woven, lighter, softer, and smoother than anything on the market. The only problem was none of us were exactly sure how to make it. This was a real crash course in product development. You always want to set the target high and then worry about execution later. We were still in the middle of trying to solve our problem when Raeford caught the eye of Spencer Love, Chairman of Burlington Industries, and the third genius of American textiles.

If Deering Milliken was Pepsi, then Burlington Industries Inc. was Coca-Cola. Like Roy Little, Spencer Love built his company steadily from a single mill into a massive company that owned hundreds of mills. Love was a generation ahead of me – a Harvard-educated World War I veteran with roots in both New England and North Carolina. His first cotton mill had been a dead duck and his second, located in Burlington, North Carolina, was barely staying afloat. That's when Love decided to take a chance on a brand new synthetic material called rayon. Needless to say, he struck gold.

From the late 1920s through the Second World War, Love's aggressive investment in synthetic yarns and swashbuckling expansions transformed Burlington Mills into a juggernaut. After the war, Burlington Mills became Burlington Industries Inc. as it gobbled every small family-owned mill it could, and soon became the largest textile manufacturing company in the world, not to mention the 48th largest company in the United States. If you were in textiles – hell, if you were in *business* – and you didn't admire the hell out of Spencer Love, you were probably unconscious.

About the time I became visible on his radar in 1956, Love had just acquired a huge group of worsted mills all over the East Coast, including Pacific Mills and some others. It didn't take long for Love to realize the woolen mills he'd bought weren't worth a damn. When he discovered my operation, he saw what he'd been missing and bought it from Little right away. Love told Little he believed he was acquiring the greatest worsted operation in the world. Then Love told me that if I worked for him, he would make me the president of Pacific Mills within a few months, which he did.

My team immediately repaid Love's faith in us by finally cracking our Raeford 280 conundrum. Our solution was to buy a special kind of superfine wool that only came from Australia. Sure enough, our new fabrics turned out lighter and more comfortable than anything we had ever done for our old boss Roger Milliken. In fact, Raeford 280 was the lightest fabric ever spun on the worsted system so far. I even designed a symbol for it, because a brand always needs a logo. My logo was inspired by Sputnik, which the Russians had put up in 1957, the same year our yarn came out.

I was lucky to have Love as a mentor, but he was demanding and extremely jealous of my time. One of the first things he told me when I arrived at Burlington in 1956 was that I didn't have time to play golf and that I should give it up. Love couldn't care less about my game: he was crazy about tennis, which he played every day. His instruction to give up my legal addiction posed a huge dilemma when Bobby Jones asked me to join Augusta National Golf Club in 1957.

After growing up with Bobby Jones as my personal hero, I got to know him well after the war. When I lived in Atlanta, out of pure coincidence I was neighbors with Bobby's daughter and son-in-law, Clara and Bill Black. Bobby sent me and my wife, Jeanne, sympathetic letters when he found out Jeanne had developed multiple sclerosis in the early 1950s. A close friend of Bobby's had MS, and he himself suffered from the incurable syringomyelia, which tragically confined the world's greatest golfer to a wheelchair. However, he maintained his grace and dignity throughout, right to the end. He understood better than anyone what my wife was going through, and his empathy brought us even closer. Bobby Jones was the greatest man

I have ever known in my life. Even if he had never picked up a golf club in his life, he still would have been a great man.

In constructing his "dream course," Bobby successfully infused Augusta with the spirit of the game – or rather his own spirit (though I would argue they're one and the same). In 1955, I had lunch with Bobby, who spoke very highly of an article about Augusta and the Masters that had just been published in a new Time, Inc. magazine called *Sports Illustrated*. At the time, I wasn't a subscriber, but I knew the writer – long-time *New Yorker* golf journalist Herbert Warren Wind. I wrote to Wind and asked him to send me a copy of his article, and indeed he eloquently captured the essence of Augusta:

"While testing a pro for all he is worth, the course, as was the aim of its co-designers, is the friend of the average golfer . . . [who] generally scores three or four shots lower than on his far less lengthy and lordly home layout." Wind argued that it isn't just its beauty, prestige, or originality that makes Augusta great. It is how it challenges every aspect of a player's physical and mental skill, while making the experience of the game more satisfying; rewards a strategic mind as much as physical brawn; and humbles the golfer's ego but inspires his imagination for creative shot-making. To quote Wind again, "Instead of instantly penalizing the player whenever he strays from the straight and narrow and appointed, a golf hole of strategic design (like Augusta's) offers a player several lines of attack, permitting him, as he judges his capacities and how the hole is playing that day, to choose conservative, mildly aggressive or audacious tactics." Herb Wind's stature in the world of golf journalism is unmatched, and that's why when Callaway Golf restored and re-released Bobby Jones's instructional films in the 1980s, I reached out to him to advise us on the project, as the foremost authority on American golf and a fellow admirer of Bobby's.

But for now, imagine: the greatest golfer of all time – my hero and now my good friend – had invited me to become a member of the club that hosted the world's greatest golf tournament on what was arguably the world's greatest golf course, which he and Cliff Roberts had created in 1932 . . . in my home state, for God's sake!

Nevertheless, I turned down Bobby Jones and Cliff Roberts because my boss told me that my career was more important than the game of golf.

But I'll be honest: Spencer had a point. Augusta, for all of its enchantments, is only open a few months out of the year; I would almost never make it down there to play anyway; and the rest of the year I would be constantly hounded by people trying to wrangle an invitation.

And I'll be honest a second time: I never did quit golf as Spencer commanded, I just didn't tell him about it. In fact, that year my wife Jeanne and I won the Mixed Doubles Club Championship at our home course, Wee Burn Country Club, in Darien, Connecticut. I was also already a member of Pine Valley Golf Club in New Jersey and joined the new Eldorado Country Club in Indian Wells, California. But I was married to Burlington Industries, with the unconquerable game as my discreet mistress.

Now, 40 years later, as the Callaway of Callaway Golf (and not the Callaway of LaGrange, Georgia), and being fortunate enough to know a few members, I am occasionally invited to play Augusta as a guest before or after the Masters Tournament for a ceremonial round. In fact, two months ago I revisited this sacred ground and hit a few balls. As usual, I didn't keep score. I just hit 'til I was happy.

"The King of Pantyhose"

In 1960, I was elected vice president of Burlington and president of its Pacific Mills division. I rose rapidly through the corporate ranks during the 1960s, which might've been the only steady thing about that decade. My tumultuous decade began with my Alabama divorce from Jeanne in January of 1960 and near-simultaneous marriage to Jane Atkins. When I had arrived at Burlington in '56, about the only people who knew anything about Burlington were in the industry. I set about changing that. I wanted the public at large to know the name Burlington as a consumer-facing brand. The first way I did it was through the production and merchandising of the next evolution in women's hosiery. This product arrived on the scene in 1959 – just in time for the "culture decade."

An inventor and husband named Alan E. Gant got the idea to take a pair of nylon stockings that came up to a woman's thigh ("hose") and sew them onto a pair of panties and give them to his wife. On that day, pantyhose were born. They were sleeker, finer, more flattering, and more comfortable than any women's hosiery that had ever come before. This single product helped transform Burlington from a business-to-business company into a consumer product company.

When people saw Burlington pantyhose in the department store or in a television ad or in a magazine, that meant something to them; they associated it with the highest-quality products and with the modern, liberated woman. And for the men, we manufactured and marketed Burlington-branded socks. It was a remarkable transformation, marred only by the sudden passing of Spencer Love from a heart attack in 1962. Fittingly, the third genius of textiles died as he lived: on the tennis court.

Since Burlington was now a consumer-facing company, by 1964 I figured we ought to have a Director of Consumer Affairs. To find the right person for the job, I went right to the White House. No, I'm not talking about then First Lady Mrs. Lady Bird Johnson – though she did sit on the board of the Burlington House Interior Design Awards, along with Dina Merrill, the actress and arts advocate; Mary Lasker, the philanthropist and health activist; and future First Lady Nancy Reagan. I picked Letitia Baldridge. Tish (as everybody called her) had just been Jackie Kennedy's chief of staff and social secretary. There was no woman – besides maybe Marilyn Monroe – as influential on the tastes and style of women in the 1960s as Jackie Kennedy, and I knew that whoever planned and executed her galas, luncheons, and other social functions would be more than qualified to help Burlington engage with the American consumer.

Letitia Baldridge was the first woman executive in Burlington's history, and back then it was pretty unusual for a woman to have such a powerful position within a major corporation. I didn't give it a second thought: I picked her because she was the best. Baldridge, who stood 6 foot 1, was a sturdy, charming, and passionate woman. She later became a successful writer and America's preeminent authority on etiquette.

I wanted consumers to think of textiles as current, fashionable, and sexy – the expression of a young, energetic, and rapidly changing society. To do that, we worked with the artist Vera Neumann to create bold, colorful bed sheets (there didn't used to be much of a bed sheet business – sheets and T-shirts just came in white), and I hired the renowned graphic designer George Tscherny to make Burlington's annual reports. I increased our television ad spend tenfold, and dreamed up innovative new ways to market our brands. My marketing initiatives earned me the affectionate nickname The King of Pantyhose (my apologies to Allen E. Gant).

The great wine consultant André Tchelistcheff once asked me to describe exactly what Burlington Industries did and how large we were, and I told him, "Well, anything that's on you, it's me. Starting from your shirt, your tie, your jacket; and you're going to sit on the chair, which is me, and the rug is me." I could've given all sorts of facts and figures on market shares, stock prices, profit, the 149 plants we owned, or the 80,000 people we employed, but I think what communicated our place among corporations perhaps better than anything was Burlington's sponsorship of *The Ed Sullivan Show.*

The Ed Sullivan Show began in 1948 and was broadcast live every Sunday night until 1971, overlapping almost entirely with my career in textiles – another lucky coincidence in a life full of them. As the head of corporate advertising, I convinced Burlington to create a national ad campaign that was showcased every week on *The Ed Sullivan Show.* The campaign was produced by the legendary advertising firm Doyle Dane Bernbach (who also created the "A Man You Can Lean On" campaign for Klopman, one of our top divisions) and featured a new company logo and brand identity designed by Chermayeff & Geismar.

Every ad began or ended with a rapid-fire animation of a textile weave pattern against a heart-pounding, driving backbeat that evoked the sound of both the machinery in a textile mill and unremitting corporate energy. The baritone voiceover intoned: "If it's anything to do with fabric, we do it at Burlington. And we do more of it than anyone in the world." Never have socks been given greater standing. These commercials generated billions of memorable impressions on the American consumer, introduced the world of textile manufacturing to a mass audience, and made Burlington into a household name. We became one of the best-known companies to the American public, alongside Coca-Cola, Ford, and Campbell's Soup.

Seems Like Just Yesterday

The year 1965 was the height of Beatlemania. Sullivan had ignited it in America the year before with three appearances by The Beatles in rapid succession in '64 and '65. The Fab Four made their fourth appearance on August 14, 1965. Because Burlington was the principal sponsor of *The Ed Sullivan Show,* I was given backstage passes for me and my three kids, Reeves, Nicholas, and Lisa.

Photography was another one of my great passions, and I brought my Hasselblad 500c camera along with me because I wanted to capture what I knew was a historic event. My sister Bessie Walker was a photo-journalist, not quite as famous as Dorothea Lange or Margaret Bourke-White, but very talented, and I have always made home movies and taken still pictures (which you can see in this book).

I was photographed on three occasions by the Canadian master portraitist Yousuf Karsh, who then became a good friend. I was able to turn the tables on him when he agreed to let me take portraits of him and his wife, Estrellita. I also greatly admired Edward Steichen, whose landmark exhibition at The Museum of Modern Art, *The Family of Man,* had a big impact on me and a lot of other people – it was the most widely seen photography show in the world. I made a pilgrimage up to Redding, Connecticut (not far from my home in New Canaan), and took portraits of Steichen and his wife, Joanna.

Perhaps my most thrilling moment as an amateur photographer was November 8, 1963, when I attended a dinner at the New York Hilton sponsored by the Protestant Council of New York. President John F. Kennedy was the guest of honor that night, receiving the "Family of Man Award." I kept the Hasselblad loaded and ready and at the beginning of the dinner, I went up to the dais and snapped three rolls of photos of the president while he spoke with friends. I must've been standing about 17 feet from President Kennedy, watching the great man through my 150mm Carl Zeiss lens. I called the photos "Profile of Courage." I believe they were some of the last portraits taken of Kennedy before he was assassinated exactly two weeks later.

But back to The Beatles. We arrived at CBS Studio 50 before the sound check. The theater was mostly empty, so my kids and I took up a spot in the orchestra pit right in front of the stage. A few minutes later, the Fab Four walked out. As Paul, John, George, Ringo, and the CBS crew fiddled and fudged with the sound balance, I picked up my Hasselblad and started taking pictures. They practiced their entire set, which included a beautiful, melancholic song by Paul that my kids and I didn't recognize. We stuck around for the dress rehearsal that afternoon and then the live performance in the evening.

The Beatles' final performance on *Ed Sullivan* was broadcast a month later on August 14. The set included their chart-top-ping hits like "I Feel Fine" and "Ticket to Ride," drowned out by a chorus of hundreds of screaming girls in the live studio audience (tens of millions more were screaming from their homes). The screaming was still out of control when George stepped up to the microphone and said, "Thank you very much – We'd like to carry on now with a song from our new album in England, and it'll be out in America shortly. And it's a song featuring just Paul, and it's called 'Yesterday.' "

The lights went down except for a spotlight on Paul. The crowd of screaming girls went dead silent, and Paul performed "Yesterday" on his left-handed Epiphone Texan acoustic guitar – the first performance of that song and the first time a Beatle had played solo in America. More than 70 million people watched Paul sing and saw the Burlington commercial that followed – the largest television audience in history.

A Mind Is a Terrible Thing to Waste

In 1970, I went to Atlanta to make a speech for the United Negro College Fund's Corporate Committee, of which I was the chairman. Unfortunately, about four hours before I was supposed to get up on my feet to talk, I wasn't on my feet, and I couldn't get up. Instead, I was flat on my back in the hotel room with a kidney stone. This was totally unexpected! I suppose no kidney stones are ever scheduled in advance, but I had never had one. Luckily, who should come to my rescue that morning but Vernon Jordan, the great civil rights lawyer and my dear friend. He came and picked me up out of my bed in Atlanta and took me to the emergency room at Piedmont Hospital at 8 a.m. Needless to say, I didn't get to the luncheon.

Still, I was determined to get there in spirit and voice. I persuaded Vernon and Joe Meehan, the Fund's head of public relations for their New York office, to bring me a tape recorder. They found one and stuck a little microphone in front of me, and I made a statement about the UNCF, why I thought it was important, and why the corporations of Atlanta should give it their money, and it was the best speech I ever made. There were two reasons why it was good. Number one, I believed in what I was saying. Number two, I'd had two shots of Demerol, and I felt like I'd had seven martinis.

My work with the UNCF was one of the great passions of my life. Growing up in small-town Georgia in the 1920s, I saw how poorly Black people were treated, and how they were deprived of civil rights and justice in the courts. My home state had long been a civil rights battleground in the field of education, ever since the founding of Atlanta University in 1865, the first historically Black college in the South. When my parents grew up, it was illegal for Blacks to pursue an education altogether. I was barely out of college during the infamous Cocking affair, when Eugene Talmadge, Georgia's son-of-a-bitch governor, fired a whole bunch of professors and administrators from the state's public universities for the sin of promoting racial equality.

The forever boiling cauldron of Georgia politics was reflected in my family. Cason Callaway's son, Howard "Bo" Callaway, was a Southern Democrat who switched to the Republican party when the Democrats, led by Bo's political rival Jimmy Carter, began supporting desegregation in the early 1960s. Bo became the first Republican to represent Georgia in Congress since Reconstruction. I liked Bo as a friend and relative, but we sat on opposite sides of the political fence. I am a lifelong liberal Democrat, aligned with my friends and fellow Georgians Vernon Jordan, Senator Sam Nunn, Mayor Andrew Young, and Morris B. Abram, Sr. Morris, a brilliant attorney who fought for decades to desegregate public schools in our home state, became chairman of the UNCF in 1970, the same year I met Vernon.

Vernon could count himself among the true heroes of the civil rights movement, particularly in the field of education. He began the decade by helping integrate the University of Georgia and ended it as Executive Director of the UNCF. The UNCF was founded in 1944 by Dr. Mary Jane McLeod Bethune, William J. Trent, and Dr. Frederick Douglass Patterson, to raise money for historically Black colleges. And yet for decades, the institution was managed by white business leaders, such as John D. Rockefeller, Jr. That all changed when Vernon took over. From that moment forward, Black leaders ran the UNCF, and had total control over how it raised and allocated funds. By that point, I was president of Burlington Industries, and Vernon knew about my initiatives at Burlington to recruit employees from Black colleges. When Vernon asked me to chair the UNCF's Corporate Committee, I immediately agreed.

As chair of the Corporate Committee, I made calls, wrote letters, traveled, solicited their executives to join the cause, including GE chairman Richard Gerstenberg, and committed significant Burlington Industries resources to raise money for the UNCF. I worked closely with Vernon to convince the heads of all the major companies in America to donate to our fund, and the two of us became very close. We have golfed together for decades after, and Vernon serves on the board of directors for Callaway Golf – as a matter of fact, I think Vernon might've served on more corporate boards than any man in America. But most of all, he was the kind of friend who picked you up when you were lying in a hospital bed in excruciating pain.

When Burlington began recruiting talent from UNCF campuses in 1963, we were in really bad shape in terms of the talent we needed. That year, we had only 1,600 minority workers in all categories, from wage earners all the way up to executives, representing about three percent of our employees. There was one Black employee in a managerial role. We had zero Black employees on our technical staff. On our sales staff, we had two. That's not something I was proud of.

Donations to the Fund increased throughout the decade, as the civil rights movement placed significant pressure on the business world to support economic equality for the Black community, but those contributions were not nearly enough and arrived far too slowly. In 1970, the UNCF Corporate Committee raised over $3.5 million from 5,000 corporations, a record at the time. But there were 65,000 corporations in America, all of which benefited to some degree from what the UNCF did, meaning 60,000 of them didn't pay a nickel. Meanwhile, efforts to desegregate public schools through busing programs were being met with challenges in the courts and brutal violence in the streets.

My job was to be a salesman for the UNCF: take the messaging Vernon and the leadership developed and help tell their story to deep-pocketed corporations. The predominantly Black schools in the UNCF had long maintained that the schools were deserving, that they turned out good graduates, and that they needed money desperately. It was easy to back up these arguments with facts. In 1970, UNCF schools gave the best value per dollar of any schools in the country. Forty percent of UNCF college graduates went onto graduate studies, and 10 percent of Black PhDs came from UNCF colleges.

Black students went to both historically white and to Black colleges, but it was at the Black colleges where a higher percentage of the incoming freshmen graduated. At least at that time, the best conditions to nourish and develop young Black men and women still occurred at Black colleges, and yet they got less than one percent of what corporations gave to higher education and less than three percent of what the federal government gave from tax dollars. Most of the UNCF colleges didn't have endowments of $1 million, and some barely had endowments at all.

Then in early 1971, the U.S. Department of Labor released a report that by 1980 white-collar occupations would account for 50 percent of all jobs in the country. Professional occupations would be the fastest-growing areas, particularly in the sciences and technology. Five million more people would be needed to work in these categories, and a lot of them would be in government. There was a great need for executives, administrators, those with professional and technological skills, and the whole gamut of experts to meet the challenges of ecology, space, inner cities, poverty, and peace. For too long, Black higher education had not been considered an input source for these professions. These shifting economic realities gave the UNCF the opportunity to debut a new message.

In the early part of '72, I went down to Raleigh, North Carolina, to pitch the business leaders of that community on why they ought to donate to the UNCF. I asked them to consider what the UNCF schools offered: 40 institutions and 45,000 students; some 6,700 undergraduate and graduate degrees every year; trained engineers turned out by Clark, Morehouse, Morris Brown, and Spelman; human resources specialists from the Tuskegee Institute; communications experts from Shaw and Bishop; Atlanta University's social workers; Dillard's nurses; Xavier's pharmacists. There were thousands of skilled people coming out of these schools, and they belonged in America's corporations.

I told the North Carolina executives that when Burlington started to recruit with intention on UNCF campuses and learned about what their students could do for us, we improved. By the end of 1971, we had 75 Black executives; in professional, we had 40; in technical, we had 36; in sales, we had 23. We had 13,187 Black employees at Burlington, about 18 percent of our total workforce. Still not great, but an improvement. A young man named Clarence Finley became the divisional president of our Carpeting Division, and he was so good that 18 months later we promoted him to vice president. These figures were meaningful particularly because we believed they were good for our company. It wasn't just altruism; it was good business.

The United Negro College Fund had never been so important or so relevant. Its new advertising slogan, coined by its new president, affirmative action champion Arthur Fletcher, began to appear on television, in newspapers, in transit ads, and on bumper stickers: "A mind is a terrible thing to waste." The copy read, "There are people born every day who could cure disease, make peace, help our cities, abolish injustice, and end poverty, but if they don't get an education they may never get the chance."

The corporate committee changed its emphasis. We were not only saying you should support the UNCF because it's nice or right or just, or because it might give you a good feeling. Those things were still true, but now our message became: "Support us because it helps *you* and because it makes *us* better people." I believed then, as I do now, that good ethics is good business. So long as I was at Burlington, I was going to do everything I could to make sure our company lived up to that creed.

*"As usual, I didn't keep score.
I just hit 'til I was happy."*

CHAPTER 4

THE MADISON MATTER

The Secret I've Never Told That Forced Me to Start Over at the Age of 53

A House Divided

By the end of 1967, I was at the top of a Fortune 50 company at the height of America's post-war boom. I had grown up in a textile family in a textile town; then secured clothing for our effort in the Second World War – running the equivalent of a multi-billion-dollar business in my twenties; then been mentored in the '50s by the three geniuses of the American textile industry, Roger Milliken, Roy Little, and Spencer Love. Throughout the 1960s, I rose through the ranks of Burlington Industries: a vice president in 1960; an executive vice president and member of the Management Committee the following year; on the board of directors in 1965. Finally, in February 1968, I became president of Burlington Industries.

This was the culmination of everything I had been working toward in my career as a textile man and industrialist. Along with steel, oil, and automobiles, textiles were one of the great heavy industries of America, and I was second in command of the largest textile giant in the world. My predecessor, Charles Myers, had been appointed president and CEO in 1962 after Spencer Love died suddenly. Charles was promoted to chairman at the exact same time I became president, and he led me to believe that he would serve for five to eight years, accept the company-mandated retirement when he turned 65 in 1976, and then I would succeed him as CEO and Chairman of Burlington. The pantheon of corporate America was finally within my reach, and I was determined that nothing would stop me.

Looking back, the seeds of my own destruction were planted before I ever became president. Burlington was a house divided. We had two corporate offices: Burlington House, a still-under-construction New York City skyscraper designed by the great Emory Roth; and the first corporate headquarters in Greensboro, North Carolina, established by the founder Spencer Love around 1936. As the two top executives at the company, Charles Myers and I embodied this difference. Charles handled the financial side of the company and maintained his office in Greensboro, where he'd grown up. Meanwhile, I handled day-to-day operations and was the driving force behind the creation of the 50-story Burlington House corporate headquarters at 1345 Avenue of the Americas.

When the building opened in 1970, we had truly arrived. We were among the giants of corporate America who built gargantuan, block-long monuments to themselves in the International Style on Sixth Avenue (aka Avenue of the Americas) between 42nd Street and 57th Street, a corridor that became known as Skyscraper Alley: Raymond Hood's Rockefeller Center in 1933 between 48th and 51st; Eero Saarinen's CBS headquarters, "Black Rock," in 1965, at 51 W. 52nd Street; Wallace Harrison's Time-Life Building, still under construction at 1271 Sixth Avenue and 51st Street; and his just-completed buildings for Standard Oil Company at 1251 Sixth Avenue and 50th Street, and McGraw-Hill, located at 1221 Sixth Avenue and 49th Street.

For 10 years in the 1960s, on the way to work, I would pass a blind man named Moondog. Dressed in full Viking regalia, replete with his horned helmet, he loomed over seven feet tall. Every day, Moondog would stand sentinel with his staff in front of CBS's Black Rock at the southeast corner of 52nd Street, facing Burlington House across the street, and sing and chant his poetry. I never understood what he was singing about, but he was a mystical, Homeric presence amidst the frenetic energy of midtown. What was he trying to tell us? I didn't know, but I usually gave him a crisp new $2 bill, because I assumed that he must be mad. It was only years later I learned that Moondog was in fact a pioneering composer, musician, and poet and a legend of the New York avant-garde since the 1940s, who collaborated with an incredible array of musicians, including Arturo Toscanini, Julie Andrews, Leonard Bernstein, Janis Joplin, and Philip Glass. We had both arrived in New York in the late 1940s, and one day in 1972 I noticed that Moondog was no longer manning his daily post (he moved to Germany and never returned). Little did I know that my days on Avenue of the Americas were also numbered.

Burlington House felt like the center of the universe, and in many ways it was: just a hop, skip, and a jump from Rockefeller Center, where for years I had taken my young children, Reeves, Nicholas, and Lisa, ice-skating followed by Broadway shows – from the premiere of *The Sound of Music* with Mary Martin and Theodore Bikel in 1959 to *Hair* in 1968. I was a member of the University Club at 54th and Fifth, one block from Burlington House. And after a one-martini lunch (extra-dry with Beefeater Gin, with a twist and three olives, in an ice-cold glass), I would walk west past The Museum of Modern Art on 53rd Street back to the office, or take a detour and stroll a couple of blocks north to Tiffany's at 57th and Fifth, where I was very well known to the their salespeople. I was a regular at the Four Seasons Restaurant in the Seagram Building, Gallagher's Steakhouse, the Oyster Bar at The Plaza, the 21 Club, and the Hemisphere Club in the Time & Life Building. A decade later I would go from VIP customer to salesman, convincing the sommeliers of New York's finest establishments to take a gamble on Callaway Wines. Throughout the '60s, I had two New York addresses: first, a penthouse apartment at 420 E. 55th off Sutton Place South, where I loved to grow roses on the terrace; and 58 W. 58th Street, once Burlington House opened.

Since I was the biggest textile merchant in the world, I was always checking out the goods and buying the latest menswear (or women's fashion for my wives) from the great New York department stores like Saks Fifth Avenue, Bergdorf Goodman, Bloomingdale's, Bonwit Teller, Macy's, and Brooks Brothers.

Whether in the office, out for the evening, or on the golf course, I always paid great attention to how I dressed, and was known for my sartorial style.

Burlington's CEO and chairman, and my boss, Charles Myers, and I were also men with different temperaments and personalities. He was a former banker – an old-fashioned, soft-spoken Southern gentleman, but cool and calculating. I was a product creator, a marketing man, and a merchant. I was passionate and outspoken and chafed under hidebound corporate hierarchies. I hated bureaucracy, committees, and basically having anyone tell me what to do. I suppose my colleagues and rivals in the big corporate world thought of me as an attention-grabbing maverick and showboater who always wanted to be in the limelight.

The northern and southern headquarters also represented opposing corporate philosophies – centralized control versus decentralized management. I was and have always been for centralization. I believed the best way to run Burlington was for the New York–based executive team to have direct oversight over what *Daily News Record*'s Harry Jenkins called our "loose confederation" of divisions, which were spread all over the East Coast, particularly in the South.

These southern division heads, while being excellent factory managers, didn't have one iota of knowledge about the New York market, which was becoming increasingly driven by design, fashion, and style, rather than by materials, traditional or new. Our profits relied on anticipating and staying ahead of fashion trends, and fashion designers were beginning to determine what people wore, not manufacturers (as they had when Roger Milliken and I created Viracle suits in 1954). Can you name any American fashion designers from the 1950s? Exactly! There weren't any! On the other hand, can you name any designers of the late 1960s or '70s? Of course – Ralph Lauren, Calvin Klein, Bill Blass, and the others who spearheaded an American fashion and societal revolution.

I had to steer Burlington from being a giant business-to-business industrial manufacturer to being a nimble, consumer-facing company, at the precise moment when society and consumer tastes were changing profoundly and rapidly, and this required a dramatic shift in how, where, why, and for whom textiles were being manufactured. In my opinion, this change could only be achieved through strong, central management. And this approach won me a lot of enemies. For what it's worth, my philosophy reflected that of Spencer Love, who had imposed on his far-flung empire a highly centralized structure, with his hands in every single aspect of the business. If Roger Milliken taught me how to make innovative products, Spencer Love taught me how to build and run a large company.

When Charles Myers took over, however, he adopted a policy of decentralization. Charles and his Greensboro, North Carolina "Garden Club" (as the New York executives called them), granted more autonomy to the heads of increasingly sprawling divisions, which now included home furnishings, carpeting, upholstery, rugs, and apparel. The controller's office served as a check and balance ensuring (or at least attempting) a steady and accurate flow of information between the division heads and the executives. There were some major players among the division heads – independently minded men like Horace Jones, George Staff, Ray Kassar (the future CEO of Atari), and Bill Klopman, Jr., another pioneer in synthetic fabrics, whose father founded Klopman Mills. The Garden Club argued that with enough diversification, Burlington needn't worry about the rapidly changing winds of fashion and decor. If one mill's product fell out of favor and began losing money, another was bound to step up and fill the profit gap. The theory went: if you make everything, you're bound to sell *something.*

Despite this North vs. South rivalry, I believed Charles and I had a very positive relationship based on mutual respect and working toward a common goal. Every week or two I left our New York headquarters and took the corporate jet down to Greensboro, about as often as Charles came up to Manhattan. Our offices in Burlington House were across from each other, with the company boardroom separating us.

Still, in the spring of 1968, I hedged my bet and bought 134 acres of land in a desolate part of southern California near Palm Springs, where I planned on planting about a hundred acres of wine grapes. But I better leave that story for later.

"Y" and the "Big Question"

On July 3, 1968, only five months into my presidency, I was at my Connecticut home for what should have been a long and relaxing Independence Day weekend when I got a call from Burlington's general counsel, Bob Lynn. He relayed urgent instructions from Doug Orr, Burlington's assistant general counsel and Charles Myers's right-hand man. Orr instructed me to drive immediately to the Stamford train station, where a special messenger handed me a five-page legal document from the Federal Trade Commission, titled Agreement Containing Consent Order to Cease and Desist.

A consent decree is an agreement between a private company and the FTC ordering the company to stop doing something illegal or unethical. I had a general notion that the FTC had been looking into our purchase of Erwin Textile Company from six years earlier, but that's about as far as my knowledge of the matter went. Investigations by the FTC were not totally uncommon. Burlington had spent the better part of two decades acquiring hundreds of family-run mills, and the FTC's purpose was to curb potentially monopolistic activity.

I was given only 10 minutes to review the document before the messenger took it back to New York. As president, I put my signature on dozens of documents every day, and while this consent decree was certainly odd, there was nothing obvious to suggest it was more than an administrative formality.

I took a copy of the consent decree home for my personal records. That night, when I gave the document a closer read, the outline of a much broader investigation appeared. The first paragraph of the decree read, "It is ordered that for a period of ten years following the effective date of this Order, Burlington Industries, Inc. shall cease and desist from acquiring directly or indirectly, through subsidiaries or otherwise, without prior approval of the Commission the whole or any part of the stock or other capital of any Textile Mill Production Company in the United States."

As I read further, I realized the FTC wasn't looking just into the Erwin deal, but into a series of large acquisitions apparently going all the way back to 1950, a decade before the purchase of the Raeford divisions of Textron, the deal that had brought me to Burlington in the first place. If Burlington agreed to sign the consent decree, it meant the FTC had determined that Burlington violated the anti-trust Clayton Act. As part of signing the order, the company neither confessed guilt nor claimed innocence, and no legal or financial penalties were imposed. The consent decree closed the book on the FTC's investigation, but only on the explicit condition that Burlington would stop acquiring new textile mills. Burlington was being let off the hook with a stern warning.

The consent decree outlined an investigation of remarkable size, scope, and duration, one that I, the president of the whole darn company, was unaware of. This document now had my signature on it, and only my signature, with two lines below designated for a couple of Burlington's attorneys – James H. Rowe Jr. (who'd been a co-architect of the New Deal and a political advisor to Hubert Humphrey) and Herbert A. Bergson. Neither lawyer had yet signed, and no other officer of the company was being asked to sign at all, which made me solely responsible and liable for Burlington's actions. Furthermore, I was being railroaded – literally – by being pressured to review, sign, and return the agreement in minutes, while the courier waited next to me at the station.

Consent agreements normally follow a period of negotiations, and I wanted to know what exactly had been negotiated on my behalf. I contacted Burlington's previous chairman, the recently retired Henry Rauch, who just so happened to live nearby (in those days, almost everybody of a certain level in corporate America had a home in the Connecticut suburbs). I asked Henry if he wouldn't mind showing me Burlington's history of correspondence with the FTC. I think he was surprised I'd spent my Independence Day weekend on legal matters, but he obliged my curiosity with a memo written by Doug Orr.

The memo summarized Burlington's responses to various FTC questionnaires going all the way back to 1960 concerning our history of mergers and acquisitions since 1954. I had no idea this memo existed.

In the memo, Doug disclosed our ownership of Pacific Mills (where I had run a division 10 years earlier), Erwin Mills, and just about every other significant acquisition I could think of, with the exception of one: Madison Throwing Company. Dalton McMichael had co-founded Madison Throwing Company with C. T. Sutherland in 1947, shortly after beginning his career in textiles as an accountant for Burlington right after the war. McMichael built his North Carolina nylon maker into one of the top 25 textile companies in the country. Burlington had held stock in Madison for years before finally obtaining a majority position back in 1959. I could tell that most of Burlington's replies to the questionnaires were misleading in their omission of Madison. Its absence was glaring and incredibly concerning. I knew that at the very least we had been something less than honest with the FTC.

It became clear that our consent order had been negotiated and settled without the FTC negotiating group knowing that we had omitted Madison. I also realized that as president, I had signed a document on behalf of Burlington that the government – if they knew all the facts – would probably claim was negotiated in bad faith. Burlington was engaged in a kind of cover-up, and Charles Myers – the CEO, chairman, and my boss – was trying to make me the fall guy, which potentially could place me in legal jeopardy. This consent decree was the smoking gun, and now my fingerprints were all over it.

Over the next four days of vacation, I thought about Madison and the many problems that might arise from our history of non-disclosure. The scandal could shake the company down to its foundations, not to mention the life I'd built over the past 23 years. If this were to break wrong, it could lead, at worst, to serious legal consequences for everyone involved. At the very least, it would be a public humiliation for Burlington, for its executives, and for me personally. The FTC could sue us or try to break up the company, our stockholders might get offended and flee, I could lose my job, my reputation could be wrecked, and since 98 percent of my wealth was tied up in Burlington stock, the vast majority of my accumulated wealth could vanish.

I decided to write a letter to Charles Myers, Doug Orr, Henry Rauch, and Stephen L. Upson, another former member of the Roosevelt administration and Burlington's vice-chairman of the board. These were the only four men who I believed knew about this Madison matter. I stated explicitly and for the record that when I signed the consent order I had not been told the facts about our non-disclosure of Madison, and I certainly didn't know that the company had sent misleading reports to the FTC. If I'd known these facts, I would never have signed the order.

Then I laid out the two things I thought we needed to do next. The first was to seek the advice of outside legal counsel who could give us an objective, comprehensive assessment of what the legal repercussions might be from our failing to disclose Madison. The second and more important step was to immediately disclose our ownership of Madison to the FTC, or at the very least disclose it in our annual report. It was my strong conviction that by not disclosing Madison at the earliest possible time, we were digging our trap even deeper and increasing the likelihood of trouble with shareholders and the Justice Department. If we made the disclosure now, the FTC would likely cancel the Erwin deal, but that was likely the worst that would happen, and still highly preferable to whatever might result if we kept Madison a secret.

But to my great shock, Charles, Stephen, Henry, and Doug all immediately dismissed my concerns and insisted that we were in no legal jeopardy. Their justification for this cavalier attitude was that the consent decree only dealt with the FTC's inquiry into our purchase of Erwin, which made any mention (or not mention) of Madison irrelevant.

In all our correspondence about this, they referred to Madison only by the code name "Y." They didn't use the words "non-disclosure" or even "consent decree," instead calling it the "Big Question." At the risk of being too obvious: if someone says something isn't a big deal, but only refers to that thing in secret code, chances are it's actually a pretty damn big deal.

I insisted that we sit down and discuss my fears out in the open. No matter what the problem, I've always believed I could solve it through conversation. We were all sensible people, after all. On July 14, I had dinner with Charles and Doug at the University Club. They reiterated that because the decree I signed had nothing to do with "Y" or anything but our acquisition of Erwin, we were not in any danger. I explained to them that even if the law didn't explicitly require us to disclose (which I doubted), then at the very least Burlington's stockholders had a right to know about something as important and significant as us owning Madison.

Over the course of the dinner, I observed Doug and Charles repeatedly shift responsibility for the Madison matter. When I suggested we seek the advice of Herbert A. Bergson, another attorney for Burlington whose signature was on the consent decree just below mine, they flatly refused. If this Madison business was so above board, why did nobody want to take credit for it or tell anybody else about it?

There was one more thing that bothered me: Doug's excuse for needing my signature, "that the FTC requested it." This was either a bald-faced lie or ridiculously stupid, considering I was never even a part of the negotiations. And the timing of the signing – both the holiday weekend and the 10-minute window – felt carefully orchestrated to maximize the likelihood that I wouldn't think too hard about what I was signing and wouldn't ask too many questions afterward.

Failure to Disclose

After that unproductive dinner, I continued to badger Charles about the reality of our situation. Everything I knew about what Burlington had told the FTC was in Doug Orr's memo, and I didn't trust him. I wanted to know exactly what the company's responses had been. Charles conceded and told our general counsel Bob Lynn to examine Burlington's records of its correspondence with the FTC, which Doug Orr kept in his office. Lynn learned that in the course of the FTC's investigation into Burlington's acquisition history, the commission had sent a questionnaire to Burlington on April 5, 1960. Item 8 of that questionnaire went approximately as follows: "Please list and briefly describe any acquisition your company may have made or mergers to which it may have been party within the last 25 years."

Burlington responded by listing nearly 20 separate acquisitions. But they did not list Madison Throwing.

On two other occasions – September 23, 1962, and October 23, 1964 – the FTC again asked Burlington for a list that should have included Madison, and three times Burlington did not disclose it. Why these omissions? Charles and Doug held firm to their hard-headed belief that these questionnaires were for inquiries unrelated to our acquisition of Erwin, and therefore had no bearing on our consent decree. I guess it didn't matter to them that Burlington included Erwin in one of our responses to a questionnaire that allegedly had nothing to do with Erwin. And their explanation didn't account for why Burlington hadn't disclosed Madison when we first took a majority position back in 1959. They had woven a tangled web in their practice to deceive, which had now ensnared all of us.

In November, the FTC released new guidelines for the textile industry. They expressed their desire to discourage the merger and acquisitions craze that had dominated our industry for the past 25 years. At the same time, the commission announced the terms of Burlington's consent decree, which officially allowed the purchase of Erwin and other mills to stand.

There was one more consequence to the FTC's announcements: a withering dissent from Commissioner Mary Gardiner Jones, who criticized her own organization's guidelines. She laid into what she felt was the hypocrisy of the FTC in allowing Burlington to acquire a company while at the same time making the way we acquired it illegal. She accused her own commission of having a different standard for Burlington than it did for more moderately sized textile companies, the ones she felt were actually hurt by anti-competitive monopolistic companies like Burlington. Jones was an anti-trust crusader and consumer advocate – not the kind of person you wanted to make your enemy.

In light of Jones's dissent, Charles had no choice but to finally bring our principal outside counsel Herb Bergson, whose signature was on the consent decree, into the circle of trust. Bergson was a former assistant attorney general in charge of the anti-trust division of President Truman's Justice Department, then resigned to start his own firm representing private interests in anti-trust suits, and was then swiftly indicted for violating a conflict-of-interest law (I think he got off on a technicality).

On December 2, Doug told Bergson about the Madison matter. We feared he'd quit and go running straight to Mary Gardiner Jones. Instead, Bergson reached out to the FTC on our behalf to ascertain the full scope of their investigation. As I had suspected from the beginning, the scope of the consent decree was never merely Erwin, but all Burlington acquisitions made from 1950 to 1968. Bergson concluded that even though it was not specifically investigated, the broadness of the FTC's inquiry meant that "Y" absolutely fell within the scope of their investigation.

Surely now, with all the facts laid bare before them, Charles and his men would have no choice but to admit I was right all along and disclose Madison in our annual report. But Bergson, while agreeing with my analysis, did not agree with my recommendation. He endorsed waiting until the following year to disclose Madison, hoping we could slip it past the FTC unnoticed. In the meantime, he recommended we sell Madison at the earliest possible date.

Now that my signature on the consent order had been made public, I was being given credit – by some inside the company and by a few outsiders – for my influence in obtaining such a favorable consent order for Burlington. This was the last thing I wanted any recognition for. The end of 1968 was fast approaching, and I felt nothing but dread.

I knew we had no business releasing an annual report which denied that we owned Madison. It was both immoral and stupid. Many people in our industry knew anecdotally that we owned Madison – competitors whose way of doing business would be impacted by the new FTC guidelines, and who had every reason to resent our sweetheart deal. If our enemies read the annual report, which listed every major division of the company except Madison, they might suspect, or even conclude, that Burlington hadn't told the FTC about it during our negotiations. They might even be inspired to go to Mary Gardiner Jones with what they knew. At that point, the FTC would probably begin to take action that would do the maximum harm to Burlington and the individuals involved, including me. But everyone else at the company who knew about Madison was against disclosure.

It is fascinating to see the way people respond in times of crisis. It's a test of our character. Most people won't call themselves out for violating the rules, as Bobby Jones had done. And when someone is caught in a lie, most people will deny it. They fear consequences and they fear the truth – I know I did. But the only solution when you tell a lie or make a mistake is to admit that you were wrong immediately and try to make it right. Of course, this carries its own risks, but the alternative is to perpetuate a lie, which usually requires telling an additional lie to justify the first one. That's what our annual report was: a lie to cover up a lie. The longer we waited, the more lies we would have to pile on top of each other to keep the whole thing going, and the harder it would become to finally tell the truth.

Nobody seemed to have a good answer for why we hadn't disclosed when the FTC first gave us the opportunity. But I suspect it began when Spencer Love made the decision not to divulge Madison way back in April 1960, and he set the precedent for his successor Henry Rauch and now for Charles Myers.

This was a hard pill for me to swallow. I had revered Spencer Love. He was a father figure to me, but he did not do the right thing when he failed to report an acquisition to the shareholders of our public company. I don't know Love's reasons, but I will go to my grave wondering to what extent Love was complicit in the Madison matter going back to 1960. Did he know that his acquisition of Madison would run afoul with the FTC, and might that have been the reason he chose to reveal nothing about it?

Doug Orr floated the idea of shifting blame for Burlington's misleading negotiations back to Spencer Love, even though he had been six feet under for six years – an idea so preposterous that even Charles couldn't get behind it. It would be great if all subsequent decisions and events and actions could be blamed on the dead. But we know better.

If only one of our lawyers had had the wisdom and the guts to speak up and convince Spencer Love to disclose Madison, it would have spared us a lot of trouble. But they hadn't spoken up. That was perhaps the thing I failed to understand at the time. My involvement in the Madison matter had not begun until the moment I unwittingly signed the consent decree. Charles, on the other hand, had been at least privy to this knowledge for years, and perhaps had been Love's enabler his entire career, as Burlington's head of finance in 1947 and Love's chosen successor as CEO in 1962. Charles wasn't about to change his M.O. (modus operandi) because of my M.O. (moral objections).

When Burlington released the 1968 annual report, it listed every one of the company's divisions except Madison. Charles promised me that we would disclose it in the first quarterly report of 1969, then in September, then in the next annual report. There was always some justification for kicking the can further down the road. And because none of our competitors raised hell with Commissioner Jones, the company's business carried on as usual.

Playing Chicken with Charles

The success of Charles's lies must've emboldened him. Otherwise, why would he have tried to buy the rest of Madison's stock in early 1970? By then, Burlington was losing its market share to cheaper products made by Japanese monopolies, and our profits were down across the board. We had seen this crisis looming on the horizon for well over a decade. In fact, I was one of the first people to sound the alarm about America's trade problem all the way back in 1959 (funnily enough, the same year Burlington had acquired Madison).

Charles's solution was to follow the Spencer Love playbook and continue to grow by swallowing up smaller mills. But while the consent order did technically allow us to acquire textile mills with the FTC's permission, in practical terms this was impossible. These circumstances frustrated the board of directors and the divisional heads who Charles counted on as allies. We could only expand through diversification, internally through the mills we already owned, or via international growth. This made acquiring the rest of Madison almost inevitable, except for the fact that the FTC didn't know it would be an internal expansion because they didn't know we owned it in the first place. If we had come clean about Madison back in '68, and if the FTC had allowed us to keep it, we probably could've bought the rest of it now without much trouble, but that was water under the bridge.

The plan to purchase the rest of Madison was Charles's most corrupt move yet. I implored him to contact the FTC for their permission before purchasing the rest of its stock. But he would've had to disclose that we already owned the majority, which he found unacceptable. See what I mean about one lie requiring another? I thought I had convinced Charles to disclose Madison in our first quarterly report of 1970, only for Doug and Bergson to talk him out of it at the last second. I couldn't sit by this time and let Charles continue unencumbered. I needed to respond.

Independent of the Madison fiasco, I had already taken measures to counter the Garden Club's decentralist agenda. I helped spearhead a broad restructuring of Burlington's management in January of 1970, which included establishing a New York–based executive committee to set and implement policy across the sprawling behemoth that Burlington had become. This committee was effective, but it drove a lot of the division heads nuts. The committee had 11 members: five vice presidents, three directors, Charles, Doug, and me. Three of the committee members – Vice President of Finance John Cave and outside directors Harry Knight and William T. French – were friends and allies who I knew would support me.

The establishment of this executive committee gave me the opening I needed to bring the Madison matter before top management. For the past 18 months, Charles had told me that I was blowing this whole mess out of proportion. I had privately and repeatedly urged him to allow Burlington's outside and inside directors and the rest of our executive committee to participate in our decision-making process for this terribly complex problem – a problem with far greater implications than our usual business decisions. I hadn't had much success. But I felt it was unfair to continue to withhold this secret from the executive committee. It was time to break our closed circle of trust.

I disclosed the full Madison saga to Harry Knight, Bill French, and John Cave. Understandably, they were incensed; I doubt any of our executives except for Charles and Doug truly understood the extent of this situation before I revealed it to them.

At the next executive committee meeting on February 11, Harry and Bill ambushed Doug Orr, who by this point had been appointed to the vital role of controller. They expressed their concerns over our failure to disclose Madison, and supported my idea to disclose Madison in our first quarterly report of 1970. They also insisted that at the very least we seek the objective opinion of outside counsel, for which I had been advocating since June of 1968, and which the company had still never truly done.

Charles just so happened to be on a two-week vacation in Jamaica and missed the meeting. When Doug told Charles what

Harry and Bill had pulled, Charles correctly suspected that I was the man who'd clued them in. Word quickly got back to me that Charles was not happy. All along, Charles had insisted that we keep the circle of people who knew about the Madison matter as tight as possible, and now I had opened that circle to include the entire New York executive committee. Doug clearly thought the idea of a new study was ridiculous and hoped the whole thing would have gone away by now, and Charles wasn't in favor of a new study either. Over the phone, he repeated his tired accusation that I was making something out of nothing. He criticized me for talking to Harry Knight and Bill French, something he should have done with all of Burlington's directors back in 1968 before negotiations for the consent decree were settled.

Nevertheless, the executive committee recognized the wisdom of my arguments and voted to disclose Madison. Doug Orr, Herb Bergson, Charles Myers, John Cave, and I adopted the following attachment to the annual report: "The company in late January made organizational changes in addition to those discussed in the annual report. Those included realignment of divisional reporting assignments for Atwater Throwing Co., Madison Throwing Co., United Furniture Co., and Globe Furniture Co. . . . These companies were previously operated on a relatively autonomous basis."

And there it was. Burlington finally slipped Madison Throwing Company into the middle of an amendment to its 1969 annual report, attributed the previous omission of Madison to "reorganization," and left it at that. The question now was: Would the FTC catch on? Or our stockholders? Or the employees of Madison Throwing Company, for God's sake?

After my move with the executive committee, my relationship with Charles was never the same. This now became a death match for the soul of the company. Either Charles or I could survive this stand-off, but not both. The events of early 1970 had brought into focus a dynamic I long suspected – Charles wanted to push me out of Burlington. Since the day Charles had been elevated to chairman, he saw me as his strategic antagonist within the company because I actively promoted a centralist agenda. Furthermore, I was known for doing whatever the hell I wanted, while he was the ultimate company man, having risen methodically through the ranks of Burlington for over 20 years by being Spencer Love's unfailingly loyal lieutenant.

It is my sincere belief that Charles was behind an intentional scheme to get my signature on that consent decree, thereby rendering me responsible and liable for the Madison matter. At the very least, Charles made a conscious decision to keep his signature *off* the consent decree. Charles never wanted to dirty his hands himself, so he had his bagman Doug Orr do it for him, setting me up as the fall guy. My efforts to appeal to Charles's sense of integrity were probably always going to be fruitless.

If I was to survive this, I needed proof positive that I'd been ignorant of this entire Madison business before I signed the decree. After much back and forth between Manhattan and Greensboro, I finally got from Charles the memo I had been demanding since July of 1968. In August 1970, Charles confirmed in an official memorandum that I had not personally participated in the negotiations with the FTC. My signing of the decree in my capacity as president was a mere matter of convenience for the company, "a purely ministerial act," as he wrote.

With Charles's indemnification in my hands, I focused my energy for the next two years on the UNCF, the U.S.-Japan trade issues, my fledgling vineyard in California, and a brand new interactive exhibition called "The Mill." Adjacent to the three-story lobby of Burlington House, and designed by the preeminent corporate branding and design firm of Chermayeff & Geismar, The Mill was one of the very first multimedia, immersive, interactive, edutainment experiences. In three sections, The Mill traced the history, manufacturing, and finishing of textiles, carrying visitors on a moving walkway past giant screens with a collage of photos and films, mirrors, and music. Nobody understood how textiles are made and how fascinating they are. I'm afraid in a lot of people's minds it was nothing but little old ladies working away on an assembly line. I wanted to give the general public an unforgettable experience that would bring textiles to a mass audience. It was my answer to Disney rides like GE's Carousel of Progress, which I remembered being impressed by at the 1964 World's Fair in Queens.

Mayor John Lindsay cut the ribbon on opening day, September 9, 1970, and for its first few years, The Mill was a blockbuster attraction in New York City, attracting 4,000 visitors per day – at times more than the Statue of Liberty, the city's number one attraction. Six million people visited The Mill during its decade-long run.

Burlington's marketing triumph was immediately followed by a truly stinkin' financial year. An industry-wide downturn in 1971 pummeled our profits and stock price. Meanwhile, our Japanese and European competitors were coming in fast with textured yarns, further eating into our sales and sparking an industry-wide shift from woven to knitted goods. To meet this sudden demand for knitted fabrics, textile companies bought knitted machinery at black market prices and faced delivery backlogs of 18 months to three years. I am glad to say I turned down all such offers to price gouge us. I beefed up our knitted operations, sure, but I didn't want to put all our eggs in one knitted basket. I believed the future of Burlington was a reasonable mix of both ways of making fabrics.

Burlington clawed through a sluggish recovery in 1972. Tensions between the executive committee and divisional heads were at an all-time high. I suddenly found myself pilloried for a litany of professional mistakes and personal misdeeds from unnamed sources: I faced criticism in the press for my "brashness and obvious belief in [my] own personality," which "appear inconsistent with a Southern-based textile company"; I was called a "marketing man" and a "showman" without enough business sense; I was taken to task for my personal life, including my impending divorce from my second wife, Jane. As one of my lieutenants opined when asked about my management style, "Let me put it this way: it was no democracy." It was even implied that I had lost focus because I had bought a vineyard in California in 1968.

In operational terms, I was blamed for being too slow to respond to the knit boom; I was criticized for my long-standing obsession with U.S.-Japan trade issues; and worst of all, I was dragged through the mud pushing this newfangled centralization.

These critics were usually identified by the press as something like "well-respected industry sources." I wondered who those "sources" could've been. A proxy war was being waged in the press, and a narrative began to take shape, driven home in a June 1972 exposé by *The New York Times*'s influential textile reporter, Isadore Barmash. Charles was given credit for virtually all of Burlington's successes, and I was held responsible for most of its failures.

Charles and I worked hard to maintain the appearance of a unified front and categorically denied all reports of a feud. Behind the facade, it was clear our relationship was cold, bitter, and distant. He took measures to rein in my independence, cut costs, further decentralize the company, and undermine me. My corporate public relations department was gutted, our television advertising budget slashed, our research center in Greensboro closed and all R&D reallocated to individual divisions, with several executives shown the door. Meanwhile, in 1971 he had opened a modern new corporate headquarters in Greensboro, designed by Arthur G. Odell – which I'm sure was a direct response to Burlington House. It was death by a thousand committees, cuts, and cutthroats.

But despite Charles's efforts to get me to resign, I had no plans on going anywhere. For one thing, I couldn't afford to resign. For another, I loved my job. I hoped I could outlast Charles in our game of corporate chicken. If I did, if I survived until Charles's pre-planned retirement, which was only a few years away, I believed I could still become chairman and run Burlington Industries the way I saw fit. I had a clear vision for the company, for the textile industry, and for American business. If I could only stay in the fight just a little longer, I wagered, I could still realize my vision. All I had to do was not blink first.

In the middle of all this, Bobby Jones had passed away after a long battle with syringomyelia on December 18, 1971. In the darkest moments of my life and career, my good friend and guiding light was gone.

Confidential and Privileged

On the morning of Tuesday, February 20, 1973, I walked a few blocks from my apartment in Tower 58 to my office at Burlington House. When I arrived, my executive assistant, Karen Stokes, informed me that Charles Myers, who was in town, had scheduled a meeting just between the two of us at 2 p.m. I thanked Karen and asked her to bring me a little piece of coffee cake, like I did every morning. I didn't think much about the meeting – Charles and I talked almost every day. I didn't even suspect anything when I first walked into his office. He had a famously cool manner about him, so it wasn't until he informed me he was giving me first notice about my breach of contract that it dawned on me: I was being fired.

Fired?! "With cause"?! Charles hoped I would resign quietly and save myself the public humiliation of being fired.

I replied, "I need to talk to my lawyer." Despite his gentlemanly demeanor, Charles could be a real son-of-a-bitch. Yes, he was chairman, but I don't think he would have had the wherewithal to fire me without having already lined up allies on the board of directors. If he successfully fired me for cause, I might not get a dime of severance. Charles had just seized the reins of power and held my net worth and my recently renewed five-year employment contract hostage. We were suddenly in the endgame.

Meanwhile, I was in the middle of divorce proceedings from my second wife, Jane, while still in litigation with my first wife, Jeanne. I was about to be on the hook for two alimony payments while already paying for the apartment of my new girlfriend Nancy (more on her in a bit!), and had put my New Canaan estate on the market to raise cash. Furthermore, I still had almost all of my net worth invested in Burlington stock and the rest in a patch of desert in Southern California, which had yet to produce a first vintage from the grapes I'd planted five years earlier. If Burlington's stock price suffered, and I was without a severance, I would face financial ruin. On top of all that, two of my three children were in college.

Charles wanted to move fast. He instructed me to fly immediately down to Washington, D.C., to meet with Walter L. Lingle Jr., former executive vice president of Procter & Gamble and outside member of Burlington's board of directors, whom Charles had already appointed chair of the search committee to find my replacement. Charles wanted to announce my replacement at the same time he announced my resignation, and he didn't want to give the press time to jump the gun and break the news.

I flew back to New York on Thursday night and met Cuz Hardee for lunch on Friday. I didn't mention the purpose of this meeting in my office desk agenda, which Karen kept. However, in my personal agenda, which I kept in my pocket, I wrote "severance" beside the entry. I didn't tell anybody that I had been fired, except for Cuz, but I wanted to be sure to continue my detailed off-the-record record of everything that was happening.

When I had first found out about Burlington's failure to disclose in the summer of '68, Cuz had urged me to keep a meticulous record at home of everything from then on. And by God, I heeded my friend and lawyer's advice. Over the next five years, I preserved every letter, both handwritten and typed, that

I had written to Charles about the Madison matter (including drafts I never sent), laying out in painstaking detail every conversation, meeting, and decision between Charles, me, Doug Orr, Henry Rauch, Bob Lynn, Herb Bergson, and anyone else involved. I kept a copy of documents regarding the FTC and relevant internal memos. I kept a copy of the consent decree. I kept a copy of Charles's memo indemnifying me from any knowledge or complicity in the consent decree negotiations. In my desk drawer at home was a 200-page truthful, accurate, and verifiable record of Burlington's cover-up. My conscience was clear that I had done everything to get Burlington to do the right thing, and I had the evidence of it.

Over the three-day weekend, Cuz and I held round-the-clock strategy meetings at his home in Connecticut. We put together the Madison dossier and devised our plan. In spite of how hurt I was by what Charles had done – over the past few days and the past five years – I did not want to seek vengeance or retribution against him or the company. I was ready to put this dirty business behind me, but by God, I wasn't about to be hornswoggled. There was no way I was going to let Charles fire me under false pretenses or take the fall, once again, for the company's malfeasance. Until the bitter end, I was determined to do the right thing.

But I was on the horns of a dilemma: if any of this conflict became public, it would almost inevitably result in mutually assured destruction for Charles, for myself, for the top management, and perhaps for the entire company, its 80,000 employees, and its shareholders. The two of us shared a desire to resolve this matter immediately but quietly.

Cuz and I set a meeting with Charles for Tuesday, February

27, exactly one week after I was fired. Once again, Charles did not have any lawyers in the room. Cuz calmly informed Charles that we totally rejected his claim that I had violated my employment contract. On the contrary, he said that Charles damn well knew that I had not only carried out my duties as president ethically and responsibly, but had devoted my entire life to the interests of the company. If Charles followed through with his bogus threat, we were prepared to contest it before the board. A civil war would break out in the boardroom between Charles and me. Then Cuz told Charles that ever since July 4, 1968, he had advised me to keep a detailed dossier, which we were prepared to submit as a matter of record at the next board meeting in a week's time.

Charles was flabbergasted. Cuz recommended that severance negotiations begin at once between us and Burlington's lawyers. Charles immediately agreed. We both affirmed that we shared a fiduciary responsibility to the stockholders and that we should do everything humanly possible to avoid hurting the company. This conversation was conducted in a very gentlemanly and cordial manner. But we both knew that everything was at stake. We had our arms around each other's shoulders, but a knife in our pockets.

Less than 18 hours later, intensive negotiations began at the University Club two blocks away between myself, Cuz, Bob Lynn, and Charles McLendon (Burlington's director of personnel), with an outside attorney, Thornton H. Brooks, providing mediation. Charles Myers did not attend. The need to stay ahead of the press was paramount. A story had just been published speculating that I was leaving the company, which we flatly denied. But the race was on.

Less than 24 hours after we began, Cuz secured a massive severance package worth approximately $1.5 million, to be paid out over the next 10 years – a mixture of fixed payments and bonuses based on company performance. I was also able to negotiate a six-month severance for my assistant Karen.

The severance agreement, dated March 7, the same day as the press announcement, contained several key provisions, including a no-poach agreement and a non-disparagement clause "expressly agreeing that Callaway will at all times evidence a spirit of friendship and good will towards the Corporation in contacts, correspondence, acts, and the like." It mutually released both parties from any and all obligations and liabilities of whatever nature. Finally, there was no mention of any breach of contract.

They bought my silence and in so doing thought that they were burying the Madison matter and the circumstances of my departure. However, I went to Karen to make sure that she knew the truth. I told her, "No matter what else you hear, I've been fired." Then I asked her off-handedly if we had a secure filing room near my executive suite.

"As a matter of fact," she said, "we do."

I signed the severance agreement on Friday, March 2, and flew to Palm Beach, Florida, to hide from the newspaper men and sidestep any circumstance where I might have to be less than fully truthful. The negotiations continued furiously until Cuz was finally able to secure the final deal. On March 6, the board voted to accept my resignation effective September 30, 1973, and elected my replacement, Horace Jones. I voted "yes" in absentia.

The story printed in the papers on March 7 was that I had been passed over for CEO of Burlington and therefore took early retirement. Charles Myers was quoted as saying, "[Ely's] resignation has been accepted with regret and with an expression of deep appreciation for the very significant contribution he has made to the success of the company." In a prepared statement, I expressed similar sentiments of gratitude and respect.

Between February 20 and March 7, Cuz and I had turned the table on Charles, from firing me "with cause" to granting me a seven-figure "early retirement" package. My best friend since college, personal lawyer, and the executor of my estate saved me with his brilliant lawyering.

My sudden departure sent shockwaves through the company and the entire textile industry. But Cuz and I did one more thing. On March 15, at my request, Cuz delivered a copy of the Madison dossier to Bob Lynn, Burlington's general counsel. I always thought of Bob as a friend and an honest broker, even though he had got himself caught up in this Madison fiasco.

I had to ensure that no matter what might transpire in the days, months, or years to come, the dossier would provide an inviolable account of the Madison matter preserved for posterity. And we placed a second copy in a secured room in the executive suite at Burlington House. For five years, I had fought like hell to get Burlington to do the right thing. I had failed. But I left the company knowing I had done everything I possibly could, that I had upheld my integrity and belief that good ethics is good business. And I left the written record of the truth as a legacy if my honor was ever called into question.

"The only solution when you tell a lie or make a mistake is to admit that you were wrong immediately and try to make it right."

CHAPTER 5

GROWING GRAPES IN THE DESERT

The Start-up Years of Callaway Vineyard & Winery (and All Its Travails)

I Wanted to Become a Farmer . . .

Five years before I left Burlington involuntarily, I'd bought 134 acres of California desert and planted 105 acres of grapes in it. Now that I was out of a job, I had the urge to leave the corporate establishment behind, go back to the land, and become a farmer. Perhaps I was burned out on double knits. I remembered my first farming venture at age 10, selling peaches from my father's grove in LaGrange. Even as a textile executive, I loved growing tomatoes in my penthouse garden in the city and in my country house in New Canaan, and I've always had a green thumb. But I had no interest in returning to the scene of the peaches or the tomatoes. I was interested in wine.

At the time, all I knew about wine was that I liked to drink it – a great Bordeaux like Château Mouton Rothschild or a Robert Mondavi Cabernet Sauvignon from Napa. Beyond that, I was sketchy on the fine points, such as what makes a Riesling a Riesling. But it occurred to me that wine is one of the few products that a farmer can control from start to finish, and put his name on it. Unless you're as big as Hormel, you can't raise pigs and expect to have a private label. Unless you're as big as Nabisco, you can't grow wheat, run a bakery, and put your name on the cookies. But anybody can grow grapes, make wine, and bottle and label it with their own appellation.

Years of decisions by committee had taken their toll on me, especially at Burlington, where a memo might have a hundred recipients, and a contract more signatories than the Declaration of Independence. In those last few years at Burlington, I felt completely out of control as the future of the company, my career, and my livelihood were in the hands of other people. I remembered something Roger Milliken once told me: "Ely, you were never cut out to work for anybody but Ely Callaway." After nearly three decades of working for Uncle Sam, Roger Milliken, Roy Little, Spencer Love, and Charles Myers, I was looking for a way to express myself.

Throughout my textile career in the 1950s and 1960s, I would travel back and forth to California to play golf at the Eldorado Country Club in Indian Wells, near Palm Springs. On those vacations, I would pass a potato farm and think about being a potato farmer. I visited Napa Valley in 1968 after playing in the Bing Crosby Pro-Am at Pebble Beach with sports agent Mark McCormack and his client Arnold Palmer, and imagined what it might be like to become a California winemaker. But I was not alone. In the late 1960s, corporate executives of my ilk had migrated to Napa to plant vineyards during what was called the "Wine Rush." I'd bet two-thirds of the 856 California wineries in existence today were started by those Park Avenue pioneers.

During my trip to Napa, I learned that Hanzell Vineyards, founded in 1953, was for sale. James Zellerbach helped to revolutionize California winemaking with techniques like stainless-steel temperature-controlled tanks for fermentation and aging the wine in French oak barrels. James had died in 1963, and his widow Hana was anxious to sell. It was an innovative and ready-made operation in a perfect location, and the price was right, but I couldn't bring myself to make the deal. I didn't want to be another stop on the Napa/Sonoma tasting tour. I didn't want to go to local grape stompings and see the same faces I saw at the Four Seasons.

In the course of my research, I sought out the advice of the three great experts of California winemaking: Leon Adams, Harold Berg, and André Tchelistcheff. Leon Adams was a historian, journalist, and the author of the definitive history and survey *The Wines of America.* Professor Harold Berg was from the University of California at Davis, which had the best enology department in the country. André Tchelistcheff was the diminutive (4′11″) Russian oracle of California wine and the Balanchine of viticulture. The son of aristocracy, Tchelistcheff had fled during the Russian Civil War, bringing his remarkable winemaking skill and impeccable palate to California. He was simply the most influential winemaker in America. All three masters told me of a remote area in Southern California that for certain reasons had a northern California "microclimate." This was an area of beer drinkers where the cattle outnumbered the grapevines by several thousand to one. It was called Temecula, for the Indian name Temeku, which means "land where the sun shines through the white mist."

There had been vineyards in Southern California since Father Junipero Serra planted the first vines in San Diego in 1769, but 200 years later their grapes were regarded with suspicion. A couple of Hollywood retirees, Vince and Audrey Cilurzo, put up an experimental vineyard in Temecula to prove that Southern California could grow fine grapes. Northern California wine snobs didn't believe this. In their opinion, Southern California grapes were only good for making rotgut wine that came in screwcap bottles.

The way business is often written about, you'd think that success requires planning, forethought, and organization. But my greatest successes, such as they are, have happened because I stumble onto something and sink all my resources into it – and then I'm motivated to make it work. That's my key to "successful planning": if you're in deep enough, you'll figure out a way to dig yourself out.

It was Easter 1968, a few months before I discovered Burlington's Madison shenanigans, but I was already convinced that I was going to go into the Temecula wine "cottage industry." A real estate agent from Coldwell Banker was driving me around the hills. We were on a dirt road somewhere when he honked his horn at a pickup truck heading the opposite way. A tall, craggily handsome, wavy-haired chap emerged from the cab in his cowboy boots. His skin had the color and texture of sun-dried tomatoes. The real estate agent said he was a wine grape expert. We shook hands in the middle of the road.

"John Moramarco," he said.

Moramarco gave me the lay of the land. A couple of miles away was the Cilurzos' experimental vineyard. Moramarco had worked there. Brookside, the established winery in the neighborhood based some 50 miles north in Cucamonga, was planting 20-acre vineyard plots in the same vicinity. Moramarco had worked there, too. Not far from where we stood, the former owner of an LA radio station, John Poole, had planted a 150-acre vineyard called Mount Palomar that year. Wouldn't you know it, Moramarco was also working for Poole. As far as I could tell, he was working for everybody. He came from three generations of grape farmers and had moved to Temecula to get away from vineyards, but the vineyards had caught up to him. He was Italian, but he'd picked up a lot of Mexican aphorisms, such as: "Wherever people complain the loudest, you're near the spot where the gold is buried." I found out later that his wife and daughter had died, so he had other things to escape from besides the family business; he was also escaping pain.

Over the years, I'd developed a technique for how to talk to an expert, which Moramarco obviously was. Instead of asking the expert what I should do about such-and-such, I always asked what *he* would do about such-and-such. Any expert is bound to prescribe the best course of action for himself, but he might settle for something less when advising a stranger. So there, in the middle of the road, I posed a question to Moramarco: "If you were planting a vineyard for yourself, and you could buy any piece of land in this area, which piece would you buy?"

"I'll show you," he said.

The real estate agent and I followed in Moramarco's dust trail as he led us to the crest of a ridge with a great view of the valleys on both sides. We were standing in the Rainbow Gap, which served as a funnel for the ocean breeze that blew through every afternoon on its daily commute from the Pacific to a low-pressure area near Palm Springs, 100 miles to the east.

The same breeze that often knocked my ball out of the fairway on the back nine at the Eldorado was coming through here and creating this Napa-esque microclimate. Except for Poole's vines, the only vegetation in sight was clumps of prairie grass and scrub brush, but Moramarco said the soil was good, the drainage was good, and the underground water supply was excellent. The agent sensed she had a sale. This was clearly the spot to be if you wanted to grow quality grapes in the wrong part of California.

Water, Wine, and Oil

Conventional thinkers would have rejected Temecula out of hand. They would have looked around and said, "This isn't Napa." They would have focused on the not-Napaness of the place and ignored its good points. That's the tyranny of habit: it stunts the imagination. Mine was working overtime as I stood on that ridge. We were 23 miles away from the Pacific Coast and less than four gallons of gas from the Los Angeles sprawl. I imagined the millions of wine drinkers down there, in Los Angeles, Newport Beach, Riverside, and San Diego. I imagined what would happen if you could make a decent wine in Temecula, deliver it to those people, and get them to identify with it as their local antidote to Northern wine snobbery.

With a vineyard in Napa, I could have guaranteed myself a modest success, but a spectacular success was close to impossible. How could I produce a distinctive product when other winemakers had descended on the same area to plant the same vines in the same conditions? Wine is a story business, unlike, say, sheets of aluminum. Aluminum is aluminum, so there's no story to tell, except the price. Customers will almost always buy the cheapest. But in wine, they're buying the story, and the better the story, the more they'll pay for the bottle. Temecula offered a chance for total failure, but also the chance for spectacular success, and a great story, if somebody could pull it off.

It turns out I was buying the property from the Atlantic Richfield Oil Company, hardly the lineage one would want to advertise on a wine bottle. Who would drink ARCO Chardonnay? Back in the 1920s, Los Angeles produced a quarter of the world's oil. Companies like Standard Oil of California (which became Chevron) and the Shell Company of California drilled all over the Los Angeles Basin, and the city formed around those drilling sites. The saying goes that Hollywood's streets were paved with gold. But really they were paved with oil. After Richfield Oil Company merged with Atlantic Refining Company in 1966, ARCO established its corporate offices in Los Angeles, building two modern new towers in place of the more aesthetically pleasing but asbestos-filled Richfield Oil Building. But they were late arrivals to the party, as Southern California oil was already on the decline.

The land I had my eye on had played the role of a cattle ranch and then failed subdivision until ARCO repackaged it as frost-free farms for citrus growers. A year after the growers moved in, a frost killed the trees and the growers demanded their money back. By 1968, ARCO had turned its attention away from California to a recently discovered little oil field in Alaska called Prudhoe Bay. As the entire industry headed north, ARCO seemed perfectly happy to unload their cursed plot onto a foolhardy textile man from Manhattan.

After that Easter weekend of 1969, I returned to New York, but being back on 1345 Avenue of the Americas felt like being on another planet. Before I even had time to clean the sand out of my trousers, I was back in Temecula. The town had maybe 15 stores and no traffic lights, even in the business district. With 500 inhabitants, mostly ranchers and their families, it didn't need a traffic light. Its major attributes were wide-open spaces, cheap land, and fresh air. Two companies from back East, Kaiser Aluminum Company and Penn Central Transportation Company, had created a new subdivision, Rancho California. After Penn Central dropped out, Kaiser got a new partner, Aetna Insurance Company, but the houses in Rancho California weren't selling. Temecula had been passed around from an oil behemoth to a railroad giant to an aluminum corporation and an insurance company, and now finally to me. It was a ghost suburb, reminding every business person who passed through here of the risks of local commerce.

John Moramarco met me at a restaurant in the only hotel in town, which was part of the only golf resort in town. I wanted to pick his brain a bit more, but the real reason I invited him to lunch was to hire him. If you want to succeed in business, you have to surround yourself with the best people. Some companies hire headhunters and consultants; I run into the talent as I go. What Supreme Court Justice William O. Douglas once said about pornography also applies to talent: nobody can define it, but they know it when they see it. I knew John Moramarco was exceptional the minute I met him. He was already working for John Poole in the vineyard next door, but he agreed to split time between Poole's grapes and mine, an arrangement that did not sit well with Poole, who felt I had stolen Moramarco away.

In order to grow grapes on my patch of rocks and sand, I needed to find water to irrigate the land I'd bought. I asked John Moramarco how I'd do that in the middle of the desert, and John said, "Well, you gotta drill." So I started drilling a thousand feet into the earth and soon enough found a bountiful underground reservoir of pure spring water. I had the water tested for safety, and would you believe it, the groundwater in my desolate desert plot spot was some of the purest water in the world. I had been worried it wouldn't be safe for irrigation, but it turned out to be the highest-quality mineral water you'd ever seen in your whole damn life! I had planned to build a wine empire, but now I'd stumbled upon the perfect natural springs for a bottled water business.

In fact, my watershed was so huge that it extended well beyond my property line. This presented a real problem. I went back to ARCO or Kaiser or whoever owned the real estate around my plot, and asked if they wouldn't mind me doing a little wildcat water drilling. I said, "Look, you aren't even using this land. Why don't you let me drill some of this water? You don't need it, right?"

And ARCO came back to me and said, "Hell no!" After perusing the logistical and legal hoops I would have had to jump through to harvest that water, I decided it just wasn't worth it.

If I had really made up my mind to pursue it, I might have become Monsieur Perrier. I bought an additional 175 acres of land, but if I had been really smart, I would've bought the tens of thousands of acres around me for $800 to $1,000 an acre, which is about what it was worth back then, and made billions as a real estate mogul. I can't say the thought didn't cross my mind, but I didn't think anybody would be interested. I figured I was probably the greatest fool in a long line of greater fools, and was better off focusing on making just one thing, and that thing would be wine. Looking back, maybe I should have de-worsified after all.

A New Life, a New Wife

By 1971, I was still at Burlington but feeling the westward pull of California. My grapes were getting more mature every year, but my relationship with Charles Myers was withering on the vine, as was my marriage to Jane. There are all kinds of things that get in the way of a successful long-term man/woman relationship. Jane and I were married 12 years, and she was a wonderful woman. But she was not meant to be a corporate wife.

Jane was only 21 when we got married, while I was already 40 and the head of the biggest textile company in the world. She did not feel comfortable being with the president of Burlington Industries and everything that came with it. I was married to my business – meeting and working all the time. I couldn't help myself, and I still can't. Jane put on a great front and I don't think she held any animosity toward me, but we slowly and subtly moved away from each other.

I met my third wife, Nancy, that same year under tragic circumstances. I've already talked a bit about my first half-cousin once removed, Fuller Callaway III, who was very handsome, very rich, but beset by demons.

He had married three times before the age of 40. One of his wives was Pia Lindstrom, daughter of Hollywood royalty Ingrid Bergman. Fuller competed in the Tahiti Race aboard his hundred-foot sailboat Morningstar and raced from Newport Beach to Tahiti. Pia flew there to meet him at the finish, but by the time she arrived Pia decided she didn't love him anymore.

We spoke often, and after Pia left him Fuller kept calling me and telling me about a girl who he was in love with named Nancy Jacobs. They weren't married yet because she was scared of his substance abuse. On the afternoon of September 21, 1971, Nancy came back to his home in Atherton, CA to find that Fuller had committed suicide from an overdose of drugs and alcohol combined. He was only 39 years old.

The family had a funeral for him in LaGrange the following weekend. I flew down for the service, and afterward went back to my uncle Fuller Sr.'s home, a magnificent estate across the street from my father's house. I went upstairs to one of the bedrooms where I saw a beautiful lady sitting on the bed crying with great force.

I turned to the late Fuller III's mother Alice and asked, "Who is that?"

And she replied, "Well, that's Fuller's girlfriend."

I walked over, sat down beside her, put my arm around her, and tried to console her a little bit. She was terribly distraught over the death of her boyfriend – having watched him die in front of her only a couple of days earlier. I showed a little sympathy and kindness, then went back to New York.

About three weeks later, Nancy sent me a message that she wanted to give me a special box of Fuller's wine, of which he was an avid collector. I wrote back and said I would love to have it, and that we should get together the next time I was in California. About three months later, I was out on the West Coast, and we met at the Fairmont Hotel in San Francisco. We talked about the case of wine, and drank a whole lot of it. When Jane and I separated in the fall of '72, Nancy moved into a love nest that I personally paid for secretly in Tower 58, below the Burlington corporate apartment.

After Burlington Industries fired me in March of '73, I immediately decided to do two things: marry Nancy and move to California to become a full-time grape grower. I spent the ensuing months running all over the state, visiting the Gallo Brothers in Modesto, Sterling, Beaulieu, Cresta Blanca, Hanzell, and other great wine estates from San Diego to Sacramento to learn as much as I could as quickly as I could.

Nancy's parents were highly suspicious of me and my motives. I was 53, 21 years Nancy's senior, and still technically married to Jane. Because I had just been sacked, I had no dependable income. Because I was determined to grow grapes in the middle of nowhere, I had very little hope for any income in the future.

Nevertheless, I trained all my salesmanship and negotiation skills on Nancy's father. Justin Jacobs was a prominent lawyer and, along with his business partner, one of the key real estate developers of the just-coined Silicon Valley. They took plum fields and peach tree orchards and built plants and factories for Hewlett-Packard, General Electric, Fairchild Semiconductor,

Varian Associates, and Intel. The hardest part was assuring Mr. Jacobs that I was not after his large fortune. I backed this up by signing a prenup and adding codicils to my will.

Two days after I finalized my divorce from Jane, I took Nancy on a whirlwind six-week European tour, which included stops at some of France's finest vignobles. We finally tied the knot in Palm Desert on August 8th. I sold Nancy on me, but I'm not sure I ever convinced her parents. In fact, I know I didn't. When Nancy and I eventually divorced, my former father-in-law convinced his daughter to sue me for more alimony.

For most of the first year in California, Nancy and I lived out of a hotel room at the Rancho California Golf Resort. Then I bought a $32,000 one-bedroom tract house in one of Temecula's prime residential areas, which lacked residents. I had a neighbor on each side, with only a few feet between our doors. All around us was empty prairie land. This was quite a downsizing from the 20-acre estate in New Canaan. The Temecula house was roughly the size of the garage of my Connecticut house, but it suited me fine. Some people might think of this as a comedown, but I didn't. I was too busy running the vineyard and starting a new life with Nancy.

I was starting over in every aspect of my life. Whenever you do that, and you make a break, it's better to make a clean break. Drop out, cash out, put all your resources into the new project, and don't overload yourself with baggage from your past. "Be here now," the hippie motto of the 1960s, ought to be an entrepreneurial motto as well. If part of you is back there, you aren't all here. My new job was so demanding, and so exciting, that I even gave up golf – again . . . sort of.

The Noble Rot, or: How Disaster Led to a Great Product

Having sunk nearly all of my severance pay from Burlington into this vineyard, I was highly motivated to learn as much as I could about the economics of my new industry. Grapes are the cheapest part of making wine. If you pay $10 for a nice bottle, the purchase price goes for the bottle, the label, and the fermentation, plus the advertising, packaging, and delivery. You're buying about 25 cents' worth of grapes. It's hard to make a living selling them, as I learned after the first harvest.

That harvest had a catastrophic beginning. It rained so hard in 1973 that we watched chunks of our vineyard sliding down the slope as an entire hillside eroded. Half the grapes were rotten (a blessing in disguise, as it turned out), and I couldn't unload the other half at a decent price. Brookside bought 50 percent of the undamaged grapes, but there were no takers for the rest until I made a phone call to Bob Mondavi.

If you're any sort of wine drinker, then you've tasted Mondavi's product (on the label he's called Robert, not Bob). The son of Italian immigrants, "The Patriarch," as he was known, built Napa Valley's international prestige almost by himself. After falling out with his brother and long-time business partner, Peter, Bob founded his namesake winery in 1966, the first major new Napa winery built in the post-Prohibition era. That winery quickly became renowned for producing some of the finest Sauvignon blanc grapes in the world, which he labeled "Fumé Blanc." Besides good grapes, his clever technological and marketing practices, along with his love for educating people about the joys of wine, all but invented modern American wine culture. "The Ambassador of Wine" (as he was also known) was probably the most important winemaker in the country's history. So imagine his skepticism when he received a long-distance cold call from one Ely Callaway, offering to sell him tons of grapes from Temecula, which Mondavi had to be told was a small wine-growing region 500 miles south of Napa Valley.

I try never to take no for an answer, but a lot of people who make that claim are constantly taking no's for answers: from their bosses, their wives, their husbands, and even their children. That's because they don't anticipate the no in advance, and fail to devise a strategy to head it off. I try to prepare for rejection beforehand, so I always have an argument to launch against the naysayers. I'm already armed with a reason they should change their mind and say yes.

When I called Mondavi out of the blue to ask him to buy the first batch of grapes from my unknown vineyard, this was a strong candidate for a no answer. Therefore, I had to offer him a reason why he would want to buy these unknown grapes against his better judgment. The only reason I could come up with was that Callaway grapes could be his alternate supply in case there was a blight or some similar calamity in Napa. Someday, there would be a shortage and he might need our grapes, so he was doing himself a favor by evaluating them now.

Normally, grapes are transported in large open trucks, where they get jostled around and crushed by their own weight. This causes them to juice and oxidize. Our plan (mostly it was John Moramarco's) was to ship the grapes in such a careful way that they would arrive on Mondavi's doorstep, a 500-mile-or-so drive up Interstate 5, looking better than the grapes picked that morning from his own vineyards.

One hundred tons is a lot of grapes, but we treated them like a shipment of nitroglycerin or rare duck eggs. We repacked the bunches into the 35-pound lug boxes the workers used to pick the grapes off the vines. We stacked the boxes in such a way that the weight of each box was carried by the edges of the boxes below and didn't squash or bruise the contents. When the moving van was loaded, we closed the door and filled the cavity with 1,000 pounds of dry ice. This created an anaerobic condition. There was no air inside, just the carbon dioxide coming from the ice. The driver left in the middle of the night so the grapes would arrive at Mondavi's place by daybreak.

I called Mondavi at 6 a.m. to ask if he had received the shipment, but the real purpose of the call was to get his reaction. Michael Mondavi, Bob's son, answered the phone. "They got here all right," he said. "Nobody can believe it. These grapes look like they belong in a flower arrangement." Our stunt worked so well that not only did Mondavi agree to buy 80 tons of Temecula's finest, he agreed to turn them into six kinds of wine and bottle them under the Callaway label. The great Mondavi was to become our surrogate winemaker. This, I thought, was no small triumph.

A couple of days later, it rained especially hard. I was wandering the vineyard with Leon Adams, who I'd brought on as a consultant, surveying rows of rotten grapes that accounted for half the first year's output. When Leon saw the tainted crop he could hardly contain his enthusiasm. "You have something amazing here," he said. "You have what the French called La Pourriture Noble . . . the Noble Rot." This was a different Noble Rot than the kind that afflicts European aristocracy after centuries of inbreeding. It was *Botrytis cinerea*, a mold that thrives on moist air. Mold causes grapes to dehydrate, which raises their sugar content, which generally is a bad thing – except in the rare situation where *Botrytis* mold appears and the afflicted grapes can be turned into sweet Sauternes, an exquisite dessert wine with a golden honey-colored hue.

In Adams's opinion, finding *Botrytis* in Southern California was nothing short of a miracle. We'd already shipped Mondavi our healthy grapes, but Adams convinced me to ship him a batch of the sick grapes as well. We let the grapes hang on the vines until the Santa Ana winds dried them out and stopped the *Botrytis* from spreading. Then we sent them along to Mondavi, so his German winemaker, Karl Werner, could ferment them into the kind that produces Sauternes. Few winemakers in the world know how to take advantage of Noble Rot, and many experts come from Germany, where Noble Rot is quite common. That Mondavi's winemaker was German was a lucky coincidence.

Mondavi crushed our grapes in October, and the juice was fermented in different tanks: Riesling, Chenin Blanc, Sauvignon Blanc, Cabernet Sauvignon, and Zinfandel. In February, the wine was far enough along that Mondavi's people could taste it and figure out whether it was any good. I drove up there to get the verdict. Mondavi said the wine was progressing well so far, before turning me over to Karl Werner for further details.

Werner was optimistic about all our wines and ecstatic about the one we made from our Noble Rot, which we decided to call Sweet Nancy, in honor of my wife. Within a decade the marriage would turn into sour grapes, but the wine was a triumph. We had no trouble selling the entire lot at $15 wholesale, three times the price we could get for wines made from our healthy grapes. Sweet Nancy helped put Callaway Wines on the map. The apparent misfortune of rain and rot was the best thing to have happened at the vineyard to date.

Sweet Nancy reaped another reward: I was able to sweet-talk Karl Werner into divorcing Mondavi and coming to work for me. The German winemaker moved into a house two doors down from mine and Nancy's. Right away, he said he was lonely and wanted to return to Napa. We fixed that by bringing his girlfriend to Temecula. In a moment of candor, she tipped me off to Karl's serious vodka habit. Why would he drink vodka in a winery? He probably thought he could get away with it because it didn't have a detectable odor. Or maybe it was to show he wasn't tempted by the wine. If he'd been hired to run a Russian vodka farm, he might've preferred Chardonnay. Whatever the reason, for five years I had an alcoholic running the winery, though with a temperament like Winston Churchill – functioned very well while totally tanked fairly often.

We lost Werner to a cult five years later, which was par for the course in California. This was the 1970s, after all, the heyday of Hare Krishna, the Moonies, and The Family, to name a few. In 1972, the notorious People's Temple opened up their Los Angeles location; their leader, the Reverend Jim Jones, would go on to murder all of his followers with a different sort of beverage. I never knew for certain what kind of cult Werner joined, but I suspected it was Dionysian. As soon as he joined, they made him the leader. Fortunately, he never traded cultivating wine for Kool-Aid.

Can a Bank Loan Be a Matter of Taste?

I could see that selling grapes was a tough way to make a living and that our survival depended on turning grapes into wine as quickly as possible. Since we couldn't expect Mondavi to continue as our surrogate winery, we had to build our own. This meant we needed money, and as my bank balance was on a steep descent, I had no choice but to seek an alternate source. In early 1974, I undertook the greatest challenge an entrepreneur can face: raising money.

The trick to raising money is to convince investors that even though you're currently losing money, it's a reasonable risk to invest in you. The vineyard was far from profitable, so I decided against trying to attract investors by selling shares in the operation (besides, so far the only investor I'd attracted was me). Instead, I approached Bank of America for a loan. The winery already had an account there, meaning at least the bank knew who we were. I also knew Tom Clausen, the CEO, who had sat with me on the U.S.-Japan Economic Council a few years earlier, but I didn't expect my $1 million loan request to reach his level. The real reason I chose Bank of America was its willingness to make wine loans. Already, it had financed pretty much all of Napa Valley, and if they ever called in their Napa loans, the majority of the California wine industry would shutter and the nation would face a serious Chardonnay shortage.

I worked my way through San Bernardino and into the Los Angeles office. I began to record our complex negotiations in a diary, writing everything down on yellow pads in red ink. When you're dealing with a bank, it's a good idea to take notes. My loan application was approved very quickly. The LA office allowed me to believe that a check was almost in the mail. All that was required was a rubber stamp from the San Francisco office. I appreciated this prompt service, because the bills were mounting.

Machiavelli warns that the faster you get what you want, the more trouble you'll have holding onto it once you do. He was talking about Italian politics, but he might as well have been talking about a loan approval from Bank of America. As my paperwork traveled up the line of desks in the San Francisco office, where the top brass had final approval, the word was traveling down the line that the bank was going to halt nearly all small business lending. This was because of the Arab oil embargo, which began suddenly in October of '73. Saudi Arabia wanted to punish America for sending military aid to Israel. The embargo sent the price of oil sky-high and created long lines at gas stations. The bank was worried the embargo would lead to economic chaos, causing a lot of people to go out of business and default on their loans. This was no help to me. I was going to go out of business if I *didn't* get the loan. Of all the possible snags in this wine affair, I never imagined it would be undone by Arab oil.

I went to the San Francisco office, with notes in hand, to remind them of the commitment I had gotten from the Los Angeles office. They told me no, but I refused to take it. I reminded them that their bank already had lost billions lending money to foreign governments, on the theory that countries don't go broke. As Bank of America had found out the hard way, countries might not go broke, but they often refuse to make their payments. My point was that lending $1 million to a local winery with trustworthy management was a safer bet than lending billions to defaulting governments, or to companies the bank knew little about.

Changing that subject, they told me they had no confidence that a winery in Temecula could produce a saleable product that was good enough to deserve a cork. So I said, "What if we could prove that we had a saleable product, would you give us the loan then?"

"Maybe," they replied, "but how could you prove it?"

That's when it came to me: *we could have a wine tasting!*

My proposal went as follows: The bank could pick a couple of experts, and I would do the same. Then we'd sit them down and have them rate the Callaway wines bottled by Mondavi against a group of the best wines from Napa. If the Callaway wines measured up, the bank would lend me the $1 million, and if our wines didn't measure up, I'd go away quietly and never bother the bank again. That part appealed to the bankers, and they agreed to my proposal, strange as it was. This had to be the first time in history a bank loan was predicated on a wine tasting.

I chose the location of the motel in Temecula, in a room that held meetings of the Rotary Club (of which I was a member). For my two experts, I invited Leon Adams, by now my good friend and the foremost authority on American wine who had discovered our Noble Rot; and Harold Berg from UC Davis, the mecca of enology. The bank chose André Tchelistcheff, the white Russian "dean of American winemakers." I couldn't believe my luck – this was the troika that had advised me to go to Temecula in the first place, and now here they were on the jury that was to decide my vinicultural fate.

The wines were as distinguished as the panel. Top brands from Mondavi, Christian Brothers, Charles Krug, and Louis Martini were placed on the table, a formidable line-up stacked against the six varieties from Callaway's rookie year. Numerous bankers, local dignitaries, and wine enthusiasts sat in metal folding chairs and watched the experts sniff, sip, spit, and nod their heads. There were no reporters in attendance; the bank didn't even put out a press release. I guess they wanted it kept quiet that they were considering a $1 million loan based on something as highly subjective as a blind wine tasting.

Not to be left out, our winemaker Karl Werner had conducted his own private vodka tasting in the parking lot or the men's room and was so far gone he had lost his Churchillian control. He nervously made loud comments from the sidelines as the tasters sniffed and sipped. Werner was prone to sweating, and he must have sweated off 20 pounds in the three hours it took the experts to finish their judging.

We left the motel, piled into cars, and drove to the vineyard to have lunch on picnic tables set up outside. It was a fantastic Mexican-inspired meal of chicken barbecued with wood, plus corn, tortillas, and beans prepared by John Moramarco and his staff. It also planted the seeds in my mind for the Callaway Winery restaurant, our farm-to-table, get-'em-tipsy, exit-through-the-gift-shop concept.

At the end of the lunch, Leon Adams got up to announce the verdict of the tasters. He said they'd arrived at a unanimous conclusion: Callaway wines held their own against the leading wines from Napa. The bankers from the San Francisco office were amazed, and the bankers from the Los Angeles office, who had approved the loan in the first place, were vindicated. I was relieved, and Karl Werner was overjoyed.

This was more than a triumph for our winery; it was a triumph for the whole region. Everybody in the wine business now realized that Southern California could produce fine wines. It was also the first of many struggles I had to raise money, for the winery and later for the golf clubs. A bank's primary purpose in life is to lend money to people who don't need it. When you need it, it's never easy to pry it out of them. They'd certainly never predicated a loan on a wine tasting before, and I don't think they've ever done it since, but that's what happened, and we got the money.

The Contrarian Path

With the winery now flush with cash, Werner wasted no time designing it and ordering the equipment: German fermentation tanks, German oak barrels, German everything. He was meticulous, a stickler for details, and he had all the skills: crushing, fermenting, bottling. I can't imagine we could have gotten as far as fast as we did if we had any other winemaker.

I let Werner and Moramarco try out new ideas; I always let everybody try out new ideas. A lot of companies make a big show of hiring brilliant creative minds and then don't actually let them do anything creative. They box them in and stifle their imagination. I wasn't about to do that. Besides, since I knew more about textiles than about wine, I was more open to experimentation than the winemakers who were stuck in tradition.

We did a lot of unusual things for that time: Werner put Chenin Blanc and Sauvignon Blanc in oak barrels, and we got good results; he also aged our red wine in oak barrels, which was almost unheard of. Most significantly for the business, Moramarco had a screwy notion of grafting one variety of grapes onto the root system of another and getting two varieties from the same vine. For instance, you take Chenin Blanc and graft it onto the root system of the Zinfandel, then train the Chenin Blanc to grow left and the Zinfandel to grow right. When the public starts to drink more Zinfandel, you cut back on the left side of the plant and encourage the right, and when the public rediscovers Chenin Blanc, you do the reverse. In thousands of years of grape growing, not many winemakers had done this.

A great winemaker from the Chablis region in France, Jean-Jacques Moreau of the storied J. Moreau & Fils, whom I'd met on my prenuptial honeymoon through French wine country the previous year, sent one of his sons to Temecula for training. We sent a couple of our people over there too, in a sort of mini-exchange program. We adopted Moreau's technique of leaving the yeast residue in the bottom of the fermentation tank for several months, to add flavor to the wine.

We were the first to allow weeds to grow around the vines, to attract insects that feed on the insects that feed on the grapes. That way, we could keep the pests down without using pesticides. Our operation was environmentally conscious before it was in vogue, and we got a better product to boot. I'm sure there's a lesson in there somewhere. Every year, we dumped 500 truckloads of cow manure on the land.

We paid our pickers by the hour instead of by the weight of the bunches they picked, so they no longer had the incentive to do a rush job and bruise the grapes. Instead of giving them the usual linoleum knives for cutting the bunches, we gave them shears, which saved more grapes from being damaged in the picking. The gondolas we used to ferry the grapes from the field to the winery were small and were left half-empty to keep weight off the grapes. That way, fewer grapes got squashed. Squashed grapes start to oxidize, and while oxidization is a necessary part of the winemaking process, if they oxidize too soon they lose their aroma, color, and flavor.

We had an unusual drip irrigation system, and an unusual way of pruning the vines in a wishbone pattern, to expose more grapes to the air. We planted our grapes on their own rootstock, which they didn't do in Napa. We used Moreau's Westphalian centrifuge machine and Hausenblase method of "fining," where you add pizzazz to the wine by pouring a potion made from the flotation bladder of a Black Sea sturgeon into the vat. Whoever thought of this one, I'd like to meet them.

All these innovations, on top of the innovation of starting a vineyard in Temecula, went into the six original Callaway Wines: Chenin Blanc, Sauvignon Blanc, White Riesling, Cabernet Sauvignon, Petite Syrah, and Zinfandel. Later, we added Chardonnay, for which the demand became quite large.

Since wine is a story business, it was important to have a label that helped tell the story of Callaway Wines. That's why I wanted to hire Sebastian Titus, the most famous label designer in Napa, to create my label. Once again, I prepared myself so I wouldn't have to take no for an answer, which of course is what I got. Titus said he was too busy to drive 500 miles to a place he'd never heard of to see a vineyard in the wrong part of California, and he wouldn't design a label sight unseen.

"Why don't you send your assistant, then?"

The assistant came down and was so impressed with our operation that he convinced Titus to make the trip two weeks later. That's how we got our wonderful Titus label with the drawing of the Rainbow Gap, where the ocean breeze is funneled through the mountain on its way to the low-pressure Salton Sea near the deserts of Palm Springs. This was the zephyr that cooled our grapes and kept them from generating too much sugar, which is the ruination of dry white wine. Since we couldn't count on the Noble Rot making a repeat appearance, dry white wine was our principal product.

On the back label, where you often find exaggerated claims, we stuck to the facts: our location. And the breeze through the Rainbow Gap that was like an air conditioner for our grapes. To add scholarly weight to the data, I hired meteorologist Irving P. Krick, who'd helped General Eisenhower with the weather forecasts before the Normandy landing in 1944. In Krick's expert opinion, we had our own microclimate.

What I suspected the first day I stood with Moramarco at Rainbow Gap was true. We had made a wine that was sound, pleasing, and impressive to the experts in an area nobody expected, which therefore gave us a unique merchandising opportunity. Southern California's population had exploded again in the 1960s, as Los Angeles County built 76 percent more houses than the previous decade, pushing the suburbs deeper and deeper into the desert. I figured there were enough wine drinkers among the 11 million people in our neighborhood to make Southern California the biggest wine market on Earth. And we had no competition, at least in the beginning. The trick was how to get our wine to the consumer.

The normal route was to go through the wholesale wine distributors who buy wine from vineyards and then sell it to restaurants and retailers. I had avoided the normal route in every other aspect of planning the vineyard, so I wasn't about to take it now. My strategy was to sell Callaway Wines directly to restaurants and retailers. Over the preceding five years, the number of dual-earner families had skyrocketed. There were now millions of couples where the husband and wife both worked. At least twice a week, that couple would eat dinner at a restaurant and order wine with their meal. If I got the restaurants to put Callaway on their wine lists, and the waiters recommended it, then customers would try it and probably want it again. They would learn to associate Callaway with a pleasant night on the town. The next time they went to the wine store, the couple would ask for Callaway. Pretty soon the stores would not only be stocking it, but they would also be selling large quantities.

This is an example of using a product to create demand, and not just to satisfy the demand that's already out there. With bottles in hand, I made the rounds of the fancy restaurants in Los Angeles, San Diego, and Newport Beach, offering on-site tastings to the management. My promotional tour ran into two obstacles. First, the market was glutted with wines from Napa because all the ex-CEOs with vineyards were coming out with new labels at the same time. Second, although I had convinced the bankers that there was merit to Southern California wine, many restaurant owners and retailers didn't believe it.

I could have brought them the greatest wine in the world, and they wouldn't have bought it unless they knew that the restaurants in San Francisco closer to Napa Valley had bought it first. Meanwhile, the fancy restaurants in San Francisco were taking their cues from the fancy restaurants in New York. That left me with only one choice: take the samples to New York.

Less than three years after I left Burlington, I was back in town, selling wine to the same establishments where I previously met over lunch and dinner on the corporate expense account. These contacts came in handy, although I wondered what they thought of me, the Pantyhose King, as I was once called, walking through the door with an armload of Callaway

Sauvignon and Chenin Blanc. At the Four Seasons, where I'd been a frequent patron, I convinced Paul Kovi to give my wine a tryout, and I had similar success with Jerry Berns at the 21 Club and Sam Aaron, the owner of Sherry-Lehmann, then the most prestigious wine retailer in New York City. All three of them wrote complimentary letters that I took back to California, where doors began to open.

By the third year, refrigerated Callaway Wines trucks were leaving Temecula every morning and making the rounds to our restaurant and wine shops through the LA, Riverside, Orange County, and San Diego areas. Our trucks were visible proof it was possible to get back and forth from Temecula to Los Angeles or Newport Beach in one day, and soon enough, commuters were buying houses in Temecula and driving back and forth right along with the wine. That little village, which had had less than 500 residents, became one of California's fastest-growing cities, with over 100,000 residents by the end of 1998.

Having refrigerated trucks was another feature that was unheard of in the business. Our bottles were rolling along in refrigerated wine cellars on wheels, while the competitors' wines were delivered in hot trucks from hot climates. We could truthfully claim the wine was kept cool from the moment the grapes were picked, crushed, and placed from the small gondolas into nearby fermentation tanks, all the way through the time it was served at the restaurant table.

We promoted the wine by hosting weekly barbecues and wine tastings, similar to the one we'd done for Bank of America. These were held under a trellis on the far side of the parking lot. Restaurant managers sent their waiters to these outings, to learn something about which wines go with what food, so they would know which wines to recommend to their customers. This educational approach, partly inspired by Mondavi, was very effective. Hundreds of restaurant employees "graduated" from our afternoon picnics. They all could tell a Chardonnay from a Chenin Blanc, and most importantly, they could recommend a Callaway Wine for any sort of meal.

I hired a sales manager, Ed Russell, from Sequoia, a fine wine shop in Newport Beach. Then the sales picked up considerably when we switched to a nearly all-female sales staff. Women have a definite advantage in selling most things, especially selling wine to restaurants and hotels, where 90 percent of the managers are men.

In the 11 years I owned the winery, we only spent $345 on advertising. We ran an ad or two in the local *Temecula Bugle*, and a couple of ads in the trade journals, but that was it. We never put an ad in the major newspapers or magazines, or on TV. At first, we couldn't afford to advertise, but later, when we could have afforded it, we still didn't do it. That's because the product was selling itself – mainly by word of mouth and free publicity.

If you've got a lousy product, no matter how much advertising you do, you'll have trouble selling it; and if you have a mediocre product, the advertising probably won't do as much good as you expected. If you have a great product, and it's pleasingly different, it will sell itself. Good advertising will move it along, but you can do just fine without it. At that point, it depends on your objective. If your objective is to sell 60,000 cases of wine a year, as ours was, then you can do it without paying for ads. If your objective is to be the next Ernest and Julio Gallo and capture 40 percent of the wine market, then you'll have to advertise, but without a distinctive and superior product, you're likely lost either way.

We made a fine wine that was very palatable. That's where the naysayer comes in. One of the benefits of doing it in Temecula was that nobody expected a Southern California wine to be any good, so if it was, then it would be surprisingly so. Our wine turned out to be superb, which was an automatic publicity factor. If wine drinkers already expect something to be good, then good is actually disappointing. We got a lot of publicity simply by subverting people's low expectations. We turned a perceived negative into a positive.

But the most important thing is that we were located in the biggest wine market in the world with no competition, and everybody was talking about us. If we had produced our Callaway Wines in Napa – same grapes, same fermentation, same quality – I doubt we would have gotten a tenth of the publicity we got by producing them in Temecula. It was our improbable location and our oddball methods that got the attention of the wine writers, who gave us more free publicity than we could have bought with a $10 million ad budget.

God Serve the Queen

In April 1976, Moramarco and I were sitting in the trailer outside the main building when I got a call from Grayson Kirk. I'd never met him, but I knew he was president of Columbia University. More important to the future of Callaway Vineyard & Winery, he was also a member of two wine committees: the Pilgrim Society of the United States and the University Club of New York, of which I was a long-standing member.

"Mr. Callaway," he said.

"Yes."

"Last night we had a meeting of the wine committee of the University Club, and we picked your 1974 white Reisling to go on our wine list."

"That's great."

"I knew you'd like that, but that's not why I called. How much of that White Riesling have you got left?"

"About 60 cases." (I didn't tell Kirk the reason we had 60 cases was the stuff wasn't selling.) "Why do you want to know?"

He told me about the upcoming Bicentennial celebration at the Waldorf-Astoria in New York, where Her Majesty the Queen of England and Prince Philip would be in attendance, along with 1,500 lesser luminaries. "The Pilgrim Society," he explained, "is sponsoring the Royal Family's visit to New York. No member of the British Monarchy has ever been served an American wine on American soil at an official function. We'd like to do just that at the queen's luncheon on July 3, and I'm pushing for yours to be selected. Don't count on it, because I'm only one vote on the committee. But will you hold those cases for a couple of weeks?"

"Certainly, I'll hold them," I said.

Meanwhile, word got around that one wine would be picked for this great event. Everybody in the industry wanted their wine to be it. Gallo or Mondavi would have paid handsomely for this chance, but our White Riesling got chosen. We didn't try to pay anybody, lobby anybody, or twist any arms – it just turned out that Dr. Kirk was an influential man on the scene. He liked the product, and he fought for it. As I've said, a good product promotes itself.

The Waldorf-Astoria wasn't too pleased. They wanted the committee to select from their own wine list. Since Callaway wasn't on that list, the Waldorf asked me to donate the 60 cases, but I refused. We weren't giving free tastings at the winery, so why should we give a free tasting to 1,500 people, even if one of those people happened to be the Queen of England?

We worked out a deal in which the Waldorf would buy the 60 cases at our regular price, and we would pay them a corkage fee, the same as they charged any customer who walked into the restaurant with his own bottle. I also insisted that the wine be served without white napkins wrapped around the bottles and that the bottles be left on the tables so everybody could see the label. They agreed to everything, but they forgot to invite me and Nancy.

A week before the event, somebody remembered. They called and said, "Oh, by the way, would you and Mrs. Callaway like to attend? You won't be in the receiving line to meet the queen, because it's too late for that, but we'll sit you at a nice table with a good view of everything."

"We'd be delighted," I said. Nancy was very excited about the whole thing. She bought white gloves and everything else a woman might buy if they're about to be presented to the queen, even though we were not to be in the receiving line.

The 1,500 guests filled the entire ballroom at the Waldorf. Nancy and I found our places at a table for 12, next to the queen's doctor. HRH herself was on a raised dais about 50 feet away, along with Vice President Nelson Rockefeller and assorted dignitaries.

Halfway through lunch, I got a tap on the shoulder. It was a messenger sent by Lord Ramsbotham, the British Ambassador to the United States, who was sitting on the platform. "Lord Ramsbotham," the envoy said, "wants to inform you that Her Majesty is enjoying your wine very much. After she's given her speech, if you and your wife stand over there at the end of the stage, the queen would like to meet you."

So Nancy and I met the queen and her husband. Nice lady! I almost felt like singing Paul McCartney's song from Abbey Road, "Her Majesty." Like the song, the whole thing took about 30 seconds, and she and Prince Philip made their exit with their entourage. At that point, Dr. Kirk appeared to tell me that during lunch, the queen had asked for a second glass of wine. A few reporters were standing within earshot and overheard Dr. Kirk's remark. The news went out over the wires, and the next morning the item was carried in papers across the country: "The Queen Has Refill of Unknown Wine."

Of course, no one could have bought that kind of advertising at any price. I was so excited the queen had asked for a second glass, I wanted to take home the glass. It was still sitting there on the table where she sat, and I tried to get the maître d' to sell it to me, but he refused. He said it was part of a special set of glasses the Waldorf used for royal visitors. I went over his head to the hotel manager, who gave me the glass without a fuss.

The day after lunch, there was a reception for Prince Charles at a famous New York restaurant. Having heard the queen liked the Callaway wine, the restaurant expected me to send over a few leftover cases for free. I refused. Just because the mother liked it didn't mean I had to give it away to the son.

After my disastrous end at Burlington, the young, trailblazing attitude of 1970s California revived my spirit and gave me new life. The Golden State was the mecca of a seismic economic and cultural revolution, driven by pioneers half my age in food, entertainment, and technology. If a 50-something winemaker from Georgia played a role in this renaissance, it was, along with my Napa contemporaries, to take what had been considered by Americans to be an elitist European pretension and make it an everyday part of American lifestyle.

I imagine if you asked almost any entrepreneur how they did what they did, their story would not be fundamentally different from Callaway Vineyard & Winery's. It happened the way most things happen in life: somebody showed up and knew what they wanted to accomplish; tried hard, tried again, and tried one more time; listened to what was going on around them; was ready when opportunity knocked; and, most importantly, was not afraid to take a chance. Time after time, I have chosen the contrarian path, which you always must do, so long as you're on the right path.

When Hiram Walker & Sons bought my business in 1981 for $14 million, our annual production was 65,000 cases per year. Though Callaway Vineyard & Winery had never made a profit except for one year, I had built a business literally from the ground up, creating for the first time a Callaway brand that was diffrunt and bettuh, had my name on it, and enhanced people's enjoyment of life. I look back on this era as perhaps the happiest and most rewarding time of my life.

"The faster you get what you want, the more trouble you'll have holding onto it once you do."

CHAPTER 6

ONE MAN'S FEAR IS ANOTHER MAN'S OPPORTUNITY

The Early Years of Callaway Golf

Starting From Scratch At 63

There's always a certain amount of fear in the beginning before you've accomplished anything and before you have any substance to offer. I used to be scared to death that I was going to fail a test in high school or fail to impress a girl or fail to please my parents. I'm not sure I ever got over any of my failures – not my four failed marriages, being fired from

Milliken, the Madison matter, or a million other things that didn't work out how I planned. I suppose I had experienced so much failure that by the time I bought Hickory Stick, USA in 1982 at the age of 63, I no longer had any fear of it.

Everybody I knew thought I was crazy, getting involved in a business like this at my age, two years short of retirement. But you see, I didn't think I was 63. I thought I was 36. I'm serious, that's the difference. I'm telling you before you get to 63 that if you're lucky enough to be healthy and if you've got a constructive attitude, you're going to feel like you're 36. You're going to consider yourself ageless. You'll feel that way in every phase of life, even with romance, as I learned in 1981 when I met and married my fourth wife, Lucinda Villa, who worked in the restaurant at Callaway Vineyard & Winery.

Everything is determined by a person's attitude – how they react to an event or situation. I don't think about my age in terms of being over the hill or ready to be put out to pasture; in fact, I don't think of it all, except in terms of the knowledge and experience that can only be acquired with age.

With Hickory Stick, USA, I saw the opportunity to create something new. I didn't have any great vision that in 10 years it would become the biggest golf company in the world. If someone had made that claim to me, I would've told them to get a drug test. But I didn't have any visions of failure, either. I believed we could take this semi-good, cockamamie concept and make a quality product that would sell for a reasonable profit, and at worst I'd have modest success. I guess I'm just built in such a way that I look more at the opportunity than the risks in any situation. I can see what others can't. I believe most successful entrepreneurs – heck, even most successful people –

have that in common; another man's fear is our opportunity.

From the very start, the opportunity that set apart Hickory Stick, USA from our competitors was that almost nobody out there, except for PING, was willing to take a risk on a radical new design. For most of the owners of the big golf club companies at the time – Titleist, MacGregor, Wilson Staff, Lynx, and Ben Hogan, among others – their main purpose was to avoid losing money on their golf clubs rather than making money, because it was deemed too risky. Since 1932, when Wilson Staff invented the sand wedge, I didn't feel anybody had made any genuine innovations – and I knew because I'd played with just about every club invented *since* that year. We recognized that very early and said, "Well, let's take a risk."

That was our business plan: take a risk on something different and see what happens. I'm not joking, it really was that simple. This flew in the face of the standard way of thinking at the Harvard Business School, not to mention among most investment bankers. I strongly believe that you shouldn't have a business plan. It's too easy to get discouraged because if you realize what you're up against, you'll never take the risk.

Think of it in terms of golf. There are two kinds of players: feel players and mechanical players. The mechanical player takes into account every single individual factor before hitting their shot – the lie, the distance, the wind, the weather, the trees, the bunkers, the hole position on the green, all the angles, and everything else. Meanwhile, the feel player gets a brief, overall impression of the situation, chooses their club, steps up, and just swings. I'm the ultimate feel player in business. I had a general sense that the golf club industry was a sleepy business in need of a wake-up call, so I went all in. I took a big swing.

Going all in meant investing my own money. I bought a 50 percent stake in the company for $400,000 in 1982, became president and CEO of the company in 1983, and bought the rest for another $400,000 a year later. If they can do it, I think it's best in new ventures for founders to take most of the financial risk themselves. It gives you a lot of motivation, and a lot of control, and keeps you from dragging down your friends into losing money. I like to build a small team around me, get a product started, learn how to manufacture it, and get it accepted by the consumer, all at my own risk. If there's a little bit of evidence of its potential, then I bring in capital investment.

My whole career, I've believed in the principle that management and ownership should be one and the same, which means management should have a major amount of their own money in their company. When I worked at Burlington, 98 percent of every penny I ever earned was in Burlington stock. When I founded Callaway Vineyard & Winery, it was 100 percent, or nearly that amount. I financed Callaway Golf by myself for four years, and I didn't take a nickel of my salary for the first eight. All told, I put about $2.8 million into the company before taking a cent of private placement money. I was willing to commit my money, but not like a gambler. I committed my money with assurance, because I had a feeling this was going to work. I had no fear.

We started out with just putters and wedges. I thought they had modest potential. For one thing, the Hickory Stick had a different feel from other clubs. This feel was an advantage for wedges and putters, where you're not looking for distance but for comfort, control, and accuracy, all of which the Hickory Stick had. Another distinguishing factor was their appearance, which is what caught my eye from the start. Appearance is a big part of selling anything.

Those first few years at Callaway Hickory Stick, as it was now called, were a relentless grind. I went around to all the golf clubs within a day's drive of Cathedral City (where I'd moved our offices and built our first plant) and personally sold Hickory Sticks in the parking lot out of the back of my Cadillac. We didn't have money for advertisements, placement in major retailers, name recognition, or the backing of a major financial institution. All we could do was convince consumers to test our product, one course at a time, with the belief that once they did, and realized what we were offering was better than what they already had, we'd have a sale.

By this point, this was a tried and true strategy. At my winery, I had personally hosted a tasting and changed the attitudes of the greatest influencers in wine, not to mention an international bank. At Milliken, I had personally shown my Viracle to clothing manufacturers and convinced them to reverse a thousand years of precedent. As a child in LaGrange, I had convinced my neighbors to buy peaches. I was confident the same principles would apply here, as they likely do in any industry.

Most new entrepreneurs don't have that confidence, because they've never actually done it before, and as a result, they waste time and money trying to manufacture that confidence by doing market studies, hiring consultants, spending too much on advertising, doing 10 things at once when all you really need to do is one thing right. I tell people one of the greatest strengths Callaway Golf ever had was that I had already done this at least two other times. That's too simplistic, but then again business really can be quite simple, at least when it's done correctly.

I tried to instill this same confidence in my team. A leader who inspires belief in any human endeavor increases immeasurably its chances for success. For an entrepreneur, surrounding themself with the best people is second only to having a great product. I needed people who believed in Hickory Stick as much as I did and would work hard, albeit never as hard as me, but pretty darn close. All leaders have blind spots, even the best ones. General Grant needed Joshua Chamberlain covering his flank at Little Round Top, and while I could always count on my right-hand man and personal attorney Don Dye, I needed a team of people filled with creativity and initiative, as I'd had in my two previous industries, who were willing to fix their bayonets and charge headfirst against the status quo.

At first, I did not have much success. I hired a team of independent sales reps who sold many lines of golf merchandise but had no particular interest in Hickory Stick. They couldn't make a damn sale. They told me the problem was my product, but I suspected the problem was them. My suspicions were proven right when I discovered my ace in the hole, my sales wizard, Bruce Parker.

I heard about Bruce through my usual headhunting channel: the golf course. I was playing a round at Palm Springs with a friend of mine, also in the business, telling him the problems I'd been having with a sales staff that couldn't sell Hickory Sticks. "You gotta meet Bruce Parker," he said. "He's been selling golf clubs for me on the telephone and getting hundreds of orders a week."

As soon as we got off the 18th hole, I called Bruce to invite him to Palm Springs for an interview. He arrived the next day with a fat box of three-by-five cards. These were all his contacts in the so-called off-course golf shops. While other salesmen – and perhaps I should include myself in that group – were wasting time visiting golf courses and selling the pros a few clubs per visit, Bruce had tapped into the huge off-course market. On the phone, he was outselling 10 salesmen on the road. I didn't need a testing service to tell me this guy was a terrific resource, and I hired him on the spot.

Because Bruce never went to college, the standard personnel director would have rejected him as sales manager material. This brings us to an important aspect of my managerial philosophy: don't get caught up in credentials. It was all those Harvard graduates in the Kennedy administration who got us into Vietnam. You can bet they had all kinds of credentials, and not a lick of sense or integrity among them. Bruce had something far more important than an Ivy League diploma: he had street smarts and a maverick's distaste for business as usual.

The day after we met, he was at a desk at Callaway Hickory Stick headquarters, crammed in between the president and the accountant. He had to vacate the desk at 2 p.m. so somebody else could use the phone and the typewriter. That was the situation back then – musical desks. Within a month, Bruce had moved up to sales manager, and we gave him his own office and a permanent desk. This 28-year-old convinced us to dismiss the entire independent sales force and hire five full-time Hickory Stick salesmen instead. Sales increased dramatically. I was inspired by Bruce and began to work the phones myself.

It should be clear by now that I've never been much of a fan of convention in any aspect of business, and my methods for hiring people were no different. I would say that in my whole career, in textiles, wine, and golf, of all the people I've ever hired, only three came from one of those outside agency executive search management consultant companies. Instead, I found talent by getting to know everybody in the business myself. An entrepreneur has to know his business from top to bottom, and that starts with knowing, at the top executive level, who's who, who's able, and who isn't.

When I identified someone I thought might be a good fit for my company, I would get to know them, or at least know about them, through a substantial amount of investigation. I contacted people who knew them well and had evaluated them. I collected as much information as possible, like some old gumshoe detective, and finally, I'd make my own judgment. I'd say 97 percent of the people I've ever hired to top executive positions have been people I assessed myself, either rightly or wrongly, correctly or incorrectly.

Perhaps the best evaluation I ever made was of Dick Helmstetter, a billiards cue designer who became my lead club designer in 1985. Dick was another man who never would've made it past the first screening in a traditional job application process. He was another hidden talent whose arrival would change Callaway Hickory Stick for good.

History is obsessed with stories of great leaders who inspired their plucky band of troops to improbable victories over vastly superior opponents, offering immortal orations like Henry V at Agincourt or Churchill before the Battle of Britain. I was never one for big speeches, though I've been asked to make plenty in my life, and I've certainly been known to dominate dinner conversation with a long-winded but (to my mind at least) endlessly fascinating yarn. But my method for galvanizing the troops was to pay people more than they asked for and give them the freedom to try out their ideas. This is the opposite of normal corporate behavior, which is to get things done as cheaply as possible and not pursue any idea that wasn't approved by three committees.

That's my theory of management: be generous. You won't learn this at the business schools when they talk about rates of return, but you get a very high rate of return on generosity and kindness. We've lost the sense of value in the noble gesture and the kind word. They don't show up in the cost-benefit analysis, but I'm convinced that generosity and kindness can boost productivity and add to corporate earnings. Don't be a pig and try to keep all the money, or all the interest, for yourself. It's bad manners. It's bad morals. It's bad business.

Whatever I've spent on bonuses, surprise gifts, and paying people more than they expected, that generosity has come back many times over in hard work and loyalty. Any employee who is made to feel like a valuable asset is more likely to end up becoming one. If people are well rewarded for what they do, they have a natural tendency to want to prove they're worth it. They work overtime to solve problems. They're always thinking about ways to do things better. They get up to brainstorm in the middle of the night.

The merits of hard-nosed bargaining over compensation are overrated. My negotiation philosophy is: drive a soft bargain. You may haggle and quibble and get somebody to perform a service for less, and congratulate yourself on saving a few bucks, but what have you really accomplished? You've fixed it so you're sure to get second-rate service. I'm reminded of the parable of the pool man in the hurricane. After the wind blows leaves and branches into all his customers' pools, whose pool does he clean up first? Not the customer who pays late and asks for discounts, but the customer who pays on time and sends a Christmas bonus.

We hear a lot these days about companies downsizing and rightsizing to improve the bottom line – that's what the guillotine did in the French Revolution: it *downsized* the opposition. But what about a kindness motive instead of a profit motive? These days we don't usually associate the words goodness, generosity, or the golden rule with the business world – quite the contrary. But the principles I learned in kindergarten were the ones that helped me get ahead in the wine business, the golf business, and the getting-through-the-day business. Years later, in early 1995, when Callaway's stock price was down and morale was dropping on the golf club assembly line, we gave all Callaway Golf employees a bonus. This made our 2,000 workers feel good about themselves and good about the future of the company, all at once.

In the start-up years, when the company was smaller and far less solvent, I brought the key employees into my office every November to discuss their compensation. One at a time, I asked them how they wanted to be paid: in cash, in stock, or some of each. If you want to know your staff's true opinion of how things are going, give them this choice. Incidentally, this is why Callaway has produced so many millionaires over the years: I offered a lot of stock early on, almost all of it out of my own shares.

In the fall of 1986, we were at a trade show in Las Vegas and I asked Bruce Parker: cash or stock? This was before we went public, so our shares weren't trading on the stock market. Being less than 30 years old, preferring to invest in Saturday night dates, and lacking a conviction that Callaway shares would ever amount to anything, Bruce chose all cash. When he opened his pay envelope, he found his cash, plus a few shares I gave him on the side. "Someday," I said, "I hope this will mean something to you." Bruce was already a workaholic, but after receiving this token of appreciation, if his office had been locked, he would have crawled through the heating system to get into it.

In my opinion, we gotta get a lot better at recognizing and appreciating human talent – selecting it, taking a gamble on the person, then giving them free rein and rewards. Business is often told as a story of products and numbers, profit margins, and rates of returns. But the early story of Callaway Golf is really about a million moments of inspiration from a small group of hardworking and innovative people: Don Dye, Bruce Parker, Dick Helmstetter, and Hickory Stick's founders, Richard Parente and Dick De La Cruz. It was their fortitude that allowed us to survive those precarious start-up years and slowly but surely build my company into a sustainable business. They meticulously and relentlessly built a rocket ship so that when the fuse was finally lit, the whole thing would take off.

S2H2, or: Innovation by Accident

The Hickory Stick as a concept had limited potential. I knew that going in. Still, after three years, it was bigger than I expected it to be. I figured the best we could hope for was $15 million in annual sales. We could make 15 percent after taxes, and end with a $2.2 million annual profit. By the time 1985 was over, I had put in $2.5 million, and we had raised $3 million of private placement from personal friends.

Without even fully realizing it, we had put certain structures in place that would aid in our coming leap. We had built a computer system for a much, much larger company than anybody would have contemplated. I also brought in Price Waterhouse to do our financial services, knowing that there might come a time when I would need to raise money or go to the public markets, where working with a major financial firm would be an advantage.

The other key to making a big business out of a small business is flexibility. The ability to pivot in business is as important as it is in the golf swing. If you come up with a better product than the one you're making, you've got to be willing to seize the opportunity and change direction quickly. This is where strategic, long-term planning can get in the way of progress. A lot of companies hire expensive consultants to make them a five-year plan or a ten-year plan, with everything figured out in advance. They get so tied up in the plan that when a fabulous opportunity comes along, they don't notice it, or they ignore it in favor of business as usual. My approach has always been: take it one step at a time and be willing to turn on a dime.

We were making Hickory Sticks, but we weren't necessarily locked into Hickory Sticks. I always encouraged people around me to come up with innovations, and I always backed my team's ideas, no matter how crazy they sounded. That's what happened with the S2H2, which was Callaway's first genuine innovation. Like so many inventions, it happened by accident. At the time, Hickory Stick was making a putter out of a raw chunk of metal, called a billet. It was the first time anybody had produced putters where each head was carved out of a single steel block, one at a time.

Parente and De La Cruz had the idea to make a wedge with this same technique. They'd take a forged piece of steel, clamp it, and shave it down. It had to be a thick piece of metal, because thin pieces would vibrate so much that they couldn't handle the machining. The result was a wedge with a very fat head, and very heavy. To take some of the weight off, Parente and De La Cruz decided to reduce the length of the hosel – the metal neck that connects the clubhead to the shaft. Reducing the length of the hosel was a bit unusual, but it wasn't revolutionary. Other golf club companies made clubs with shorter hosels. They realized a golf club didn't need to have a long neck like a rake or a shovel, which was how it had been made for hundreds of years.

Even with the shorter hosel, our new wedges were too heavy. To solve that problem, we decided to drill a hole into the hosel. Golf clubs in general already had a small hole at the bottom of the clubhead, to let the air out when the shaft was inserted, but nobody had tried to lop off the neck entirely and connect the shaft and clubhead directly through a big hole. That's what we did to take the weight off the wedge.

This created another problem: how to keep the clubhead from flying off the shaft and hitting somebody. By this time, a better class of glue had come onto the market, and these new epoxies did the trick. Our wedges held together pretty well, but the most important thing was how they played. I tested the new wedges myself – they had a different feel from your run-of-the-mill wedge, but they played great.

The important thing to understand is it wasn't some epiphany to make a better golf club by taking weight out of the hosel and moving it down into the head. It was entirely serendipitous. In trying to solve a machine-tool problem – how to compensate for a heavy billet – we invented a superior golf club.

The short hosel with the hole drilled through it immediately became the cornerstone of Callaway Golf. The Hickory Stick was on the way out.

The new wedges were so successful that we decided to make an entire set of short-hosel irons. We started with the 5 iron. We carved it different ways, adding weight here, taking weight off there, until we got it right. We tried it out on the golf course, and we couldn't believe how well it played. The next iron we made played even better.

My son Ely Reeves Callaway III, known as Reeves, was key to the design and manufacturing of the iron and christened it S2H2, which stood for "short straight hollow hosel." It was his riff on R2-D2, the little droid of *Star Wars* fame.

Engineering a golf club was tiddlywinks for Reeves, who has designed, built, and raced high-performance vehicles, both terrestrial and airborne, since the age of 11, when he built his first fire-engine red Royal Norseman Convertible Pushmobile Go Kart. It was obvious even then that the need for speed was his "legal addiction" and his destiny. Knowing that there was nothing I could do about it, I resigned myself to being his transporter and pit crew, taking him to local tracks to race the Go Karts he built. He has a huge talent for making things with his hands, and I have no idea where he got that skill – certainly not from me.

By the time of his 17th birthday in 1964, he had already rebuilt a British Racing Green '64 Shelby Cobra and a '56 Thunderbird. In 1970, for his senior fine arts thesis in "sculpture" at Amherst, he rebuilt the Ferrari 375 Plus that had won the 1954 24 Hours of LeMans. In 1988, his 898-horsepower Callaway C-4 "Sledgehammer" became the fastest street vehicle in the

PICTURES FROM ELY CALLAWAY'S PERSONAL ARCHIVE

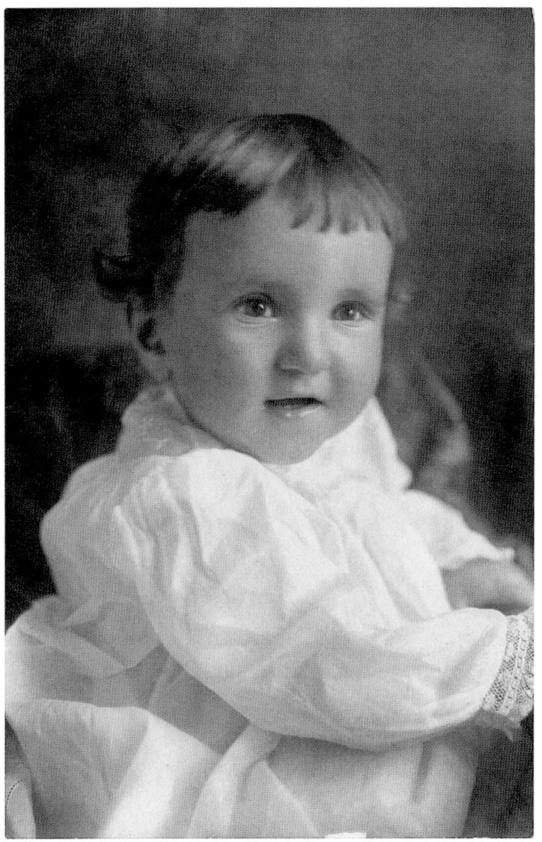

Ely, age 1, LaGrange, Georgia, 1920

Ely, age 3, Central Park, New York, 1922

Ely, age 3, Brooklyn, New York, 1922

Ely shooting for the stars, age 4,
Brooklyn, New York, 1923

Ely's parents, Ely Reeves Callaway, Sr., and Loula Walker Callaway, late 1940s

MOTHER AND SISTERS HAIL NEW CHAMPION Aug-1938

LAGRANGE.—When Ely Callaway, Jr., finished on top of the ninety-six entries to win the 1938 Highland Country Club invitation tourney Friday, it brought great joy to his mother and sisters, who are shown here greeting him at the finish. There is one young lady outside the family in the picture, namely, Miss Margaret Palmer, of Atlanta, daughter of Charles F. (Chuck) Palmer, president of the Chamber of Commerce, who was just as ardent a rooter for Ely as the rest of them. From left to right in the picture: Mrs. Mary Crim, Miss Palmer, Miss Bessie Walker Callaway, best of the women players at the Highland Club; Ely Callaway, Jr., Mrs. Ely Callaway, Sr., and Mrs. Phillip Albright.—Journal staff photo by Walter Sparks.

Ely, age 19, Highland Country Club champion, with his sisters and mother, LaGrange, Georgia, August 1938

Ely, age 17, high school graduation portrait, LaGrange, Georgia, 1936

Ely, age 17, Highland Country Club, LaGrange, Georgia, c. 1936

Ely (left) with his two best friends and classmates at Emory University, Atlanta, Georgia : James "Jimmy" Wilson (center) and Covington "Cuz" Hardee (right). Late 1930s. Jimmy and Cuz went on to become brilliant lawyers and provided counsel to Ely at critical times in his life. The three remained lifelong close friends.

Ely (right) and Covington "Cuz" Hardee (left). Emory University, Atlanta, Georgia, 1940

Ely with his first car just before leaving to enlist in the U.S. Army, LaGrange, Georgia, 1940

BACK ROW L TO R: Ely Reeves Callaway, Jr., Mary Ely Callaway (sister), Benjamin Phillips Albright, Sr. (brother-in-law).
FRONT ROW L TO R: Ely Callaway Crim (nephew), Loula Callaway Albright (sister), Loula Walker Callaway (mother), Benjamin Phillips Albright, Jr. (nephew), Ely Reeves Callaway, Sr. (father), LaGrange, Georgia, 1940. Photograph by Bessie Walker Callaway (sister)

THIS PAGE: Ely and Jeanne, newlyweds in uniform, Philadelphia, 1942

FACING PAGE: Portrait of Jeanne Wiler Callaway, Philadelphia, 1941

L TO R: Lisa (daughter), Jeanne (first wife), Nicholas (son), Ely, and Reeves (son), Darien, Connecticut, 1956

Ely with Reeves, 1949

Ely with Lisa, Nicholas, and Reeves, 1954

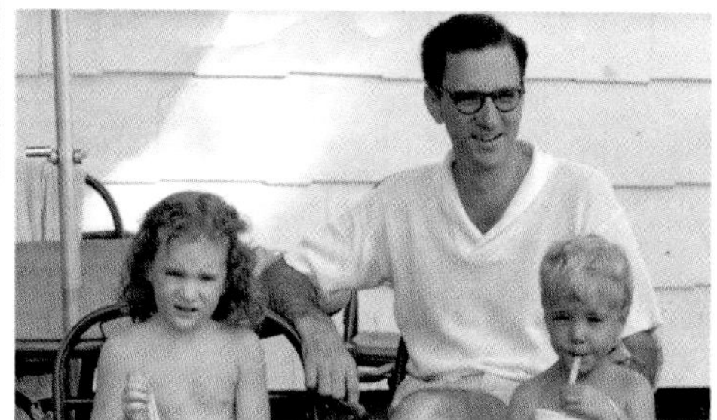

Ely with Lisa and Nicholas, Darien, Connecticut, 1957

Ely and Jeanne, La Coquille Club, Manalapan, Florida, 1958

Ely and Jeanne, The Patio, Palm Beach, Florida, 1958

Ely's hero, Bobby Jones, 1927 U.S. Amateur champion, Minikahda Club, Minneapolis, Minnesota

Photograph inscribed by Bobby Jones "For Jeanne and Ely Callaway / Two of my very favorite young friends, Bob Jones," early 1950s

ROBERT TYRE JONES, JR.
1425 C. & S. BANK BLDG.
ATLANTA, GEORGIA

March 21, 1952

Mr. Ely Callaway
Deering,Milliken & Co.
261 Fifth Avenue
New York,N.Y.

My dear Ely:

I was grateful indeed for your very nice letter and delighted with the VISA material. I shall certainly have it made up and, according to its virtues, of which I have no doubt, I will enjoy it immensely.

We often think and talk of you and Jeanne. We hope you will both be down here before long and will come to see us.

Billy is going home today from the hospital, after a minor but fairly uncomfortable operation. He had a cyst removed from the base of his spine. Otherwise all are well and all send their best to you both.

With many thanks,

Most sincerely,

Bob

RTJ-j.

The One really great man I've ever known well. He would be great even if he had never seen a golf stick. I want to talk with you about him. He's probably the best loved, most respected sports figure to come out of the Golden Age of Sports – the 1920's. You would love this man.

Letter to Ely from Bobby Jones, March 21, 1952, with Ely's handwritten note on bottom of page: "The one really great man I've ever known well. He would be great even if he had never seen a golf stick. I want to talk with you about him. He is probably the best loved, most respected sports figure to come out of the Golden Age of Sports – the 1920s. You would love this man."

Ely at textile showroom, New York, 1950s

Ely, late 1950s

Ely at opening ceremony of a Burlington Industries textile plant, 1960s

Ely in his office, New York, late 1950s

"Profile of Courage," portrait of President John F. Kennedy, Jr., Grand Ballroom, Hilton Hotel, New York, November 8, 1963. One of the last portraits of JFK before his assassination two weeks later. Photographs by Ely Callaway

ABOVE AND BELOW: The Beatles's fourth and final appearance on *The Ed Sullivan Show*, New York, August 14, 1965. Photographs by Ely Callaway

Ely's second wife, Jane Atkins Callaway, New Canaan, Connecticut, 1966. Photograph by Ely Callaway

Jane Atkins Callaway, New York, 1962. Photograph by Ely Callaway

Ely's mid-century modern house, New Canaan, Connecticut, 1967. Photographs by Ely Callaway

Portrait of Ely by Yousuf Karsh, New York, 1968

Ely (right) with Arnold Palmer at the 1968 Bing Crosby National Pro-Am. BELOW: note from Bing Crosby, Pebble Beach Golf Links, Pebble Beach, California

Bing Crosby
Hollywood

Getting Arnold all straightened out, are you?

Yours
Bing Crosby

PEBBLE BEACH GOLF LINKS

PLEASE REPLACE TURF
LEVEL SAND IN BUNKERS

HOLES	YARDS LONG TEES	YARDS SHORT TEES	PAR	WOMEN'S PAR	HANDICAP STROKES
1	385	375	4	4	8
2	497	450	5	5	10
3	355	320	4	4	12
4	325	300	4	4	16
5	160	160	3	3	14
6	515	470	5	5	2
7	110	110	3	3	18
8	425	400	4	4	6
9	450	425	4	4	4
TOTAL OUT	3222	3010	36	36	
10	421	365	4	4	7
11	380	380	4	4	5
12	205	185	3	3	17
13	400	380	4	4	9
14	555	545	5	5	1
15	406	360	4	4	13
16	400	375	4	4	11
17	218	190	3	3	15
18	540	530	5	5	3
TOTAL IN	3525	3310	36	36	
TOTAL OUT	3222	3010	36	36	
TOTAL	6747	6320	72	72	
SELF					
OPPONENT					

DATE

1968 Bing Crosby National Pro-Am final round scorecard of Ely Callaway, Bill Parker, Arnold Palmer, and Mark McCormack, founder of IMG, Pebble Beach Golf Links, Pebble Beach, California

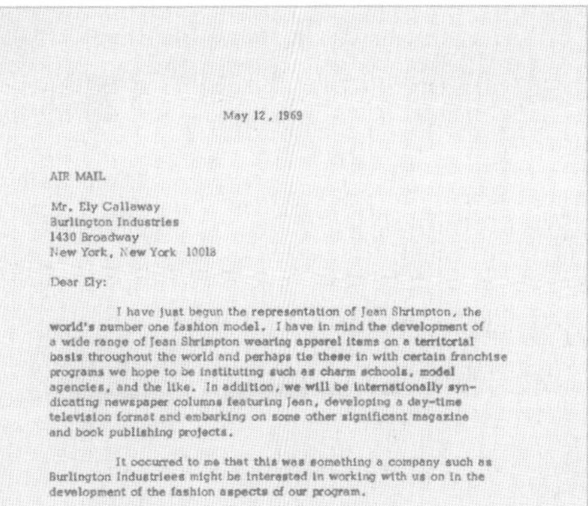

May 12, 1969

AIR MAIL

Mr. Ely Callaway
Burlington Industries
1430 Broadway
New York, New York 10018

Dear Ely:

I have just begun the representation of Jean Shrimpton, the world's number one fashion model. I have in mind the development of a wide range of Jean Shrimpton wearing apparel items on a territorial basis throughout the world and perhaps tie these in with certain franchise programs we hope to be instituting such as charm schools, model agencies, and the like. In addition, we will be internationally syndicating newspaper columns featuring Jean, developing a day-time television format and embarking on some other significant magazine and book publishing projects.

It occurred to me that this was something a company such as Burlington Industriees might be interested in working with us on in the development of the fashion aspects of our program.

Mr. Ely Callaway
Page 2
May 12, 1969

With this in mind, I thought I might drop you a note to see if you would have any interest.

I hope we will have a chance to get another golf game together before too very long.

Looking forward to hearing from you, I am

Sincerely yours,

Mark H. McCormack

MHMc:jac

Letter to Ely from Mark McCormack, founder of IMG, May 12, 1969

Ely at the Greater Greensboro Open Pro-Am, Sedgefield Country Club, Greensboro, North Carolina, 1972

The Mill at Burlington House, a 10,000-square-foot permanent exhibition designed by Chermayeff & Geismar, New York, 1970

Ely at inauguration of The Mill at Burlington House, Avenue of the Americas at 54th Street, New York, September 10, 1970

Lobby of corporate headquarters of Burlington Industries, 1345 Avenue of the Americas, New York, 1970. Logo design by Chermayeff & Geismar

Ely with Mayor John Lindsay on opening day at The Mill at Burlington House, New York, September 10, 1970

Installation, The Mill at Burlington House, New York, 1970

1965 Burlington Annual Report designed by Chermayeff & Geismar

Exhibition detail, The Mill at Burlington House, New York, 1970

To CFM 10/30/69

Re. Madison — My 10/30 Report to You.

The subject of divisional listings in annual report is before us again.

I continue to feel that we should disclose our ownership in Madison. I think we should list Madison in our '69 annual report — just as I felt we should do in the '68 report.

I realize that when we do disclose, it's going to cause the company some embarrassment and probably some real problems. But I honestly and strongly continue to feel that these problems will only get bigger as time passes, and that the embarrassment will only increase with time. That has been the history so far — in my view.

And I feel I must say to you again that, regardless of legalities or technicalities I'm convinced that it's wrong, dead wrong, for Burlington to continue to mislead and lie to our own people and to the outside world about our ownership of this big and significant part of our company.

ERC Jr

Letter to Charles Myers from Ely, October 30, 1969

Charles Myers, CEO of Burlington Industries, New York, c. 1970. Photograph by Ely Callaway

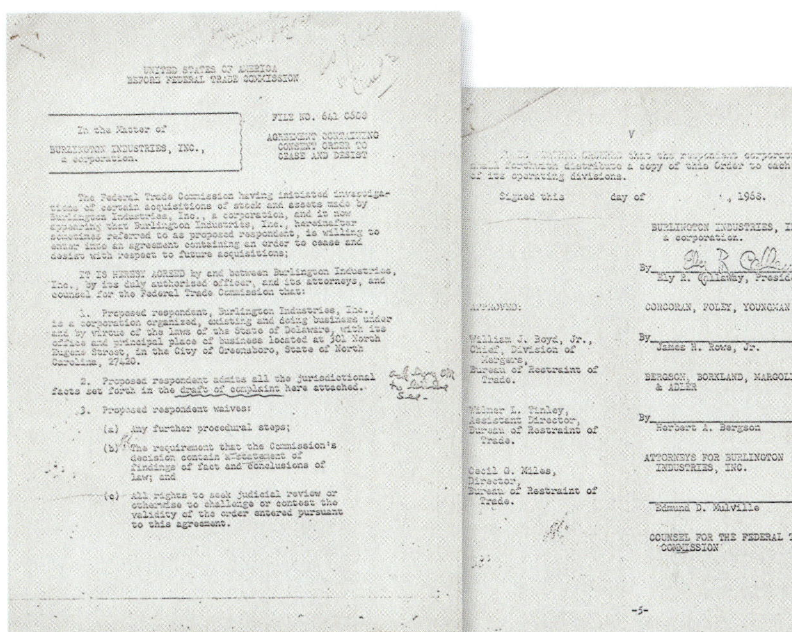

UNITED STATES OF AMERICA
BEFORE FEDERAL TRADE COMMISSION

In the Matter of BURLINGTON INDUSTRIES, INC., a corporation.	FILE NO. 641 0608 AGREEMENT CONTAINING CONSENT ORDER TO CEASE AND DESIST

The Federal Trade Commission having initiated investigations of certain acquisitions of stock and assets made by Burlington Industries, Inc., a corporation, and it now appearing that Burlington Industries, Inc., hereinafter sometimes referred to as proposed respondent, is willing to enter into an agreement containing an order to cease and desist with respect to future acquisitions;

IT IS HEREBY AGREED by and between Burlington Industries, Inc., by its duly authorised officer, and its attorneys, and counsel for the Federal Trade Commission that:

1. Proposed respondent, Burlington Industries, Inc., is a corporation organized, existing and doing business under and by virtue of the laws of the State of Delaware, with its office and principal place of business located at 301 North Eugene Street, in the City of Greensboro, State of North Carolina, 27420.

2. Proposed respondent admits all the jurisdictional facts set forth in the draft of complaint here attached.

3. Proposed respondent waives:

(a) Any further procedural steps;

(b) The requirement that the Commission's decision contain a statement of findings of fact and conclusions of law; and

(c) All rights to seek judicial review or otherwise to challenge or contest the validity of the order entered pursuant to this agreement.

V

[illegible] that the respondent corporation [illegible] distribute a copy of this Order to each of its operating divisions.

Signed this day of , 1968.

BURLINGTON INDUSTRIES, INC.,
a corporation.

By Ely R. Callaway
Ely R. Callaway, President

APPROVED:

William J. Boyd, Jr.,
Chief, Division of Mergers,
Bureau of Restraint of Trade.

Wilmer L. Tinley,
Assistant Director,
Bureau of Restraint of Trade.

Cecil G. Miles,
Director,
Bureau of Restraint of Trade.

CORCORAN, FOLEY, YOUNGMAN & ROWE

By
James H. Rowe, Jr.

BERGSON, BORKLAND, MARGOLIS & ADLER

By
Herbert A. Bergson

ATTORNEYS FOR BURLINGTON INDUSTRIES, INC.

Edmund D. Mulville

COUNSEL FOR THE FEDERAL TRADE COMMISSION

-5-

Consent decree issued by the Federal Trade Commission (FTC) demanding Burlington Industries cease and desist, as a result of investigations of Burlington's acquisitions from 1950 to 1968, July 1968

Signature page of FTC consent decree, with only Ely Callaway's signature, as instructed by Burlington's corporate counsel, July 1968

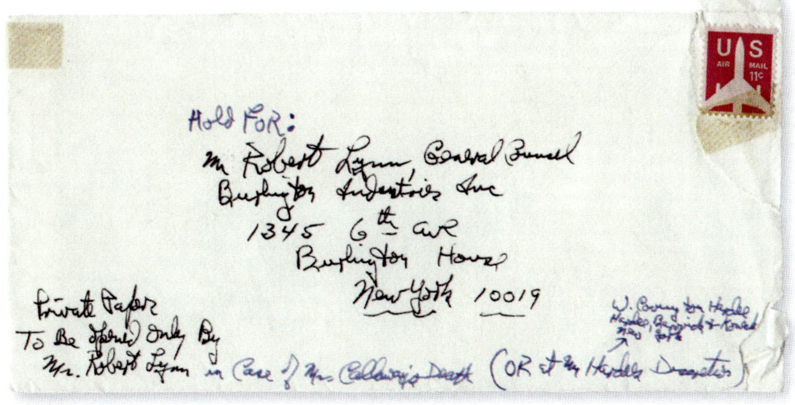

Envelope containing Ely's account of the Madison matter written in his hand in 1973, with instructions to Robert Lynn, the general counsel of Burlington Industries, to not open the dossier until after his death. Documents found for the first time in the Ely Callaway archives, 2023

Two Southern California wine industry pioneers: (left) Ely Callaway, founder of Callaway Vineyard & Winery and (right) John Moramarco, 10th generation viniculturist and Senior Vice President.

Callaway was built from the ground down.

CALLAWAY
Vineyard & Winery

When Ely Callaway chose to plant his vineyards near Southern California's beautiful Rainbow Gap, he was on to something big. It began with the remarkable soil, granitic and well drained. Then the nurturing temperate climate. Over the years, it has allowed us to produce some of the finest white wines in California. Fresh from our vineyards to your table.

Callaway Vineyard & Winery advertisement, 1991

Blind wine tasting for $1 million bank loan, Temecula, California, 1974

Queen Elizabeth II drinking Callaway estate bottled 1974 White Riesling wine at the Bicentennial Luncheon, Waldorf-Astoria Hotel, New York, July 9, 1976

Callaway estate bottled Chenin Blanc and red vintage wines, 1976

E II R

LUNCHEON FOR

HER MAJESTY QUEEN ELIZABETH II

AND

HIS ROYAL HIGHNESS

THE PRINCE PHILIP, DUKE OF EDINBURGH

NEW YORK · JULY 9 · 1976

Program for Bicentennial Luncheon, Waldorf-Astoria Hotel, New York, July 9, 1976

Ely with his third wife, Nancy Jacobs Callaway, Callaway Vineyard & Winery, Temecula, California, 1974

Callaway Vineyard & Winery Vintage 1980 Chardonnay, Temecula, California

Ely at wine tasting, late 1970s

Ely with Callaway Vineyard & Winery management team (L to R): John Moramarco, Ely, Edward Russell, Karl Werner, and Robert Norton, Temecula, California, 1975

Ely at Callaway Vineyard & Winery, Temecula, California, early 1980s

FACING PAGE: Ely testing the Little Poison II Hickory Stick putter, The Vintage Club, Indian Wells, California, 1983

Ely with first Hickory Sticks, The Vintage Club, Indian Wells, California, 1983

Callaway Hickory Stick wedge and putter, 1983

First Big Bertha logo designs, 1991

World War I cannon "Big Bertha"

ABOVE AND FACING PAGE: First Callaway Big Bertha driver and fairway woods, 1991

Callaway
DRIVER
10°
BIG BERTHA
USA
Callaway
DRIVER
9°
BIG BERTHA
USA
Callaway
DRIVER
8°
BIG BERTHA
Callaway
DRIVER
11°
RTHA
Callaway
5
BIG BERTHA
Callaway
3
BIG BERTHA
USA

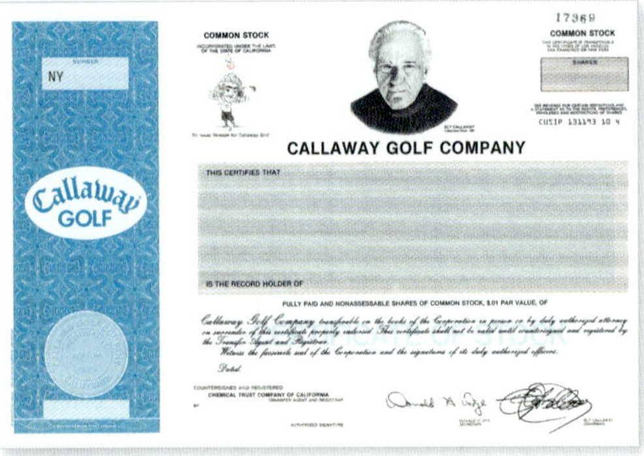

COMMON STOCK

17369

COMMON STOCK

NY

SHARES

CUSIP 131193 10 4

CALLAWAY GOLF COMPANY

THIS CERTIFIES THAT

IS THE RECORD HOLDER OF

FULLY PAID AND NONASSESSABLE SHARES OF COMMON STOCK, $.01 PAR VALUE, OF

Callaway Golf Company transferable on the books of the Corporation in person or by duly authorized attorney on surrender of this certificate properly endorsed. This certificate shall not be valid until countersigned and registered by the Transfer Agent and Registrar.

Witness the facsimile seal of the Corporation and the signatures of its duly authorized officers.

Dated

COUNTERSIGNED AND REGISTERED
CHEMICAL TRUST COMPANY OF CALIFORNIA

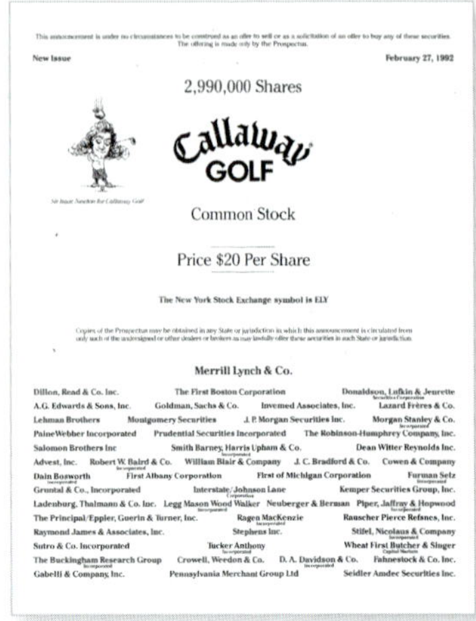

This announcement is under no circumstances to be construed as an offer to sell or as a solicitation of an offer to buy any of these securities. The offering is made only by the Prospectus.

New Issue — February 27, 1992

2,990,000 Shares

Callaway GOLF

Common Stock

Price $20 Per Share

The New York Stock Exchange symbol is ELY

Copies of the Prospectus may be obtained in any State or jurisdiction in which this announcement is circulated from only such of the undersigned or other dealers or brokers as may lawfully offer these securities in such State or jurisdiction.

Merrill Lynch & Co.

Dillon, Read & Co. Inc. — The First Boston Corporation — Donaldson, Lufkin & Jenrette Securities Corporation

A.G. Edwards & Sons, Inc. — Goldman, Sachs & Co. — Invemed Associates, Inc. — Lazard Frères & Co.

Lehman Brothers — Montgomery Securities — J. P. Morgan Securities Inc. — Morgan Stanley & Co. Incorporated

PaineWebber Incorporated — Prudential Securities Incorporated — The Robinson-Humphrey Company, Inc.

Salomon Brothers Inc — Smith Barney, Harris Upham & Co. Incorporated — Dean Witter Reynolds Inc.

Advest, Inc. — Robert W. Baird & Co. Incorporated — William Blair & Company — J. C. Bradford & Co. — Cowen & Company

Dain Bosworth Incorporated — First Albany Corporation — First of Michigan Corporation — Furman Selz Incorporated

Gruntal & Co., Incorporated — Interstate/Johnson Lane Corporation — Kemper Securities Group, Inc.

Ladenburg, Thalmann & Co. Inc. — Legg Mason Wood Walker Incorporated — Neuberger & Berman — Piper, Jaffray & Hopwood Incorporated

The Principal/Eppler, Guerin & Turner, Inc. — Ragen MacKenzie Incorporated — Rauscher Pierce Refsnes, Inc.

Raymond James & Associates, Inc. — Stephens Inc. — Stifel, Nicolaus & Company Incorporated

Sutro & Co. Incorporated — Tucker Anthony Incorporated — Wheat First Butcher & Singer Capital Markets

The Buckingham Research Group Incorporated — Crowell, Weedon & Co. — D. A. Davidson & Co. Incorporated — Fahnestock & Co. Inc.

Gabelli & Company, Inc. — Pennsylvania Merchant Group Ltd — Seidler Amdec Securities Inc.

ABOVE AND RIGHT: Callaway Golf company stock certificate and IPO prospectus cover, 1992

Diana Duvall, Ely's executive assistant, 2000

Warren Buffett and Ely, early 1990s

Opening bell, Callaway Golf IPO, New York Stock Exchange, New York, March 3, 2000

ABOVE AND BELOW: Ely and Cindy Callaway meeting the Emperor and Empress of Japan with President Bill Clinton and First Lady Hillary Clinton at the White House, Washington, D.C., June 13, 1994

THE PRESIDENT
AND MRS. CLINTON
welcome
THEIR MAJESTIES
THE EMPEROR AND EMPRESS
OF JAPAN

The White House
Monday, June 13, 1994

July 22, 1955

Mr. Herbert Warren Wind,
Editor
Sports Illustrated
9 Rockefeller Plaza
New York City, New York

Dear Herb,

Yesterday, I had the pleasure of lunching with Bob Jones. He spoke very highly of your writings on golf in general, and particularly in regard to the piece you wrote for Sports Illustrated in advance of this year's Masters Tournament at Augusta.

Unfortunately, I missed that issue. Since Bob stated that this issue of yours was the very best analysis he has yet read regarding the real purpose behind the Master's, I want to read it. If convenient for you, please send a copy to me.

With best wishes to you for continued success and good health.

Cordially,

ERC:pk

Ely R. Callaway, Jr.

Lettter to Herbert Warren Wind from Ely, July 22, 1955

THE NEW YORKER
25 WEST 43RD STREET
NEW YORK, N. Y. 10036

EDITORIAL OFFICES
(212) 840-3800

September 22, 1983

Dear Ely,

I am sorry to be this slow getting back to you for both your letter and the arrival of the two Hickory Sticks. I have been slow, because my time has been taken up by the tennis piece I have been working on this summer, then by the U.S. Tennis Open, and the wrap-up of the piece. This same preoccupation with tennis has prevented me from actually trying out the sticks on a golf course, but I can tell from just tapping and clipping ball around the office that they are first-rate. Of course, they look superb -- what hickory shaft doesn't ! -- but I have the feeling that they will play just as handsomely as they look. I want to thank you both for your thoughtfulness and your generosity.

What interests me, of course, is your ability to understand and create in totally different fields -- Burlington Mills, your vineyard, and now your steel-core clubs. That really is something ! It is very unusual for a man to combine the creative and administrative abilities in the first place, but to move into totally disparate fields and come up with something of quality both times is remarkable. And , to be sure, all the things you accomplish have that rare thing called taste. Nice going.

The photographs I have seen of the Vintage Club make it easy for me to understand why you have settled there. You can be certain that should my work take me into that vicinity, I will look forward to see you. And I hope that if you come to New York, you will get in touch with me. It is much too loong since we last talked.

All good luck on the new project.

Yours very truly

Herb

Herb Wind

Letter to Ely from Herbert Warren Wind, September 22, 1983

OFFICERS
ROBERT TYRE JONES, JR.
PRESIDENT
LEWIS B. MAYTAG
VICE-PRESIDENT
CLARENCE J. SCHOO
VICE-PRESIDENT
JOHN D. AMES
TREASURER
CHARLES R. YATES
SECRETARY

AUGUSTA, GEORGIA

EXECUTIVE COMMITTEE
CLIFFORD ROBERTS, CHAIRMAN
FRANK B. EDWARDS
ROBERT TYRE JONES, JR.
BARRY T. LEITHEAD
LEWIS B. MAYTAG
PHILIP D. REED
WALTER N. THAYER

February 8, 1963

Mr. Ely R. Callaway, Jr.
Burlington Industries, Inc.
261 Fifth Avenue
New York 16, New York

Dear Mr. Callaway:

I want to thank you once more for your courtesy in furnishing me with a ride to Los Angeles when we were stranded at that airport -- the name of which I do not even know.

In view of the fact that you evidenced such an interest in the Masters Tournament, I am forwarding to you today a copy of a plaque which the Club gave to the players and press people last year. I am in hopes it will serve as a reminder of our meeting in California.

Best regards.

Yours sincerely,

Clifford Roberts

CR:wg

Letter to Ely from Clifford Roberts, chairman of Augusta National Golf Club, February 8, 1963

Ely at Augusta National Golf Club, the day after the 58th Master's Tournament, April 11, 1994

Ely Callaway
Chairman - CEO

August 27, 1996

VIA FACSIMILE

Mr. Phil Knight
Chairman and CEO, Nike
1 Bowerman Drive
Beaverton, Oregon 97005

Dear Mr. Knight,

Perhaps we are incorrect but we have been informed that Mr. Tiger Woods has publicly announced that he has now become a golf professional and that IMG and Nike will announce tomorrow that Mr. Woods will use and endorse products specified by Nike.

If these things are true, we offer our congratulations to Nike. We also want to state to you that Tiger Woods can be of great value to Callaway Golf under certain conditions.

These conditions are:

1). That Mr. Woods make a serious and thorough evaluation of our Big Bertha Drivers in any current or future model of his choice. This evaluation to begin at any time he chooses between now and the next 12 months.

2). That Mr. Woods then becomes convinced that one or more of the Callaway drivers of his choice is the best driver to enhance his skills, and for him consistently to use in competition and for him to endorse, exclusive of any other driver.

If Mr. Woods enters into such an agreement with Callaway, we would agree to pay Nike or Woods the annual sum of $ 1.5 — 3.0 million plus bonuses for the three years following his first and continued use of any Callaway driver chosen by Mr. Woods. We would not require him to use and endorse any other Callaway golf club during the three year period.

We feel you should know that the degree of use of Callaway drivers is unprecedented not only among your own Nike Tour professionals but also on the four other significant tours. Attached are the Darrell Survey figures showing professionals use of driver brands for the tournaments held this past weekend, and cumulative for 1996 to date, as well as pertinent figures for 1995.

We also want you to know that not more than 15% of all of these pros competing that are using our clubs in all of these tournaments this year have been paid endorsement fees by Callaway.

We will be happy to discuss this matter further with you and/or Mr. Hughes Norton or Mark McCormack any time convenient for you.

Sincerely,

Donald H. Dye
President and CEO

Ely Callaway
Founder and Chairman

2285 Rutherford Road • Carlsbad, CA 92008-8815
Telephone: 619-931-1771 • Outside California: 1-800-228-2767
Facsimile: 619-929-8120

Letter to Phil Knight, CEO of Nike, from Ely and Don Dye, August 27, 1996

Ely, Carlsbad, California, 1994. Photograph by Dudley Reed

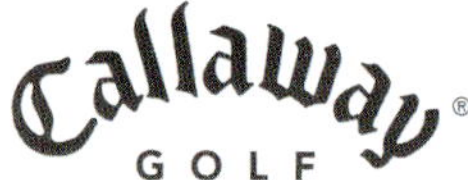

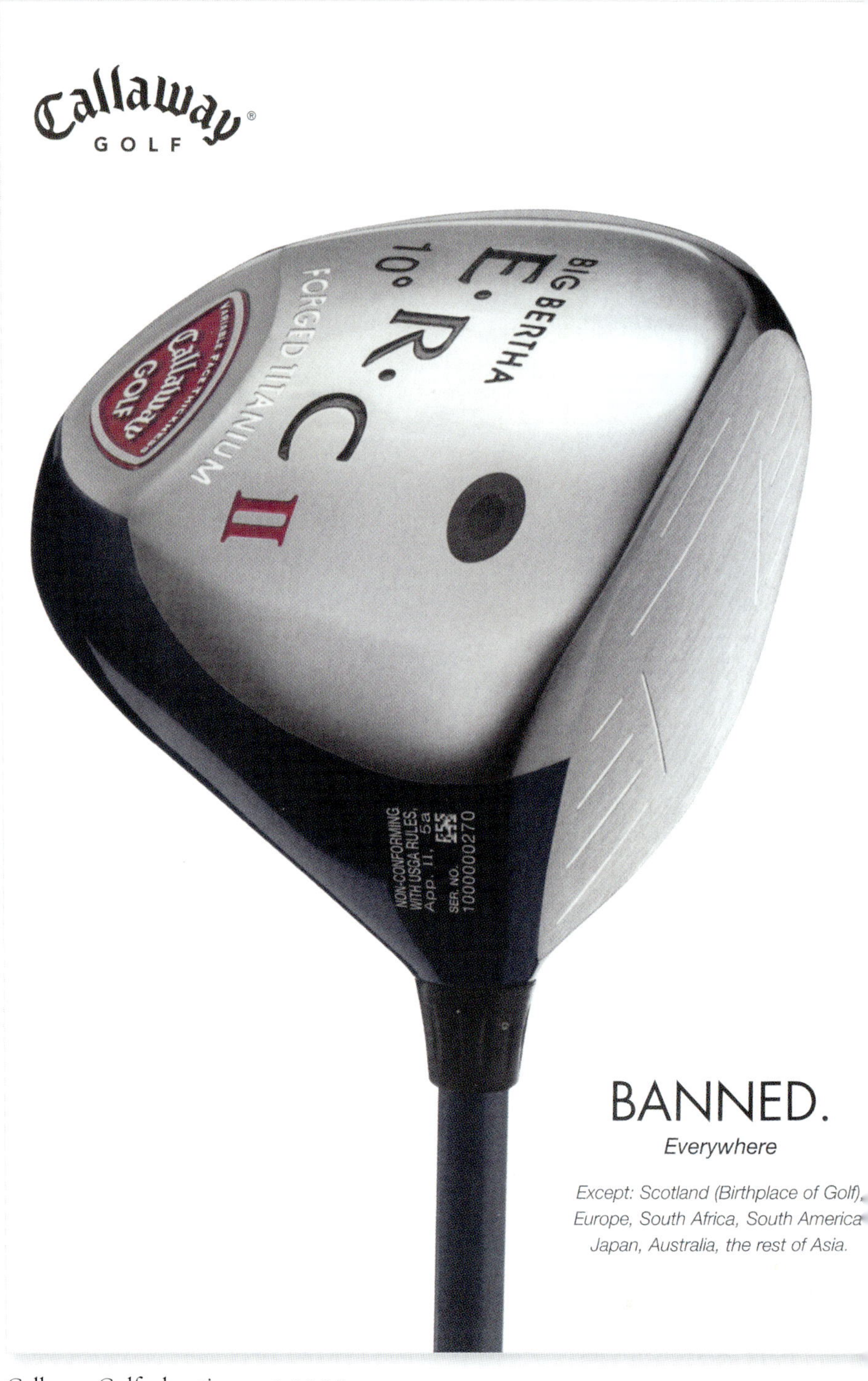
Callaway
GOLF
BIG BERTHA
10°
E.R.C
II
FORGED TITANIUM
NON-CONFORMING
WITH USGA RULES,
App. II, 5a
SER. NO. 1000000270
BANNED.
Everywhere
Except: Scotland (Birthplace of Golf),
Europe, South Africa, South America,
Japan, Australia, the rest of Asia.

Callaway Golf advertisement, 2000

BIG BERTHA
HAWK EYE
VFT-TITANIUM
10°
CONFORMS WITH
USGA RULES
SER. NO.
3000003172
BLESSED.
Everywhere

Colin Montgomerie

L TO R: ChiChi Rodriguez,
John Daly, Johnny Miller

Arnold Palmer

Patty Sheehan

Paul Azinger

TOP L TO R: Jim Dent, Bob Murphy
BOTTOM L TO R: ChiChi Rodriguez, Johnny Miller, Jim Colbert

Ely, Del Mar Country Club, Rancho Santa Fe, California, 1994 Photograph© by Mark Hanauer. All rights reserved.

Annika Sörenstam, Moon Valley Country Club, Phoenix, Arizona, 2001

Jack Nicklaus

Gary Player

Arnold Palmer

DRAFT OF ERC LETTER TO BIG 3

Dear Arnold, Jack and Gary,

For a few weeks now, even before I got sick, I have been pondering a vision of a remarkable, interesting and unique concept – probably one of the best profit potential business concepts in golf's future.

This concept involves all three of you and Callaway Golf, joined together in a variety of creative and profitable ways. I think the age, achievements and emotional growth that I expect is developing in each party involved is the key to creating this unusual opportunity for development.

Without attempting to identify or recognize some of the challenges this venture will face, I believe the benefits are so clear and unusual that the four of us should begin serious consideration immediately for creating and establishing a brand new company or division which would put Arnold Palmer, Jack Nicklaus, Gary Player and Callaway Golf Company solidly in business together. The first objective would be to design, manufacture, produce and sell full lines of golf clubs and golf balls that would be clearly and very actively promoted exclusively under the name of the new company – especially featuring the names of the individual "Big Three."

Planned and executed properly, each of these Callaway "Big Three" lines could include special design features as might be wanted by the respective divisional chief, i.e., Palmer, Nicklaus and Player. In my book, this concept is sound and doable, and can be very personally rewarding in many ways to each of you great champions. I believe that this could not have been done at any time before.

Good things have changed in all of us, so I believe the time is now for action and reward. With your advise and counsel and enthusiasm, our company will take the signal from you and will begin to bring together in many details the small and big things that have to be agreed upon and envisioned as being worthwhile objectives.

Despite my illness, and even if things don't go as well as expected with my health, the basic idea I am presenting is more doable and more likely to succeed under the conditions I see for our company in the future. And I feel pretty sure this could not have been done in the past.

I look forward to your reactions and comments as soon as is practicable.

With warm regards,

Ely

Draft of letter from Ely to the Big Three – Arnold Palmer, Jack Nicklaus, and Gary Player, May 2001

Portrait of Ely. Photograph by Mariana Cook, 1992.

world, setting a speed record of 254.76 mph. I am hugely proud of Reeves for doing what he loves and for following my diffrunt and bettuh philosophy – there may even be more Callaway Cars nuts than Callaway Golf nuts.

The year was 1987, and I saw immediately that we had a winner on our hands. Once again, we were looking to make demonstrably superior and pleasingly different products, and the S2H2 club was both. We were golfers, so we had an in-house testing department. This was also an important aspect of Callaway's success. If we had invented a superior Cuisinart by accident, we wouldn't have known it was superior. But since we were golfers (and two or three of our salesmen were golfers) we could trust our reaction, and that faith prevented us from second-guessing ourselves when we faced difficult times.

We shifted production entirely to steel-end graphite-shaft S2H2 irons and phased out the Hickory Stick irons (but kept the Hickory Stick putters and wedges). To accomplish this, we had to remake the company: we needed new equipment, new tools, a new factory, new people, and a lot of new money. We even changed our name; Callaway Hickory Stick became Callaway Golf. This was a thrilling moment; for the first time, we saw just how big this enterprise could become. It also signaled the arrival of the dreaded, inevitable moment I had spent my own money trying to delay. It was time to raise private capital investment.

The Hardest Thing in Business

The single biggest problem I've ever had to overcome is financing. No matter how much success I've had before, it's never been easy for me to get money the next time. I'm not sure it's ever been easy for any entrepreneur. Many promising companies collapse before their time simply because they could not get the money they needed. The fundamental problem is that the more you grow, the more capital you need. When a company is growing, it takes years to become profitable, because the costs are constantly increasing.

Take our S2H2 irons, which were immediately in demand. We needed to order enough raw materials and clubheads to fulfill the orders, and that was expensive as hell. S2H2 had a minimum lead time of 26 weeks – more than six months between placing the initial purchase order and the product arriving on the shelves – let alone the time it took to get paid on the road to breaking even. If a successful product could be instantaneously turned into cash flow and profit, then you wouldn't need all that outside money to expand. That would be lovely, wouldn't it? But that ain't the way it works.

After two private placements that raised $2 million, once again we were running low on cash. We lost nearly $1 million in 1987, and I wrote a $900,000 check to the company to keep it going. I didn't ask for more shares; I didn't even ask for interest. It wasn't everything I had, but it was a large chunk. I made this personal loan to the company without hesitation because I believed in the golf clubs. That's what entrepreneurs have to do. They have to be so convinced of the virtue of their product that they empty their wallets and don't lose any sleep over it. An entrepreneur who is not willing to spend their last dollar should stick with the job they've got, take up fishing in their spare time, and save themselves a lot of grief.

My $900,000 was enough to carry us for a few months,

but to go into full production with these new irons we needed additional millions – $4 million, by my estimate. That's a fairly substantial chunk of change, four million bucks. I thought we should try to get the financing from a company that might be a potential strategic buyer for Callaway Golf somewhere down the road. The company was valued at $20 million, and we were willing to sell 20 percent of the company for $4 million. By the way, we did the valuation ourselves.

Our first target was Sumitomo. Sumitomo was the oldest of the four great trading companies of Japan, known as the *zaibatsu*, dating back to the 19th-century Imperial era, along with Mitsui, Mitsubishi, and Yasuda. Sumitomo was also the biggest bank in the world, and that's only one of about 15 different areas in which they dominated. They were the biggest shipbuilders in the world, the largest copper producers, and ironically enough the world's number one textile producer (by this point, Burlington was shrinking fast). Sumitomo was the biggest in everything.

We already had a fine relationship with Sumitomo. Among its many divisions was Sumitomo Rubber Industries, which made Dunlop golf balls. Sumitomo Rubber had taken over as the distributor for Callaway clubs in Japan, and we were about to sign them up as our exclusive sales reps over there, doing our small part to try to undo the massive U.S. trade deficit. We had already shown Sumitomo prototypes of the S2H2 irons, and they were impressed.

This was all somewhat ironic, given that I had grown up fighting Japan as America's mortal enemy in war, and then in the post-war era as an adversary who decimated the textile industry through unfair trade practices. In fact, over 20 years earlier in

1959 I had sat across the table from Japan's business leaders and tried to negotiate more balanced international trade deals as part of the U.S.-Japan Economic Trade Council. And now, I was asking them to invest in my upstart golf club company.

In 1987, Japan was still riding high off its economic miracle. With Japan now firmly established as the second-largest economy in the world, everybody there was trying to invest in the United States, and Sumitomo was no different. They were looking for new ventures, and we were becoming prominent in a tiny way, so it was a real no-brainer. Not to mention, Japan revered American brands and was a golf-obsessed nation. They loved the precision, power, and privilege associated with golf. Sumitomo already loved distributing our clubs and believed in our future, so they made a deal with us.

Don Dye and I decided to offer to sell Sumitomo 25 percent of Callaway for $5 million, giving us a $1 million cushion over what we thought we needed (we'd been underestimating our cash needs all along, so this was really a cushion against ourselves). Sumitomo would also get an option to buy more shares later. We were dealing with Sumitomo's regional director in Denver, Isao "Kami" Kamitani. He handled the joint venture with Coors, which had a distribution agreement with Kirin Beer, another subsidiary of Sumitomo.

Once we had Kamitani-san on our side, we had to convince his bosses in the Sumitomo New York office, and then their bosses at Sumitomo Rubber in Japan. Everybody agreed it was a wonderful investment for Sumitomo. By this time, the deal had been pared down so we were selling 20 percent of the company for $4 million, the amount we thought we needed in the first place. The letters of intent were drawn up, representatives from

Sumitomo New York flew out to California to visit our plant, and the deal was progressing along without a hitch.

We scheduled a ceremony to consummate the marriage in April 1988 at the factory in Carlsbad. Sumitomo sent a large contingent that included Kamitani, the president of Sumitomo USA, Sadao Taura, and a couple of top people from Sumitomo Rubber in Tokyo. We played golf together and had a dinner party to celebrate the closing – except there was no closing. This turned out to be a kind of practice signing, with the real one scheduled for a week later, when I would fly to New York to meet with Taura in his office. It seemed a bit strange, since the president of Sumitomo USA was already sitting right next to me at the dinner in Carlsbad, but I didn't think much of it.

A week later, Cindy and I headed for New York for the closing. There were no issues in dispute, no points to be negotiated; it was just a matter of putting pen to paper and playing a round of golf with Taura at his club on Long Island. But when Cindy and I walked into our room at the University Club (where I had negotiated my Burlington severance two decades before), we were confronted with an urgent message from Kamitani-san in Denver. I called him and he gave me the news: Tokyo had turned down our request for the money. Kamitani was upset and deeply apologetic. Cindy was upset. I was confused. Kamitani had no explanation for how such a thing could happen at this late date.

I kept my golf date with Taura and his wife, hoping he could shed some light on this incredible situation in between strokes with his new S2H2 irons. He said very little, except that Sumitomo still wanted to distribute our golf clubs, and Tokyo's reaction was a mystery to him.

Less than two months later, Sadao Taura was fired. This is a lesson for people doing business with a company like Sumitomo. Sumitomo was obsessed with consensus. We had consensus from the bottom all the way up the company hierarchy, but in Japan, no decision is final unless it comes from the *shachou* in the head office in Japan. The president of Sumitomo USA sounded like the top, but he wasn't. What happened, I think, was that he overstepped his bounds in approving the Callaway deal without the consensus from Tokyo. Tokyo didn't like that, so they got rid of him. They sent him to Siberia – I mean, they literally sent him to their offices in Siberia.

What I failed to realize, and what I really should've known after a lifetime of dealing with Japan, was that their corporate hierarchies are strict and all-powerful. I had run up against this before at Burlington and with Milliken and had been able to navigate around them and keep my independence (until, of course, I was fired both times), but there was no such wiggle room to be found at Sumitomo. I thought I had found Callaway Golf's financial savior, but Japan left me at the altar.

Playing Hardball with Jack Welch

When the Sumitomo deal fell through, Callaway Golf was in deep trouble. It would've been easy to despair, to feel sorry for myself, to curse fate or Sumitomo or the incompetent trade policy of the United States. But I was too preoccupied to worry about that. I was busy wondering who we could approach next for the missing $4 million. My next idea was even bolder: United States Tobacco. They turned us down right away. So much for that.

In the middle of being rejected by Sumitomo and U.S. Tobacco, we got word that our board member Elmer Ward had convinced his friend Larry Carpenter to try our clubs. Carpenter loved them so much that he convinced *his* friend, GE Chairman Jack Welch, to try them too. Welch played with our new irons and thought they were terrific. At that time, General Electric was so big that out of every dollar spent in America, a penny was spent on a GE product. I'd never met Welch, but his reputation more than preceded him. Since becoming the big boss in 1981, Welch had undertaken an aggressive campaign to rapidly grow GE while making it more efficient. To those he favored, Welch could be generous with bonuses and stock options, but he was a hard-driving negotiator and ruthless cost-cutter, particularly when it came to people. He loathed red tape and bureaucracy, and his love for mergers and acquisitions made Textron's Roy Little look puny.

I wasn't going to make the same mistake with GE that I had with Sumitomo, so I sent a letter directly to Welch via Federal Express, and two days later he answered with a fax. Here's the head of one of the biggest companies in the world responding in a day and a half to a fundraising campaign from an upstart golf club maker. He never would have bothered if he hadn't liked the clubs. If an entrepreneur has a good product, they should do whatever it takes to get it into the hands of influential people. You never know when your efforts will pay off.

Welch explained that Callaway Golf wasn't a GE kind of investment, but the GE Pension Fund might be interested. He told me I'd be hearing from Dale Frey, the GE treasurer and chairman of the board of the Pension Fund. In less than a week, I got a call from Frey, who put me in touch with the president of the Fund, John Myers (no relation to Burlington's Charles).

From the way it sounded, I didn't think these two were very interested. They didn't think investors could make any money from a golf club company (and up until that point, they were right), but they invited Don Dye and me to Connecticut to meet with them anyway. I don't doubt the reason: the boss of GE had suggested it. Even though they didn't want to make an investment, they were talking to us because Jack Welch had encouraged the relationship. Whenever you're dealing with the potential source of funds, try to work from the top down, and not from the bottom up.

Don Dye, Larry Carpenter, and I flew out to Connecticut, my turf for 25 years, to visit Myers and Frey. When I had lived there decades earlier, I was a prince of the American corporate establishment; now I was returning to deal with the king of American business. Right off the bat, my suspicions were confirmed: they weren't interested in us, because we were too small for them. We wanted $4 million, and for the GE Pension Fund, $4 million was pocket change. But even though we got a no for an answer, I wasn't about to give up. I knew if Frey and Myers could find a way to justify making this investment, they would do it because, in the backs of their minds, they wanted to please Jack Welch, who liked our golf clubs.

It took a couple of visits to bring them around. I showed them the clubs. I gave them testimonials from other golfers besides Welch who had tested the clubs. The one thing I didn't want to do was let the two of them try the clubs. Myers and Frey played golf, to a point. The most optimistic thing you could say about their game was that it was consistent. New clubs, I figured, wouldn't have helped them. But soon enough, they got interested.

I had heard from friends and associates, at the top level of the corporate establishment, that GE played very hardball, and my God, were they right. From the first day of negotiations, they sent down their investigator, Wolfe "Bill" H. Bragin, the vice president of GE Asset Management. Bragin started talking about how he was going to run the show. He found fault with everything and told everybody what to do: he wanted to change the distribution system; he wanted to have something to say about clubs. He'd been there all of 20 minutes and hadn't even invested yet and already he was strong-arming us like some sort of wannabe mafioso. He fundamentally did not respect what I had built. My diagnosis of the situation was that there was a fundamental fear within GE of being taken advantage of. These people were handling giant pools of money at one of the great successful companies in the world, and they were scared to death that an upstart golf club company with a few million in annual sales was going to fleece them.

This attitude reflected the nature of Jack Welch, who was a Boston street fighter – that's literally what he was. He grew up on the streets with no money and a mother who encouraged him to be aggressive. He fought his way up and now he was brawling with us, even though ours was a little deal. The only reason it was even happening in the first place was that he had a sentimental desire to get into the golf club industry. If it failed, it was no skin off his behind; it was just something fun to do. Even still, Welch sawed the ropes to cut a very hard deal, allowing his negotiator to change two deal points at the last moment after we'd already agreed to them. I don't remember what they were; I was too upset. I do have to give Welch some credit; he ran one of the most successful corporations in the world. But I loathe these kinds of two-faced deal-makers and always have.

Fortunately for me, I was battle-tested from having gone up against the worst of the worst: Murder, Inc. in World War II; a brutal C-suite duel to the death at Burlington; moldy grapes in the Southern California desert. My war with Burlington, for instance, had given me the experience and the tools necessary to not let Neutron Jack railroad me, as he did almost everyone else in business. I may have been in the final third of my life, but Lord knows I still had the vigor to stand up to schoolyard bullies like Welch and Bragin.

If the deal with GE went through, it was going to fundamentally alter the stock structure of Callaway Golf, which meant negotiating with my own team as well as Welch's. As the terms of the deal began to take shape, Manzoni and Parente believed they were being diluted. I think they felt they were losing control of their invention. And it was true; by going out and getting the money, they were giving up the baby they'd conceived together in a garage in Temecula. We had several discussions in which I tried to convince them that what they were really getting was a smaller piece of a much bigger pie.

Parente in particular felt very insecure. He'd had a deal fall through at a previous company, and was scarred by the burden of that failure. But in my mind, that was the wrong attitude. What matters is how you react to failure. I'd taken my licks, just like Parente. Anybody who's ever risked creating something new has gotten kicked in the teeth a few times. But I wasn't going to let the fear of giving up 50 percent of my ownership of the company nor disillusionment with GE stop me from doing what I knew was necessary for the company to reach its full potential. I made the deal with GE.

The other big structural change came when GE's men joined our board of directors. This is one of my favorite subjects. The purpose of a board of directors is not to run the company, but simply to choose the chief executive and then give him or her free rein to run the company as they see fit. Most of the time when a board picks the wrong executive, they don't know it before it's too late, and if they picked the wrong one, why the hell should they pick the next one?

The problem with Callaway's board was that it was now filled with outsiders – people like Dale Frey, who had a huge financial investment in a business that he did not understand. It didn't used to be this way. In the 1920s, boards were made up of people from within the company. They echoed the philosophy of the chief executive, and he was allowed to run things as his own personal fiefdom. That's what works best in my book. Today, boards screw things up by harassing the executive and making his job six times harder than it needs to be.

We held our first board meeting with GE in Fairfield, Connecticut. Dale Frey and John Myers were there, along with other board members like Mike Sherwin, who had invested $400,000 in Callaway Golf for National City Bank of Cleveland about a year before GE came into the picture. Mike opened with, "Well, you know, I'm sure glad we got GE in this picture here because now I think we can bring some organization and discipline into the company." Mike asked Frey to ask me what our business and marketing plan was, and I revealed that we didn't have one. We didn't show Mike or the GE people one when they invested, we didn't have one now, and we were not going to have one moving forward.

Mike didn't respond, but later at lunch, he pulled me aside. "Ely, I've been trying to get you for two years to come up with a formal structured plan and a budget. We need it now."

And I replied, "Why do you need it?"

He insisted, "Because every company needs discipline. And you do too. That's the reason: it will discipline us."

And I simply said, "I do not need any discipline of that type – I really don't, Mike. If you can show me that I need it, okay. But we're going to run this company the way I feel it should be run, and we are subject to change without notice because flexibility and the ability to make a decision in the moment and go with it or not is what's going to make us successful. Besides, that's the way I operate. That's what I did at Burlington in all of my areas."

Now, it's not that we didn't really have plans or a budget – we did! But we didn't want the board to get their hands on it and say, "Here's the budget and you're not meeting it and therefore you're doing it wrong." If we were crooked or lazy or getting drunk or something like that and not meeting a budget, that would be different. But we already knew that any budget we made would change often, and we didn't want to limit our flexibility or our creativity.

And when it came to creativity, Callaway was about to make another giant leap forward. Not just for the company or even the golf club industry, but for the entire game of golf.

"The merits of hard-nosed bargaining are overrated. My negotiation philosophy is: drive a soft bargain."

CHAPTER 7

A RADICAL CHANGE IN ATTITUDE

How Big Bertha Revolutionized the Game Forever

Everybody's Least Favorite Club

Since a Scotsman invented the game of golf sometime in the 15th century, and for the next 500 years or so thereafter, the club that people liked least was the driver. Everybody was scared of it. I knew this from having played the game for half a century. Sure, people bought them, but they didn't like them because they had no confidence in their ability to hit a good drive with it, and that's not an enjoyable golf experience.

Standard drivers were made of persimmon wood, which made a great crack when you hit them – more like Hank Aaron striking a baseball than the crisp metal pings you hear at today's driving ranges. At an average of 140 cubic centimeters, the clubhead was also significantly smaller, which left an itty-bitty margin for error. If golf gives the player plenty of time to commit suicide, then hitting an old persimmon driver was like playing Russian roulette.

When Callaway set out to reimagine the driver in the late 1980s, we knew we needed to create something radically new that would significantly improve the average golfer's chances of hitting a good shot with their generally not-too-good swing. We needed a club with a larger sweet spot that remained stable at impact (particularly for off-center swings), allowing the player to make more mistakes – a club that was forgiving. The problem was fundamentally one of physics: we needed to make our existing driver clubhead design 25 percent bigger, but not heavier (otherwise it would be too cumbersome to swing and more likely to break). We were willing to gamble that if we did that, we'd have a more satisfying club that would sell at a profit.

We did not originate the oversized clubhead. Hisamitsu Ohnishi, the executive director of our Japanese distributor, Sumitomo, and one of the great figures in golf in Japan, had introduced us to an oversized driver called the Yonex. This club was big in Japan, and Ohnishi thought it might do well to add this type of design to Callaway's repertoire. Dick Helmstetter, Don Dye, Bruce Parker, and I decided to try it out. Bruce barely played golf, but it was always good to have the opinion of a typical hacker when evaluating a new club.

We liked the idea, but after three weeks of trials, we determined the Yonex was not even as good as our S2H2 driver. It didn't feel as good, and it didn't perform as well. Still, the idea of an oversized clubhead was promising. This was a critical moment: we could take the safe route and simply make an American knockoff of the Yonex and sell it right away, or spend a lot of time and money finding ways to improve it. Some say it's best to be first – that's a myth. Being first is always very short lived. The key is to be first *and* the best. We chose to take our time and make the best. Fortunately for us, nobody else was interested in oversized clubheads, so we were going to be first no matter what.

Our first problem was that the Yonex had a graphite head. Graphite was a composite material of carbon fiber and epoxy that could be stretched easily but was too prone to scuffing and caving in. We thought, "Let's try to make it out of stainless steel instead, which is a stronger metal that could better hold its shape." A steel head would require developing a whole new casting technology – a technique to stretch the walls thin enough to make it big but sturdy enough to hold up on impact. I called up Jack Welch and told him about this hot new idea we had, and asked if anybody in his R&D department could lend us a hand. Welch said, "Let me put you in touch with my aircraft department."

My design team, led by Dick Helmstetter and our toolmaker, Glenn Schmidt, with some help from GE's science and technology people, crafted a whole new clubhead mold that could produce 100,000 stainless steel heads without serious deterioration. Usually, the more you made, the more the quality of the clubheads would deteriorate over time, particularly with the size we were attempting. This mold cost twice as much as a regular mold, but in the long run would be cheaper and make a better clubhead.

I didn't want to see any of this new technology or new designs until they were done, not even a drawing. I'm not a technical person and I can't visualize anything, so I didn't want to see anything halfway through. All I wanted to see was the finished product so I could take it out and use it. Dick plopped down the first oversized stainless steel clubhead on my desk in the summer of 1990. It wasn't that big, but it was bigger than normal at the time. It was also ugly. But it pleased me in a way I couldn't quite put into words. I told Dick to stick the head on a shaft so we could take it for a spin.

Dick and I tested our new driver that weekend at The Vintage Club in Indian Wells, where I'd first discovered the Hickory Stick 10 years earlier. The first time I swung it was on the tenth hole of the Mountain Course. I hit my first shot off the tee right down the middle of the fairway. That was good, but it wasn't the clincher: on my second shot, I hit the driver off the fairway and the ball fired directly to the pin. As good a player as I was, I could not hit this kind of shot from the fairway. The trajectory as it rose into the air was more like a tee shot than an approach shot – it felt like it had been propelled out of a cannon rather than ricocheted off the club face.

Because of this feeling, the name of our new driver came to me almost immediately. I've always had a knack for naming things. Years before it was a credit card, I named a fabric Visa, because I thought the fabric traveled well. Bobby Jones had a similar knack. He named his putter Calamity Jane, after the female sharpshooter in Buffalo Bill's Wild West Show. It was not uncommon for people to name golf clubs after weapons – Spalding came out with a series of clubs called The Cannon in the mid-80s. I remembered a reference book on artillery from my days in the army during World War II. There was one image of a giant World War I German howitzer invented by Friedrich Krupp AG, the largest weapons manufacturer in Germany. The reference book claimed this particular cannon shot artillery shells further and straighter than any other. German soldiers had bestowed the cannon with a peculiar nickname.

I often went golfing with my son, Nicholas, and I brought the new Callaway driver to the Del Mar Country Club one weekend, hoping I might impress him. I told him, "Nicky, we're gonna bring out a new golf club next year, and this is the first prototype. It is going to change the game of golf. I've even given it a name. Would you like to know what it is?"

And he said, "Sure, lay it on me."

"I'm gonna call it Big Bertha."

Nicholas shot back, "Ely, that's the worst name for a product I've ever heard."

I replied, "Well, you're wrong, for two reasons. First. it's a great name because it has a story behind it. The World War I German cannon! Second, just remember: the product makes the name, the name doesn't make the product."

Nicholas retorted, "I still think it's a terrible name."

I said, "Well, why don't you try it out and then tell me what you think?" Nicholas addressed the ball on the tee and took a mighty swing. It made a very strange sound, and not just from the fact that the clubhead was stainless steel. When he looked down at the tee, the ball had dribbled just a few yards, while the clubhead had flown 30 yards down the fairway. He was left holding a headless shaft.

I turned to Nicholas and reassured him, "Well . . . we've still got a few gluing problems to solve. And I swear that in 12 months the Big Bertha is going to be the biggest-selling golf club in the world and it's going to change the game forever."

I was right.

Don't Let the Problems Kill the Promise

The truth was our problems went far beyond gluing. In order to make the clubhead bigger but not heavier, we stretched the stainless steel perimeter walls like blowing up a balloon. This had the unintended consequence of making our driver sound like an empty Campbell's Soup can every time you struck the ball.

The sound seemed like a disadvantage. Every player knows that that sound on impact is key. Or maybe they know it, but don't know they know it. Throughout his career, Ben Hogan preferred his old-fashioned forged iron clubs over the newer cast iron clubs. Hogan was famous for being able to tell a cast iron from a forged iron club by its feel alone. But was it really the feeling? I maintain there's no way for any human, no matter how good a golfer, to tell the difference between these extremely hard surfaces just by looking at the club, touching it, or even by how it feels to swing. No, I believe the difference was the sound.

Now I can't prove it more than anyone else can, but I think Hogan could recognize a subtle difference in the sound of the impact between cast and forged irons, and the sound of his old irons just pleased him more. Perhaps it reminded him of when he was a boy first learning how to golf, and the joy and innocence of youth. I still maintain it was the sound that was the difference for Ben Hogan, and I believe that most humans can tell the difference too, even if it's only subconsciously.

We worked hard to preserve that classic persimmon sound. First, we filled the heads with foam so they wouldn't sound so hollow. But the foam made the club heavier, causing our shafts to continually break. We then tried lighter foam, but that deteriorated within the clubhead after only a month. We had many problems, but they were the kind of problems you run into when you're trying to do something nobody has ever done before. The only question was whether the problems were going to kill the promise.

Eventually, I decided to get rid of the foam, in part because of the weight problem, but also because we decided we liked the sound of the early Big Berthas better. With all due respect to Ben Hogan, we were selling a whole new type of club; why should it sound like an old one? Around the time we were developing Big Bertha, our chief rival TaylorMade released their own line of metal woods. They spent God knows how much filling their clubheads with foam to maintain that pure persimmon wood sound, then a hell of a lot more money advertising that they'd done it. We didn't need to bother with that, because the Big Bertha and its unconventional sound were going to bring the golf club industry out of the Stone Age and into the Space Age. It didn't sound like a tin can anymore; it sounded like a Big Bertha. Like the location of Callaway Vineyard & Winery, we took a perceived disadvantage and turned it into an asset. We sold the difference.

I've always believed it pays to make a product that is different from what is already out there, and then promote the fact that it's different. If the product is good enough, the difference will sell it. Once upon a time back in the vineyard days, I happened to notice the label on the back of a bottle from the Chateau Ste. Michelle Winery in Yakima Valley in Washington State. Most of the label was taken up with a map that showed that the winery was on the same latitude as the Burgundy region of France. The people in charge of this advertising wanted you to think that Ste. Michelle wine would emulate the character of wines from the Burgundy region simply because the two places were located on the same degree of latitude.

I found this so interesting that I went to fetch an atlas. I followed the latitude to Washington and across the U.S. to France, where it hits Burgundy, just as the label says. But before the line gets to Burgundy, it passes through Nova Scotia and touches the edge of Greenland. In the logic of the Ste. Michelle advertising department, this means that wine from Nova Scotia and Greenland ought to be of the same high quality as wine from Burgundy and Washington. The Greenlanders and the Nova Scotians are missing a fine bet. They should get out of the fur business, or the fishing business, and plant vineyards.

I made this point with various luminaries at a Napa wine conference. Their reaction was, "Well, that's interesting," but then they let it drop. It's standard procedure for companies to try to compare their latest products to the successful brand names that are already in the marketplace. They don't realize that this is a self-defeating strategy. When the Chateau Ste. Michelle Winery produced that map, trying to make a far-fetched connection between Washington and Burgundy, it was giving a plug to Burgundy wine. It was telling you that when you bought Ste. Michelle wine, you were buying an imitation of the real thing. The label might as well have said, "Drink Burgundy."

Once my sales department got over their brief misgivings about the name, they wanted to release the Big Bertha immediately. The new club was certainly better and different than the products we had on the market, but Dick and I believed that as good as the Big Bertha was, it could be better. We still felt it was too ugly, and Dick thought we could create a new mold (what he called BB-2) that would be both bigger and more aesthetically pleasing, and that we shouldn't go to market until then. You never want your new product to have any disadvantages, and so long as we saw ways to improve Big Bertha, I wasn't going to be satisfied with just "good enough."

We got the final factory samples of Big Bertha around Christmas 1990, with clubheads a whopping 190cc. It wasn't just that it was bigger. By putting more weight around the perimeter of the clubhead, we instantly enlarged the sweet spot compared to persimmon drivers. Our designers used our patented S2H2 technology to eliminate the neck of the club by extending the shaft through the clubhead, creating more energy at impact. We tested them at Bear Creek in Temecula, next to where I lived, and at The Vintage Club. The Big Bertha performed so beautifully, we just hit balls indiscriminately into the desert for sheer pleasure.

When you're releasing a new product, you have to predict how many you're going to sell for the first six months of the next year, so you can decide how many to fabricate and therefore what the lead time must be as well as how much money you will risk on inventory. Starting from scratch, it took 26 weeks to get a clubhead after placing an order with the foundry. You don't go down to the corner store and ask for 10,000 Big Bertha clubheads and get them within two weeks. Someone suggested we order 40,000. but I said, "No, we're going to order 60,000," which at the time was a huge commitment. No customer had tried the club or even seen it, but still, we ordered 60,000 clubs.

We bet the farm on Big Bertha. Each club cost about $25 to $30 to produce, instead of the usual $12. We spent $2 million producing these funny-looking, oversized sticks. We had a feeling our casting technique would hold up to 500 clubheads before the mold deteriorated, but 60,000? We really had no idea. Meanwhile, the head of the casting plant was a heavy drinker and ran us all nuts. We couldn't kill him, we couldn't fire him, and we couldn't ignore him – we just had to work around him. Hasn't everybody encountered that kind of person in their workplace?

After we placed the order but before we debuted Big Bertha, the GE Pension Fund heard about this promising new club and wanted to have a meeting. Dale Frey told us how excited they were about our new product we were about to premiere. "Now, we know you name everything," He said, "and I hear that you're going to name it Big Bertha, and we're wondering whether or not that's the best name."

I replied, "Well, we think it is. Have you got a better one?

And he said, "No, no, it's just that some of us think it might not be the best."

"Some of us who?"

"Well, me, and John Myers and Jack Welch."

Well, that's a pretty powerful group right there. But they didn't have a substitute, so I told them the name was Big Bertha and that's the way it was. Very few people rebelled against Jack Welch, but I didn't give a damn what Jack Welch thought, and I told Dale Frey just that. Now, you can't do that unless you have a record of achievement or unless you're very foolish. But my record of achievement was such that I could reasonably take a position, and say, well, I'm going to do things my way.

Despite my bold prediction to Nicholas, I didn't know exactly how good Big Bertha was, or if it would even be successful. No matter how much confidence you have, there's no real way of knowing until a product is used by the customer. We didn't really do any market research either, at least not in the traditional sense. And why would we? If I had gone to consumers in 1991 and asked them whether or not they would buy a driver that was 25 percent bigger than the one they already had; looked totally different from anything they'd ever hit; was priced twice as high as any driver they'd ever paid for; made a peculiar sound on impact; and had a funny-sounding name to boot, they would say no. So we didn't ask them! We wanted to do it, and we knew that if we did it right, the customers would buy it and be delighted.

We debuted the Big Bertha at the PGA trade show in Orlando in January 1991. We didn't do much advertising, because we couldn't afford it. Instead, we designed our campaigns to create a maximum splash. During the week of the trade show, we took out a full-page ad in the local North Florida Edition of *The Wall Street Journal*. Our sales staff hand-delivered the paper to every hotel room in town on the second day of the show. Since nobody notices whether or not it's a local edition, these people thought they were seeing an expensive national ad. With brain power, a few sore backs, and a little money, we got a lot of high-priced exposure on the cheap.

Callaway held a press conference to discuss our revolutionary new club, and I made sure to put Jack Welch beside me at the table. I asked him to stand up and accept some recognition for helping develop Big Bertha. He hadn't really done much, but he was our money, and it's never a bad idea to let your money feel good about itself. Three years prior, our S2H2 irons had established us as a company to be reckoned with, but that was nothing compared to the enthusiasm with which the industry greeted Big Bertha.

Changing the Psychology of Golf

Big Bertha was one of those products, of which there are very few, that lit a fuse and took off like a rocket. We had fretted over our initial order of 60,000. We should've ordered 150,000. Within weeks of the trade show, before a single consumer had spent a cent on a club, pros on the PGA, Senior, and LPGA tours were teeing off with Big Bertha. President George Bush, Bill Clinton, Sean Connery, Jack Lemmon, and most of the CEOs and corporate executives at the AT&T Pro Am had a Bertha in their bag. Within a year it became the best-selling golf club in the world, favored by pros and hackers alike. Our sales that year leaped to $54 million. And during that whole first year, we ran three print ads and not one second of television ads. It was all word of mouth.

Once we sold through our initial stock, it took us the better part of three and a half years to catch up with demand. The Big Bertha catapulted us from a small golf club company into a behemoth. It also kicked off the age of stainless steel drivers and oversized clubheads, an arms race of bigger heads and lighter metals that would continue into the 21st century.

Big Bertha was truly revolutionary not only because of the innovative technology and unprecedented sales but because it forever altered the psychology of golf. The club fundamentally changed the attitude of the masses about the driver from one of fear to one of affection, because we made it so easy to use, relatively speaking. Today, it's a fact that the driver is the most favored club in the bag. People love their driver because they get more satisfaction from it. That's what we did. We took away their fear. We made a radical change in people's attitudes.

What Callaway accomplished with Big Bertha can be done in any business. Think of how the internet and email changed personal computing, or how Amazon popularized online shopping, to name just some of the inventions that hit the market within a few years of my driver. Suddenly an aspect of the game that perhaps felt too advanced for the common man became widely accessible, even beloved. It isn't that hard to do. The problem is that most people don't make up their minds to do it.

"They don't show up in the cost-benefit analysis, but I'm convinced that generosity and kindness can boost productivity and add to corporate earnings."

"Some say it's best to be first. That's a myth. That success is very short lived. The key is to be first and the best."

CHAPTER 8

DIFFRUNT AND BETTUH

How Callaway Innovated Its Way to Becoming the Biggest Golf Equipment Company in the World

The Problem Is They Fell in Love with Us

When I bought Hickory Stick in 1983, we had five employees in a 1,500-square-foot office, and our annual sales were $500,000. In 1988, the year we introduced the S2H2 irons, our sales were $5 million. By 1993, we had 1,200 workers, expanded our plant to 250,000 square feet, and hit sales of $255 million. Our income that year was $42 million, more than doubled from '92 (the year I took Callaway public). We weren't just the most successful company in our industry, we had the 7th fastest-growing revenue of any company of any kind in the entire state of California and the 14th highest in the whole country.

It took Burlington 50 years to rise from one itty-bitty mill to the largest company in its industry. Callaway took only 10 years to go from pipsqueak to gorilla. It was a meteoric rise, unprecedented in the history of golf clubs. Our success was built almost entirely on the back of Big Bertha drivers and metal woods, which accounted for roughly 75 percent of our total sales, not to mention a third of the drivers and woods used by professionals on the PGA Tour. Callaway had transformed from a dumpy little nobody to one of the biggest, most respected golf club companies, as well as one of the most recognizable brands in the world.

We were just getting started.

By the end of '91, it was obvious to GE that they hadn't been too dumb to invest in us after all. What began as a tenuous relationship became a red-hot love affair, and they fell in love with Callaway more and more every month. Why wouldn't they? GE took a chance on us in the first place because they wanted the prestige that came with owning a golf business, and Big Bertha made us the belle of the ball. They saw we knew how to manage this very fast-growth company, and profitably so. We liked that. It was wonderful! The problem was the more they fell in love with us, the more they wanted to help us, but the reality was they really couldn't help us at all.

Now it's not that the folks at GE weren't smart. It's not that they were not able, fine businessmen, and it's not that they didn't have vast experience. The problem was these people didn't know the first damn thing about the golf club business. The only things they knew about the business were in the reports we gave them, which they could read and tell were fantastic, but they knew nothing about what Callaway actually did or how we did it.

GE would harass us by sending their little minions, the number-crunchers. Every company has them, but GE's were a particular nuisance. They'd descend like locusts on our Carlsbad office and try to help us with our planning and budgeting and make everybody nervous as hell. They'd ask a bunch of questions they didn't need to know the answers to, then give a bunch of advice about marketing and spending that didn't make one iota of sense.

The main thrust of their curiosity seemed to be that they couldn't understand how we were this successful. They didn't understand how a golf company could be so much more profitable than any of our competitors, and maybe even suspected something fishy was going on; either we didn't know how to do our own books because we were stupid, or we were cooking our books because we were crooked. Bullshit! We were neither. What they couldn't comprehend was that we had an operation just as good as GE's in every way, probably better, with the highest possible level of administrative and reporting controls; superior relationships with our suppliers; and the ability to plan our business, execute, and grow by 100 percent a year, very profitably, in a flat industry.

The GE Pension Fund had a fiduciary responsibility to closely watch their roughly $40 billion of assets under management, so of course they deserved to be adequately informed about their investments. I made sure they were. Carol Kerley was our chief financial officer at the time. She'd come to us from Price Waterhouse and was smart as a whip. I gave her specific instructions: "Number one, we're going to be honest in all our reporting. We're not going to cover up a damn thing or try any tricks, and we're going to be very conservative in everything we do – on our evaluations, predictions, and everything else."

I wasn't about to repeat the malfeasances of Charles Myers and Burlington, and by keeping our prognostications conservative, we always ended up doing better than we predicted, which is just good business sense. We'd send in our quarterly reports, and every time GE would call me up and say, "Goddamn, you give us more information than anybody else does." Good, I thought, maybe now they'd stop harassing us and be satisfied just reading our reports.

But GE's harassment didn't stop. After about a year of the number-crunchers crunching everybody's sanity with their poking and prodding and micromanagement, I finally had enough and called up John Myers, the president of the Pension Fund.

I told John, "For God's sake, stop sending these people. They keep asking all these questions that insinuate we're hiding something from you. It's gotten so bad, I've told all of my people not to even talk to what's his name – Billy Joe, or whatever his name is! Besides, you keep telling us every day this is the best investment you've got, so what the hell are you trying to do?"

And Myers came back with some reply like, "We don't mean to butt into your business, but we've got standards to meet."

And I hit back with, "Well, I can tell you this, we're not paying any attention to your guys because half the time they're wrong. Because they don't know a thing about this business."

To which Myers went on and on about what sounded to me like a whole lot of GE bureaucracy, which could not have interested me less.

Finally, I told John that from now on if his men had any questions about marketing or finance or anything else, they were to talk to me first. I concluded, "And if you think I'm trying to cover up something, you're nuts!" Well, that was the basis of our relationship from then on.

I suppose I felt bad for Myers, in a certain sense. GE was a corporation run on fear – the fear of Jack Welch. At the end of every year, Welch would fire the bottom 20 percent of his managers, no matter how the company performed. If I knew my head was constantly on the chopping block, I probably would've been as neurotic as John Myers. I found GE's way of doing business fairly objectionable, but in those days I was in the minority. This was the age of the hard-edged, merciless corporate kingpin, an attitude that Welch embodied. In 1999, *Fortune Magazine* even named Welch its "Manager of the Century." Good for him! Never was much of a golfer, though.

There's almost never any point for an investor to meddle in the affairs of the company they've invested in. Their job is to pick the right company, not to manage it. If the investee is run by smart, competent people, then they've got nothing to worry about. If management is bad, the investors might think they can help, but I'm telling you right now, it won't matter a bit – the enterprise is doomed to fail. The only thing a financier should really do is listen to the people they've entrusted with their money and try to understand how and why their business works. No matter how many times we tried to educate GE about our business, they never could wrap their heads around how Callaway became Callaway, and as a result, they never trusted us.

We Made a Better Product and Outsmarted the Competition

More than anything else, Callaway's success was built entirely on two simple principles: we made a product better than anything else on the market, and we outsmarted the competition. Before going into business, an entrepreneur has to take stock of what their competition will be and determine if they have the wherewithal to beat them.

Let's say I'd gone into computers in the 1980s. I would've been up against the likes of Steve Jobs and Bill Gates –real geniuses who I wouldn't have had a chance in hell of competing against. Fortunately for me, I didn't go into computers, I went into golf clubs. Before I invested in Hickory Stick, I studied my competitors and came to the conclusion that the golf club industry was full of fundamentally incompetent people.

By incompetent, I mean lazy, dumb, unimaginative, conservative, and asleep. Let's take Spalding, TaylorMade, Hogan, Wilson Staff, and MacGregor, five of the biggest golf club manufacturers at the time. After I studied them, I realized that all their owners were based overseas, far away, doing something else. In 1984, Spalding was bought by the Cisneros family, owners of a Venezuelan supermarket empire. In 1985, TaylorMade was bought by Salomon SA, a French ski equipment manufacturer. Hogan was sold in 1984 to Minstar, a holding company owned by a man nicknamed Irv the Liquidator, then to the Japanese company Cosmo World in 1988. Wilson Staff and MacGregor, for decades perhaps the two most iconic names in golf clubs, were both sold to Helsinki-based Amer Group Ltd. in 1988. For Cisneros, Salomon, Amer, and Cosmo World, their livelihoods didn't depend on the success of the golf club business. All they wanted to do was avoid losing money. That's the difference. Their strategy was defensive and protective. They didn't go and create something new and fabulous and take a gamble on it.

I didn't mind my competition being asleep. In fact, I preferred it that way. Outsmarting my competition meant not letting on what I was going to do next, but knowing what they were going to do before they did it. How did Callaway know what our competition was going to do? Number one, I knew how they thought because I studied what they'd done before. Therefore, I had a pretty good idea of what they would do in the future, and I bet on that likelihood.

About the only thing my competitors and I shared was location. Because of our sudden success, money and talent began to pour into Carlsbad, and I inadvertently created an area known as Titanium Valley, which is now the golf manufacturing capital of the world. Pretty soon most of the top companies were headquartered within a Big Bertha drive's distance of each other. Our list of rivalrous neighbors included Cobra, TaylorMade, Titleist, Aldila, Lynx, and Odyssey (who we later bought and placed under the stewardship of Callaway's then vice president of manufacturing, Ron Drapeau). You could more or less walk from one corporate headquarters to another, and when you went out to dinner, you were likely to be seated next to Cobra's Mark McClure or TaylorMade's Chuck Yash. You had to keep shop talk to a minimum – you never knew if the maître d' might be on TaylorMade's payroll.

After Big Bertha, the first bet I made was that my competitors would try to knock me off. Now I don't mean knock me off like Joe Pesci in *Goodfellas;* I mean they would try to copy

Big Bertha. We anticipated these knockoffs and took measures to cut them off at the pass. Before we put Big Bertha on the market, we wanted an outside opinion from a few pros in the pro shops and from off-course retailers: was this club really as good as we thought it was? But we couldn't send Bertha out to be tested without running the risk it would fall into the hands of a competitor. Certain club pros and retailers, we had learned, were not above passing a prototype along to a rival manufacturer, who could make a quick study of it.

We put together a list of testers that seemed trustworthy, and we told them to try the club for a day or two, then send it straight back. That didn't guarantee that some of them didn't let Cobra, TaylorMade, or some other company have a sneak peek at Bertha. This sort of thing happens all the time, and I will admit Callaway does it right along with the rest of them. By now, everybody in the business has figured out a way to snoop on their competitors' latest products. You could write a spy novel about the intrigue in the golf industry. I wouldn't be surprised to hear that double agents have been planted in the design departments of the biggest manufacturers. We never planted spies, but it would've been an easy way to pick up information about new golf clubs.

Within a couple of years, every golf club company sold its own oversized driver and wood: Spalding's Thunder Heart; Wilson's Killer Whale; MacGregor's Mad Mac (I guess Big Mac was already taken); Founders' Judge; and Cobra's King Cobra. All of them bragged about how their oversized clubs improved upon Big Bertha. They touted features like heavier heel weight or a better sound, but none of them were as good as Bertha, and the sales numbers proved it. Besides their inferiority, the other thing the knock-offs had in common was that they were cheap. The Killer Whale, for instance, was made of aluminum and retailed for $100. This was the bet my competitors made: they let Ely Callaway spend all the money and take all the risk to see if a new product would sell, and then found a way to market it themselves for a percentage of the cost.

Well, I was not going to take this lying down! Callaway spent over $3 million in 1993 alone chasing down a variety of copyright violations and registering our rights with the United States Patent and Trademark Office. Why shouldn't we? It took us two years to develop the special technology and features of the Bertha driver, and another year to make Heavenwood, which was probably the second most popular club in the world (and used by Jack Nicklaus to boot). We spent millions of dollars and worked our tails off to create an entirely new market in a flat industry. Then my competitors think they can reverse engineer it, figure out what we did, and sell it for half the price. It's not fair.

We had a great deal of success stopping the most egregious knockoffs coming out of East Asia, Southern California, and south of the border, including one ridiculously named Big Bursar. In early 1999, our chief legal officer, Steve McCracken, and Callaway's Special Investigations Unit caught wind that someone was selling fake Callaway clubs over the internet. These knockoffs used cheap steel screws instead of our higher-quality tungsten screws. Steve's investigators tracked the counterfeit clubs down to Tijuana, Mexico, and discovered that an American golf instructor, Wayne J. Guerin, had somehow got his hands on incomplete clubheads from our Mexico supplier. Guerin combined the stolen parts with other parts obtained on the open market, then sold his Frankenstein clubs to unsuspecting customers through classified ads. After six months of diligent undercover investigation, Steve turned our evidence over to the San Diego police, who quickly busted Guerin. It was a sting operation worthy of Eliot Ness.

Despite this and other triumphs that saw counterfeiters thrown in jail, we'd never be able to shut it all down. Think about the United States trying to stop drug trafficking. They spend billions of dollars and they can't even make a dent. The fact is that as long as the product is in demand, there will be a market for cheap knockoffs. All we could hope to do was to keep the pressure on so it didn't become rampant. But the more profitable our product was, the more incentive there was for people to try to capitalize on our work.

Despite Callaway's success in the early part of the decade, I didn't feel comfortable or self-satisfied, and I never got complacent. I couldn't afford to – if we had one strong competitor yesterday, I assumed we would have 10 tomorrow. Big Bertha was the best driver in the world, but it was only a matter of time before someone came along and beat it. We ran scared by making new and better products and finding new areas to innovate.

When choosing where to innovate, an entrepreneur has to consider whether their invention actually has a chance of improving the consumer's experience. Let's say I wanted to make the next big thing in putters. If golf is 50 percent psychological and 50 percent physical, then putting is 90 percent psychological, at least. By the time a golfer's ball gets to the green, they've already navigated obstacles of distance, the rough, trees, sand traps, water, turkeys and snakes if you're in California, and alligators if you're in Florida. On the green, there are no obstacles.

It's just you, the ball, and the hole. Everything becomes psychological; even measuring the slope and firmness of the green is more mental than physical.

My point is, the kind of putter you use is not really going to help you. People still have all kinds of preferences about their putters; in fact, the relationship between a player and their putter might be the most intimate one they have. But there's not much I could do to improve a putter, at least not enough to overcome the demons inside a golfer's head.

Eventually, I wanted all 14 clubs in a player's bag to be Callaways, and since we had already conquered drivers and woods, I figured the next logical step was to work our way down to irons. We already had our S2H2 irons on the market, but I wanted a new club that would be a bestseller. Irons proved as tough a nut to crack as drivers, but for the exact opposite reason. In 1993, the iron market was already flooded with options from every major golf club manufacturer and a bunch of lesser ones too.

Even in this oversaturated market, the PING Eye2 stood above the crowd – "the pros' choice for irons," as their marketing department claimed. PING's founder was a man named Karsten Solheim, a former mechanical engineer for GE of all places, and one of the truly great innovators in the golf club business. *The New York Times* once called Solheim the Goateed Yoda of Golf Clubs, a nickname so good I wish I'd thought of it myself.

Unlike most of my competitors, PING was not owned by a conglomerate. Karsten Manufacturing Co., the Phoenix-based manufacturer, was a family-owned business. It's much easier to compete against a company owned by a big outfit than a small company owned and operated by innovators. I had studied

Solheim for years. I watched him take a full decade to get his irons accepted by golfers, and admired how he paved the way for consumers to accept radical new designs. Though I respected this Jedi Master of the unconquerable game, I believed he could be beaten.

To begin with, I didn't think PING's irons were actually all that great. Maybe they were in 1985, but by 1993 technology had leaped forward, and the PING Eye2 was yesterday's news. Solheim also did not have a successful metal wood on the market. He didn't make woods like Callaway made them; he didn't even try. Solheim was on record claiming that the oversized club craze was nothing but a fad, and once people realized larger clubheads didn't actually improve their scores, the novelty would wear off and the fad would pass. That was his weakness. He was stuck in his own idea of woods, the woods of the past, because he totally underestimated the physical and emotional pleasure of Big Bertha, which had almost nothing to do with the number of strokes it took to put the ball in the hole. In other words, he was asleep at the wheel.

Then Solheim became embroiled in a war with the USGA and PGA Tour. The PGA threatened to ban PING's irons from the tour on account of their square grooves. After he'd been fighting them for a year, I told my team, "This is great; he's not paying attention to his business anymore." I didn't know for certain, but I had heard through industry gossip that while Solheim was busy suing the USGA, he was letting his sons oversee most of his golf club business. This left an opening for Callaway to strike. As soon as Solheim started wasting his physical and psychic energy on hating the USGA, I knew we were going to win.

In 1993, we set about making the Big Bertha irons. It'd been 40 years since one company, Wilson Sporting Goods, had dominated both irons and woods, but I was determined to try. I declared, "Let's go and spend the money and do whatever it takes, because we are not going to fear Karsten Solheim." Big Bertha had come to mean something very special in our consumers' minds, and I wasn't going to compromise my own credibility by releasing an inferior iron. Like our driver, these irons would be engineered to be very forgiving of the average golfer's less-than-perfect swing. They featured Callaway's iconic S2H2 hosel, a large chunky brick of a clubhead, a bore-through shaft, and a cavity on the back of the clubhead and a deep cavity to maximize perimeter weighting and MOI, or moment of inertia. We worked with Hitchiner Manufacturing in New Hampshire and Coastcast Corporation of California on brand new casting technology. All these unique details required special manufacturing operations that were incredibly costly.

One of the best ways to beat the competition is to set up a barrier they're unwilling to cross, and for us, that barrier to entry was cost. We're reasonably cost-conscious, but we don't let that dominate our decision on what kind of products to make. I believe we spent two percent of our total revenue from 1993 just developing Big Bertha irons. Our competition looked at all the extra money we were spending to make these features with no obvious rewards, at least as far as they could see, and determined that we must be really dumb, and they thought I was nuts. They simply couldn't wrap their minds around why any single club would be worth spending all that money on, so they never did it themselves.

But the "why" was no great mystery. For one thing, we could

afford it. The success of the Big Bertha driver and Big Bertha woods in the early '90s had given us a $50 million war chest and no debt. We could take the financial risk and invest in our golf clubs without hurting our immediate profit. Callaway's claim to fame was technical innovation. What else were we going to spend that $50 million on besides making something diffrunt and bettuh?

Still, my competitors convinced themselves that the rewards and playability that Callaway achieved just simply weren't there. No matter the evidence in front of their eyes. No matter if we told them, "It's 'cause our clubs are better." They would come back with excuses like, "Oh, Ely, he's just a good merchant."

We debuted our irons at the PGA trade show in Orlando, in February of 1994. The trade show had changed quite a bit in the three years since we premiered the Big Bertha driver. It was now an extravagant affair, a testament to this boom time in our industry. There were over 700 exhibitors, including all the major golf club manufacturers and many independent inventors, and a record 35,000 people, many eager to see our secret new club – known only as Project X.

The theme of the show was "innovation," and boy, did they mean it. Companies like Cobra and Aldila bragged about hiring aerospace engineers to design their club shafts (I wonder where they got that idea!). A reporter for *Sports Illustrated* speculated that after the fall of the Berlin Wall and the swift end to the Persian Gulf War, perhaps former defense contractors needed the work. I'm still not sure if he was joking. Most of the inventions were oddities and diversions, but among the more entertaining exhibitions was a golf ball with a microchip tracker inside so it'd never get lost in the rough, a bag tag that emitted a dragonfly-like drone to ward off mosquitos, and a talking putting mat named Putty Buddy.

But for all these bells, whistles, lasers, and smoke, the centerpiece of the trade show was my unveiling of the Big Bertha irons. Our Friday morning presentation captured the imagination of the Orange County Convention Center. We brought two-time majors winner and Callaway endorser Johnny Miller on stage, and the then 47-year-old Miller vowed to "kick butt" on the Senior Tour with our irons when he became eligible in three years' time.

Despite our success at the trade show, the naysayers warned that at $140 a pop, our irons were simply too expensive. This was the common criticism hurled at Callaway – a theory based on nothing, but one I had to work my tail off to disprove.

My test marketing consisted of letting every member at my home course, the Del Mar Country Club, try out the Big Bertha irons, as I stood on the 10th tee in my suit and tie and greeted each player as they played through – by my count, 144 people over the course of five hours. I asked each one how they were enjoying the irons, what we could do differently, and how we could improve performance and satisfaction. They had their opinions, as customers always do, but the most interesting part about those discussions was that not one person out of 144 complained about the projected price. My competition might've convinced *themselves* our clubs were too expensive, sure, but they didn't convince our customers.

The fact that we did things that appeared too costly or silly turned out to be one of our great strengths. If an entrepreneur has a great product, then they shouldn't concern themselves with the cost of development, cost of production, or even cost to the consumer. The higher, the better, because it discourages almost all the competition from doing the same thing. This is a philosophy I learned from Roger Milliken: if the product satisfies enough people, then damn the torpedoes and to hell with the cost. There will always be enough people willing to pay more for better quality.

Anticipation for our irons sent our stock price up to $40 in April 1994, an all-time high. In fact, excitement was so high that we had to devise a rationing system to meet our expected demand – something that frustrated our buyers, who were accustomed to having bargaining power. One buyer, a young professional who couldn't get enough irons, quenched his thirst by buying two dozen Big Bertha hats on a whim. "You can't go wrong with the major names," he exclaimed. There was no bigger name in golf than Big Bertha.

Big Bertha irons hit the market on May 1, 1994, and were an instant success. In 1995, Callaway surpassed PING to become the best-selling (in dollars) manufacturer of woods and irons, with $550 million in total sales. I had beaten Karsten Solheim, but still, I wasn't satisfied. Before my irons were released, Helmstetter and his team had already turned their attention to improving Big Bertha. Why would we spend time and money improving what was already the best driver in the world? Because I believed there has never been a single product in the history of the world that couldn't be improved in some significant way.

For example, I don't think it's controversial to say that in America, there is no brand with a more solid-gold reputation than Coca-Cola. When I was a kid back in LaGrange, one of the great joys of my life was visiting the Coca-Cola Bottling

Company plant in the nearby town of West Point. The beverage had been invented just up the road in Atlanta in 1886, and in 1908 the company opened its first-ever bottling plant. When I was a kid, the plant was run by George S. Cobb, Sr. and Jr. The father's innovations included the coin-operated vending machine and advertisements that played before a movie – basically the precursor to television commercials. I anticipated those trips to the bottling plant with a zeal that today's kids might reserve for the family vacation to Disney World.

I would look through an observation window and watch the workers on the factory floor putting that wonderful sugar water into pristine glass bottles. The bottles had the slogan, "Every bottle sterilized." Even as a kid, that sounded right to me. My mother had taught me to drink out a clean glass instead of a dirty one, so I was impressed. I don't think anybody else in the soft drink business had a slogan about sterilizing every bottle. Maybe Pepsi did it too, but because they never advertised it, I always assumed it was a feature unique to Coca-Cola. Sometimes you can sell a difference just by having the good sense to point out something obvious that no one else seems to notice.

But that changed in 1960 when Coca-Cola introduced the aluminum can to the general consumer. Somebody at the Coca-Cola Company, or maybe Mr. August Busch out there at Budweiser, must not have been thinking, because when you open the can, the lip is sent backward, injecting whatever germs were on the lip into the fluid inside. How sterile is that? Not very! Imagine if the Coca-Cola Company got to work on this problem, solved it, and then got a strong patent on it.

To this day, Coca-Cola hasn't improved its cans, and I doubt it ever will. I call this a failure of imagination – to look at a product and think that it is as good as it can be. I didn't allow that kind of thinking at Callaway. I insisted we look for any improvement, edge, or advantage we could achieve over our competitors. I'm certain that we've spent more time and effort thinking about developing golf clubs than anybody in the history of the game.

De-worsification, or: The Importance of Sticking to Your Specialty

Big Bertha's improvement, which I named the Great Big Bertha, launched in 1995, with a whopping 253cc clubhead. Besides the increased size, the most notable change was swapping out heavy stainless steel for a lighter Ruger titanium, made exclusively for us by firearms manufacturer Sturm, Ruger & Co. Titanium meant that even though Great Big Bertha's clubhead was 25 percent larger, the club was 10 percent lighter than the previous version. We also lengthened our Japan-designed graphite shafts by a single inch – a small change, but one we thought would significantly improve the average golfer's sense of control.

The final change was cost. Steel was an industrial-age metal; titanium was space-age. In other words, it was far more expensive. We duly retailed our Great Big Bertha drivers at an unprecedented $500 a pop. Our competitors criticized that price point with no shortage of vitriol, but we sold them for $500 because that's what we thought they were worth. And good night, did we sell a lot of them! Our Great Big Bertha driver and woods quickly became the most popular golf clubs in the world.

These were years of boundless product creation. Between '95 and '96, we finally released two new putters, Big Bertha Blades and Bobby Jones. We also put out new wedges co-designed by the legendary Roger Cleveland, new "Gold" irons made of an aluminum-bronze alloy for an even softer feel, and improved Big Bertha irons. We made a few small design changes to our second-generation irons, such as an undercut cavity and increasing the sweet spot on the club face. They were more forgiving, more comfortable, and more enjoyable than anything else on the market. Former PGA champ Paul Azinger even called them the greatest irons ever made.

People thought we were crazy to still be putting out stainless steel clubs in 1996. After the Great Big Bertha, everybody was rushing to make titanium clubs, copying our drivers and woods and then selling them cheaper (except they weren't really selling so much as gathering dust). One of our competitors down the street came up with a bright idea to spend a lot of money on print ads in *Golf Digest* – a double-page spread, I believe – and hastily produced TV commercials that proclaimed, "Stainless steel is dead, and titanium is the survivor." But we didn't pay attention to general trends, we just tried to make a better club. That same year, we sold $207 million worth of stainless steel Big Bertha metal woods, which I'm fairly confident was more than the total combined shipments of the company that prematurely wrote the obituary on steel. But steel's resilience shouldn't have been too surprising. After all, remember Ben Hogan – some people just prefer the feel of their old, heavy, cumbersome clubs.

Not every product was a success – that would've been impossible – but when we fell short, I firmly believe it was never due to the quality of the club. I stand behind every club we've ever made and say with assurance that Callaway has never put out a bad product. Our only failure was one of storytelling. An entrepreneur must tell the story of their product to the general public. Our challenge was to tell a story that convinced the consumer that the benefits of our club were worth the price of exchanging their old one – which the average golfer only did every four years or so – while spending more than they would on any of our competitors' products.

In 1997, our hitting streak reached its climax with the unveiling of the Biggest Big Bertha, our largest driver of the decade, boasting a clubhead of 290cc. It was also the high-water mark for the golf industry. Business was booming everywhere in Titanium Valley.

As Callaway became more and more successful with more and more clubs, many on my team were tempted to expand our company into more novel areas. I pushed back on this. The truth is that most of the time when companies go far afield, they fail. It's baloney to think that just because they're good at one thing, and they're pretty smart people, they can do the same thing almost anywhere. If someone thought it was going to be very easy to take the Callaway image and make it work effectively in a lot of other fields, they were dead wrong. If we were going to enter a new field, I had to have pretty good evidence that I could be the absolute best. I had to know I could outsmart my competition.

This is why I resisted getting into the golf ball business for so long. It is exactly the opposite of the golf club business. The golf ball business had some very smart people in it, and I didn't want to compete against them. I considered buying one of them if the price was right because it's a great business, but I sure as hell didn't want to go against them unless I had the money and the right talent.

Companies get carried away with the need to grow. They don't need to diversify what they make; they need to focus on manufacturing and merchandising in their specialty, and to grow it profitably and soundly. Back in my winery days, some executives from Coca-Cola wanted to buy me out, but at the time I wasn't looking to sell. However, I did warn them not to go into wine. I told them that they were the undisputed kings of the soft drink business, but that for all their money and smarts, they wouldn't have a chance of competing against Ernest Gallo, because they couldn't outsmart such a ruthless operator. He didn't mind letting a small operation like mine have a piece of the market, but he'd never let a big player like Coca-Cola make any real money – he would kill them.

Coca-Cola ignored my advice, bought Sterling Vineyards in 1977, and everything played out exactly as I predicted. Gallo waged an aggressive price war against them and lost money for a few years, but he could afford to play that game. Coca-Cola's shareholders, on the other hand, could not stomach such picayune profits, and after five years the beverage king sold Sterling and got out of the wine business altogether. Fortunately for Coca-Cola, they were so damn rich they could easily survive this mistake, but most companies can't. They still do it for one reason: ego. Pure ego. Before an entrepreneur lets their unchecked ego lead them down the path of de-worsification, they ought to study their competition.

In 1996, I stepped down as CEO and president of Callaway Golf and devoted myself full time to getting our golf ball off the ground. I remained chairman of the board, and my longtime consigliere, Don Dye, succeeded me as the chief executive. My first step was to find the right talent to run the golf ball division. I found it in Chuck Yash, who had joined TaylorMade a few years earlier and helped wake them up from a lengthy hibernation. TaylorMade reemerged as one of our best competitors, behind Cobra. Before that he worked for Spalding, whose golf ball brand, Top-Flite, was the second-best-selling ball on the market. By hiring Yash, once again I stole talent from one competitor and gained valuable insight into another (from Jeanne to Raeford to Yash, I've always had a knack for stealing people right out from under my competition's nose).

Next, I built a $150 million golf ball manufacturing facility in Carlsbad. I finally had the money and the talent to compete in golf balls. Our competitors hired a helicopter to fly over the construction site and take pictures of our unfinished facility while it was being built, hoping to get a glimpse of our secrets. As Tom Preece, my new head of product development and a man who once helped engineer F-22 fighter jets, remarked, "The security here is tighter here than at Lockheed."

On Yash's recommendation, I hired Mark King away from TaylorMade and made him vice president of the golf ball division. King had been tied to TaylorMade for 16 years, but the marriage soured after King got passed over for president. He left them and got hitched to Callaway. But while he did good work for us, I don't believe he was ever truly happy. A few years later, King defected back to TaylorMade after the man who originally beat him flamed out. TaylorMade took King back and made him their president, and I felt jilted. Losing King was a damaging blow (he took a lot of our trade secrets with him!), and I blame TaylorMade as much as King for the fiasco. But it is human nature: a man never truly lets go of his first love.

Golf balls were Callaway's biggest risk yet. There were eight million golfers around the world using Callaway clubs, and I bet that at least 80 percent of them would want to try our balls. But brand recognition would only get us in the door. If we were going to beat Top-Flite and Titleist, we had to make a better ball than anything else on the market. By the dawn of the new millennium, I had spent three years and $150 million developing golf balls and had yet to put a single ball on a tee.

"The No's don't matter, only the Yes's."

"I believe there has never been a single product in the history of the world that couldn't be improved in some significant way."

CHAPTER 9

A TRAGEDY FOR THE AMERICAN INVESTMENT PUBLIC

The Agony and Ecstasy of Wall Street and My Rivalry with Cobra

To Go Public or Sell? That is the Question . . .

Executives always ask me if I think their company should go public, as Callaway did in February of 1992. But what they really want to know is, "Do you think my company has what it takes to be the next Callaway?" While on its face, Callaway was a straightforward success story of an IPO on Wall Street, the truth is something a bit more complicated. Callaway's journey through the New York Stock Exchange was full of agony and ecstasy, and my personal feelings toward that odd, all-powerful institution ran the gamut from pride to confusion to downright contempt. I once confided to a nervous shareholder that when it came to running my business, "I try not to pay any attention to Wall Street." I'd like to tell you why.

From 1981 to 1990, I did not take a nickel of salary. I put millions of my own money into Callaway, and all I got in return for my labor were stock options worth next to nothing. By June of 1991 I was 71, we had the biggest golf club in the world that was totally changing the industry, and I was ready to cash in my chips. Don Dye, Dick Helmstetter, Bruce Parker, John Duffy (our head of manufacturing), and I discussed it among ourselves, we talked with the other board members, and we concluded there were two ways to exit: go public or sell the company.

The GE men on the board, Dale Frey and John Myers, were adamant we should sell. The most obvious suitor was GE, but they nipped that idea in the bud right away, explaining it was a conflict of interest for GE to buy a corporation from the GE Pension Fund. Then without telling us, Myers went to Japan and tried to sell us to Sumitomo, our international distributor and the very company I'd tried to get to invest before GE. Fortunately, Myers was the worst salesman in the world, so the deal didn't go through.

Don and I had no contacts in the investment banking world, so we all agreed we should meet with the major firms and ask them which option – IPO or sell – to go with. We went to New York in July, where Frey and Myers hosted meetings with Morgan Stanley, JP Morgan, Lazard Frères, and Merrill Lynch.

They took different positions. Morgan Stanley believed we should make every effort to find a strategic buyer, because market conditions at the time meant we would probably get 25 percent more from selling than from going public. I was already prejudiced against Morgan Stanley because of how unfairly they'd handled a leveraged buyout for Burlington a few years back. They had practically wrecked the company with that deal.

On the other end of the spectrum was Merrill Lynch, who recommended that we go public. This was the answer I was waiting for. The truth is, Don and I had no interest in selling. From the very beginning, I knew there was nobody out there that would buy us that I would want to be owned by. The GE people and I had a real conflict over this that erupted right there in our pitch meetings. Seeing this divide, all of the investment bankers except for Morgan Stanley came to me privately and said, "You're right. To go public would be a very good idea –if you do well, you would get a lot more money in the long run." I knew we were going to do well, but the GE Pension Fund didn't. They didn't have confidence, because they were merely money managers, not merchants.

Merrill Lynch was by far the most optimistic about a public offering. Two representatives came out to Carlsbad to evaluate our situation, study our figures, and see what we had. I told them we were considering three other investment firms and it would take us a couple of weeks to decide. I could see they were excited about us because they immediately started talking about how much money they would put in to back us.

I responded, "Well, as a matter of fact, I don't really need an investment banker for this. I can raise the money and put out a little public offering to sell the stock myself."

I was partly kidding, but the Merrill Lynch guys took me dead seriously. They told me, "We think we can do a lot better raising the money than you can." They added that if I did go public, I could pick one or two firms to underwrite Callaway, but that I should do whatever I wanted because it was my deal. From that answer, I knew Merrill Lynch was the right choice. I picked them, and them alone.

At the end of the meeting, Merrill Lynch warned me that most companies don't do well their first few years on the stock market, and that I should not get discouraged.

"Don't worry," I grinned, "We're not going to have that problem."

We opened Callaway for public trading on February 28, 1992, with an initial public offering of 2.6 million shares at $20 a share for a market valuation of $52 million. Seeing ELY, our official three-letter moniker, up there on the New York Stock Exchange ticker board was the fulfillment of a lifelong dream. I think I had always romanticized the idea of taking a company public. It seemed to me that if a man was able to build something from nothing and have great success, then he should want the American investing public to own a piece of that company and share in its fortune and growth. I'm talking about the average working man or woman who sets aside a little bit of each month's paycheck, or the pensioner who entrusts his children's future to a low-risk mutual fund.

A large group of us attended the opening day: me, my wife Cindy, Dick, Don, Carol, Bruce, and some people from Merrill Lynch. When we got to the trading floor, we looked around and saw that all the traders were wearing Callaway caps. I went up to the balcony above the trading floor and everybody applauded me. My whole team was emotional – I was nearly in tears. I rang the opening bell, and Wall Street went to work.

Twenty-five minutes later, our share price had jumped all the way up to $36. I watched from the trading floor as four million shares changed hands over the next nine hours. I had enough sense to know that what I was witnessing was very special, perhaps even unprecedented for a sports apparel or luxury goods company. Callaway met the closing bell at $32.75 a share. We were the toast of Wall Street that day, and for a good deal of time thereafter.

The Weeping Investor

Despite the unmatched thrill of that first day on Wall Street, I always felt our greatest rewards, not only financially but emotionally, would come from future increases in our stock value. I didn't care about the first day's price; I cared about the price two, three, or 10 years down the road, and the returns for our investors who'd been with us since the beginning. The problem is nobody is ever sure if the future performance of a company is going to handsomely reward its shareholders. Because of that, large companies and institutional investors try to grab all the stock they can in the beginning.

Jack Welch wanted 20,000 shares set aside for him in the first offering. When his representatives asked me to do this, I balked. I didn't believe we should set aside any special shares for anyone, let alone Jack. But Welch went behind my back to Merrill Lynch, through his own broker in New York, and got them to set aside some stock for him at the IPO price. He knew Callaway would be a hot IPO, and he flipped all of his shares on the first day for a quick profit. This is the game he played.

There were few rules on Wall Street, but one was that when a company went public they had to issue a prospectus, with all sorts of details about the company's offering, including how much stock they had left. Next, they had to agree to a six-month lock-up where they couldn't sell without the permission of the underwriters, which for us meant the beginning of July. Our stock traded consistently in the high 20s for those first six months, then bumped up even higher in June, before we'd even published our quarterly figures. GE decided to pounce on this opportunity and sell a lot more of their Callaway stock – and sell it a little bit quicker than the lock-up would allow.

This practice was pretty standard. If a stock was very successful right away, like Callaway's, the investment bankers would usually let the company out of the lock-up in five months instead of six. GE informed us they were ready to completely unload their position in Callaway, which was fine by us. In fact, we were delighted. We couldn't stand GE. They had put in $4 million to begin with, followed by about $5 million a little later on, for a total of $9 million. They got back much more than that as a return on their investment. The relationship had been highly lucrative for both parties, and there was no bad blood, but everyone agreed it was time for a swift and amicable divorce.

At the same time GE was releasing its prospectus for the secondary offering a few months later, Callaway's stock was suddenly hit very hard. It dropped all the way down to $18 a share, $2 below the initial offering. There was no obvious reason for our sudden decline – we hadn't even published our first-quarter earnings yet – but it scared the hell out of GE. and everyone else. I told GE not to overreact and cancel the secondary offering. I believed our low stock price was premature and only temporary, and they should at least wait until we reported our earnings, which were sure to increase Wall Street's confidence in us and lead to a swift recovery. But GE was worried we hadn't reached rock bottom yet. They feared our stock price might drop all the way to $12, so they canceled the offering.

The weeks we were down to $18 were some of the darkest periods in Callaway's history. At that point I was the entire investor relations department, answering every investor call, institutional and individual. This was by choice. Investors were beginning to panic, and when they called us to ask what the hell was going on, I wanted to be sure that I was the one to reassure them and talk them out of abandoning a ship that wasn't even close to sinking.

I remember receiving one particularly emotional call from a woman I'd never met. I could immediately hear in her voice that she'd been crying. She said, "Mr. Callaway, I'm desperate. I inherited quite a bit of money from my father a year ago and I put 50 percent of it in your stock at $36 a share."

In between gasping sobs, the woman confessed that she'd never played golf before in her life and didn't know one thing about the game. What's more, she'd never even invested in the stock market before, but she read about Callaway in a magazine and decided to go all in, which of course I found very flattering – though if I had given her the inheritance, I probably would've had a different word for it.

"I'm worried to death!" she confided. "I don't know how to talk to my father. My husband is going to leave me. This is the worst thing that's ever happened in my life. What should I do?"

And I replied, "You should come down here to Carlsbad and talk to me in person, see firsthand what you invested in, and then you'll see the company's better off than ever and you have nothing to worry about."

The next day this particularly anxious investor drove down to our offices with her husband. She entered the office in tears. It's possible she hadn't stopped crying since our phone conversation the day before. The husband was clearly embarrassed by the whole situation and kept telling his wife to calm down – which, if you know anything about marriage or people in general, is a surefire way to just make somebody more upset. We gave the couple a private tour of the plant, and I told her all about our upcoming products and explained why the company had great prospects. We even gave her some hats to take home as souvenirs. She left our offices very happy, and her husband even asked me for a job.

I continued to get calls from her and from many other concerned investors for the next couple of months. I tried to explain that the people who bought our stock on the opening day had simply paid too much for it. It happens with lots of public offerings: people are so eager to get in on a good deal, they ignore the fact that they are paying too much for the merchandise, at least temporarily. They completely ignore the price–earnings ratio, which is one indication of whether a stock is overvalued.

In the year before we went public, Callaway Golf earned $0.85 per share, meaning the initial investors who bought the stock at $20 a share were paying roughly 23 times the prior year's earnings. This wasn't cheap, but it wasn't too expensive either for a fast-growing company like ours at that time. However, by the time the stock hit $36, buyers at that price were paying 35 times the prior year's earnings. I considered a P/E ratio of 35 for our company to be very high, and I even said so in our first report to shareholders.

As far as I know, this was one of the first cases on record where the CEO of a company complained that its stock was overpriced. We told our investors that while we were confident in our ability to increase our earnings, we doubted the stock would continue to sell at such a high P/E ratio. Sure enough, the price came down, and investors who overpaid in the first place were looking at losses.

We didn't have any legal responsibility to tell our investors they had overpaid, but I believed we had a moral responsibility. When an individual invests in Callaway, they are entrusting me with their mortgage payment, their children's college tuition, their retirement, and whatever other dreams or ambitions they might have for themselves or their families. An entrepreneur needs to personally feel the weight of that trust and take seriously the fiduciary responsibility that comes with it. It's not just good morals, it's good business. If I was unusually honest with my investors when things were good, they would be more likely to trust me and stick around when things inevitably went bad. I wanted to build long-term loyalty with my investors.

When we finally did report our first-quarter figures, the stock bounced back to $27 a share, just as I had predicted. Our earnings grew so fast the rest of the year that the stock took off again until it reached the point that shareholders doubled, tripled, and quadrupled their money, depending on the prices they had paid. Some people even made six times their initial investment. I don't know exactly how much my weeping heiress made, but I spoke with her one more time after the bounce-back, and she made out okay.

As for GE, they soon realized they'd made a misjudgment on top of a mistake and hastily layered on a private placement.

This took GE's ownership down from 40 percent a few years earlier to only about 5 percent. I suppose from GE's perspective the cancellation of the secondary public offering worked out in their favor, but because they went with a private placement instead, there was less Callaway stock available on the public market, and they likely scared away a lot of potential investors.

In 1992, an overall bullish year for the NASDAQ, our sales were $135 million, nearly triple the previous year, and yet our stock price had reached a dangerous low. I challenge any financial analyst or so-called economic expert to make sense of that. This was the first but by no means last time Wall Street's evaluation of Callaway did not shake hands with reality. The lunacy of Wall Street would later collide with my greatest rival in the golf club industry, Cobra.

Snakes in the Grass

The greatest rivalries are often defined by the two opponents' similarities as much as their differences. Cain and Abel shared parents. Hatfields and McCoys shared a river. Well, the same principle could apply, if only superficially, to Callaway and Cobra. We were the only two sports companies dedicated exclusively to golf. Like Callaway, they were nothing but an itty-bitty Carlsbad start-up well into the 1980s, before breaking through a crowded industry in the early '90s with an oversized club, the King Cobra irons.

In every other way, however, Cobra and Callaway were polar opposites. Cobra had an announced policy that they were not the kind of company to create a radically new design. They let somebody else do that, Callaway or whoever, and then their job was to come along and detect the trend and make it available their way. They didn't necessarily copy our product, but they emulated it, only with their standards and prices, which were both generally much lower than ours. They wanted to give the consumer the benefit of a trend but at a lower price. That's just a difference in business philosophy, but I'm not saying which one is right or wrong.

For a while, our relationship was very warm – more Nicklaus and Palmer than Hatfields and McCoys. As the two new kids on the block, we took pride in disrupting what for years had been an entrenched, sleepy, unglamorous, and flat industry. Long before our Golf War, Gary Biszantz, the top man running the show at Cobra, asked me to help him sell the company. Then right after we went public and had some success, Biszantz came back to me and said, "Well, do you think we ought to go public too?"

I replied, "Sure. If you're willing to take all the negatives. We're glad we went public."

Then at the end of the luncheon, he floated, "Well, why don't you buy Cobra?" As if that hadn't been the point of the lunch all along.

I chuckled, "We don't need it, that's why, but what's your price? Maybe we will. "

"$70 million."

"Okay, well, I'll talk to Don Dye about it and we'll think a little bit, but I really don't want it because we don't need it. We have different philosophies and different segments of the market."

"Okay," he said, "but do you think we'll be successful?"

I said, "Yeah, you will be."

They went public in 1993 and, just as I predicted, they were successful right away. In 1994, Bloomberg even published an article calling Cobra the next Callaway. A narrative began to take shape in the media, on Wall Street, and around Carlsbad that the golf club industry had become a two-horse race: Cobra versus Callaway. For a couple of years, there was something of a tit-for-tat rivalry with our club-making; their King Cobra driver was a direct response to our Big Bertha, while our oversized Big Bertha irons debuted the same year as their highly popular oversized King Cobra irons.

The arms race extended to endorsements. Cobra made a big splash signing Greg Norman, at the time the most popular golfer on the PGA Tour. We countered by signing Johnny Miller and John Daly. Still, the real battle was not over who had the better pros or superior clubs. No, the real war between Cobra and Callaway was a philosophical, spiritual, and even moral showdown, and our battleground was Wall Street.

Cobra knew how to spot a trend, make a golf club that took advantage of that trend, and market it effectively to the consumer. What they hadn't figured out was their obligation to the American investment public to behave responsibly – in particular, to not lie through their teeth. Cobra knew they couldn't make a golf club better than ours, and they couldn't beat us in dollar shares of the product market. They had to beat us in the stock market, and the people over there seemed to think the best way to sell Cobra stock was by *unselling* ours.

Cobra accomplished this deception by feeding their underwriter, Lehman Brothers, with misleading sales information. Lehman Brothers would then take that information and publish a misleading report, which the public largely believed because they were conditioned to trust these Wall Street firms, though I don't know why. Here's an example: Lehman Brothers put out a report to all their clients listing the top-selling golf clubs in the ladies' market, and the Great Big Bertha wasn't on it. The Great Big Bertha was the hottest-selling club in the world among women, but it didn't even show up on the list. The implication was that Cobra's clubs were the bestsellers, which of course caused people who read the Lehman report to think more highly of Cobra's stock. On the other hand, when they didn't see the Great Big Bertha on this bogus best-seller list, they thought Callaway had hit the skids and were inclined to avoid our stock.

What Lehman Brothers neglected to mention to their readers was that Cobra conducted this survey on 25 pro shops. Pro shops only accounted for 30 percent of the total golf clubs sold in the U.S., meaning this sample missed out on over two-thirds of the total market. Coincidentally, pro shops also just so happened to be where most of Cobra's business came from. Callaway's main business came from the sports stores, which accounted for the other 70 percent of golf club sales. Cobra claimed they were tops in the ladies' market? That was bullshit.

I will grant Cobra that for a while they sold more irons than us in terms of individual units, but we outpaced them on dollar sales, no doubt about it. And when it came to the ladies' market, Callaway probably shipped 30 percent more dollars than they ever did. I remember in another report, Cobra claimed they outsold us in the Senior market by 79 percent to 4 percent. The fact is Callaway shipped about twice as much in dollars' worth of clubs in the Senior market.

Lehman Brothers didn't publish these reports out of stupidity either, because we told them in person they were working from an invalid sample and misleading their shareholders, but they kept right on ahead publishing misleading reports anyway. It's no mystery why Lehman was so eager to play favorites. The folks at Lehman had a vested interest in increasing the value of Cobra's stock at the expense of Callaway's. In most cases when you've got that kind of relationship between company and underwriter, the financial analysts are going to put their own little positive spin on the facts – everybody does that – but I didn't believe Lehman Brothers would go so far as to deliberately hype up one stock and diminish another. Instead, I suspected that like most of Wall Street, Lehman simply knew next to nothing about the golf club business, and were therefore happy to gobble up and regurgitate whatever misleading statistics Cobra fed them. Why be deceitful when you can just be willfully ignorant?

These manipulated facts told a completely fictional story about Cobra and Callaway. This was a classic case of false advertising, and our investors or potential investors were fooled because of it. In 1995, our stock dropped from 32 to 20 in a matter of weeks. I can't prove it, but I would say at least six of those points were due to Cobra's manipulation.

This was the first case I knew of in which one publicly traded company sold its stock by deliberately lying about another publicly traded company. I could feel the specter of the Madison matter coming back to haunt me. Burlington had gotten away with shareholder deception two decades earlier; I did not want to let Cobra get away with similar shenanigans. I sat down with Chairman Gary Biszantz for another one of our "friendly" lunches and told him that Cobra ought to quit conducting business in this slimy way. Biszantz hemmed and hawed, claiming, "Well, we never meant to imply that Cobra was the top brand in terms of the biggest dollar volume in the business." Well, what the hell did they mean? He sounded like a used car salesman, and maybe that's because before he founded Cobra, he *was* a used car salesman.

I still hoped I could convince Biszantz that honesty and transparency were a better way of doing business. I told him about my first-ever shareholder's report when I warned Callaway's investors they'd bought our stock too high and that it was more than likely to dip over the coming months. Biszantz looked me straight in the eye and told me, "Ely, that's maybe the dumbest thing I've ever heard anybody say about their own company."

I replied, "Well, Gary, I understand that's maybe not the way you do business, but we don't want to run our company on hype, and we don't want our shareholders to have false expectations." Let's just call that good old Callaway diplomacy.

I had more fun with Cobra than any of my other competitors because I hated them. We fought our battle on multiple fronts: I got our general counsel Steve McCracken to gather all the documentation that would refute Lehman's reports and send it to Cobra, which was the legal equivalent of a warning shot. We began publishing our own financial reports with Merrill Lynch to counteract the ones Cobra was putting out through Lehman. Cobra responded by trying to hire Merrill Lynch to report for them instead. Fortunately for Callaway, Merrill Lynch refused. We retaliated by trying to convince Lehman to cover us. This was the tenor of our conflict: back and forth for several years, trading salvos on Wall Street and on the fairway. Up to that point, in the history of the golf club industry, I don't think there had ever been a rivalry quite like ours.

Short Sellers, Poison Pills, and Bad Analysts

By the middle of 1995, Callaway was winning the Golf War in the marketplace but losing it on Wall Street. We were delighted by our sales performance, but our market cap had dropped 35 percent. The gossip from New York was that Wall Street feared we couldn't sustain the continual, rapid growth we'd enjoyed the past four years. Still, such a precipitous and sudden drop-off didn't make any goddamn sense at all. Everything about my company was a hell of a lot better in the summer of 1995 than it had been in the summer of 1994, and I thought our prospects for the future were pretty good too, yet Wall Street valued us at 35 percent lower than they had before. Our stock price dropped to $15, then to an all-time low of $12. If Cobra was responsible for six points of this plummet, I lay the rest of the blame on the short sellers.

Short sellers are the leeches of Wall Street, and I hated them with every fiber of my being. The entire welfare of a short seller lies in their ability to hurt a company's value and then profit from the loss. To accomplish this, they spread destructive misinformation about our company for the explicit purpose of lowering the value of our stock, and because there's no regulation from the SEC or anybody else, they got away with it. The short sellers had no regulations, no laws, and no controls at all over what they could say about us, most of which were lies. They got rich on failure, without any accountability for how destructive they could be. When they did this, they weren't just hurting our company, they were hurting all of our other shareholders – decent, hard-working men and women who believed in our company and wanted to share in our success. If Congress had any sense, they'd pass a few laws to put some prohibitions on these short sellers.

The annual shareholder's meeting came in May of '95, and you could feel the nervousness about the company. As the public face of Callaway, I knew I had to pull out all the stops to ease the troubled minds of my investors. I invited Johnny Miller and Kenny G, the jazz saxophonist, to appear with me at the shareholders' meeting. I even singled out our youngest stockholder, a 15-year-old boy who'd owned a few shares since he was 11. My hope was to put positive energy back into Callaway to counteract the naysayers and analysts and short sellers. I wanted the shareholders to know I had their back.

At one point during my speech, I asked, rather brazenly, "How many short sellers are in this room?" The audience laughed, but I knew for a fact they were there. Nobody confessed, and I moved on.

Our stock stayed down, and the sharks began to circle. Murmurs of a hostile takeover floated through Titanium Valley. Everybody from Carlsbad to Manhattan knew American Brands Company (formerly American Tobacco Company) had just dumped their tobacco brands and were looking to fill that hole in their balance sheet with premium luxury goods brands, specifically in golf. They'd already bought Titleist, and now they had their sights set on Callaway. There was nothing wrong with American Brands – they were a fine little conglomerate and did beautifully with shoes and gloves and other accessories, but

I did not want to sell Callaway, and I particularly did not want to sell Callaway when our price was so low. That would be devastating to our long-term stockholders.

To stop American Brands from gobbling us up, the board of directors and I issued a shareholders rights program, commonly known as a poison pill. All it really did was give management time on behalf of the shareholders to get a good price for the company and not get forced into a precipitous hostile takeover. It gave Callaway a chance to demonstrate the true value of our company, not the artificially depressed value Wall Street had saddled us with.

I wanted Callaway to remain independent for the next decade and beyond, but I had to consider the price American Brands, or any potential suitor for that matter, was willing to pay. If the price was good enough and the buyer was someone who could nurture us and carry us forward, then I had an obligation to maximize the value of our shares at any given time. If the board of directors and management team, particularly our president, Don Dye, approved an offer and thought it would be a rewarding thing for themselves and the shareholders, then I would consider that a triumph.

I wasn't limited in my imagination, though. Maybe American Brands would acquire us – or maybe we could acquire them? There's no reason, if we really wanted to, that we couldn't acquire Titleist from American Brands, or Spalding. There were a lot of possible outcomes that I would've considered triumphs. This kind of thinking kept me nimble, energized, and open to new possibilities through many of the company's most tumultuous days. If American Brands bought us, or Disney for that matter, so be it.

That didn't end up happening. The poison pill scared off American Brands, who instead decided to buy – believe it or not – Cobra. I guess because American Brands couldn't get the top golf club company, they settled for number two. When American Brands bought Cobra for $700 million in December, articles were written about what a boon this would be for Cobra. Now that Cobra had a conglomerate behind them, they could spend more money on producing better clubs and on creating better marketing. Analysts assumed Callaway would have to cut our prices in order to compete. "The Golf War," one journalist declared, "has begun in earnest."

That was wrong too. American Brands purchasing Cobra wasn't the beginning of the Golf Wars, it was the end of them. American Brands quickly turned Cobra into another safe brand, like all those international corporations had done to the sleepy golf companies they'd acquired in the '80s, just as they might have tried to do to Callaway if we had not resisted their takeover. Within a couple of years, the Cobra brand had been surpassed by TaylorMade and Nike. This outcome for Cobra was not surprising – because they were never creators, they were imitators.

Over and over again, the Wall Street analysts were dead wrong about Callaway. There are many agonies about being a publicly traded company, from panicked investors to short sellers to financial manipulators, but the most difficult group to deal with were the security analysts, because they didn't have the ability to accurately evaluate a company – especially the abilities of the chief executive or the top management, which is the single most important factor to consider when predicting the future success of a company.

It is a tragedy for the American investment public that we are advised by people who don't know what the hell they're talking about. The reason these advisors are so incompetent is that they have never run companies. It isn't that they're dumb or terribly informed or lazy or negligent. It isn't that at all. They're fine people, but they simply don't understand what it takes to make a company successful, except in a very superficial way.

That's why the analysts so badly misvalued Callaway and everybody else in the golf club industry, for that matter. In 1995, people were absolutely enamored of Cobra and its co-founder and CEO, Mark McClure, and at first glance, perhaps they should have been. But in my opinion, Mark McClure didn't know what he was doing. The analysts overestimated the value of their models, which were often based on bad information, and underestimated the importance of human talent and decent, honest values.

Now, the analyst's bosses might've understood, because many of them were proper businessmen who'd run companies or been executives, but they were not willing to go out and do the spadework themselves. Instead, they hired these analysts to do their job for them, paid them very little, or at least relatively little, and low and behold, they couldn't do it. When it comes to market valuations and predictions, these "experts" at Lehman Brothers and Merrill Lynch and the rest have made some of the dumbest mistakes imaginable. We've allowed these analysts far too much influence over our economy, and too much control over how people think about, spend, and invest their money. They haven't earned the public's trust, but we've given it to them anyway.

The night before Callaway went public, a bunch of us went

out to a fine restaurant to celebrate. Around the table were some of the top analysts at Merrill Lynch, representatives from the GE Pension Fund, a few Callaway executives, and my wife, Cindy. We all had a pool – and everyone put up 10 bucks – as to what Callaway's closing price would be the following day. Cindy bet that it would be $34.50 a share. The closing price turned out to be $34.

Cindy beat the analysts.

"Business really can be quite simple, at least when it's done correctly."

"We took a perceived disadvantage and turned it into an asset. We sold the difference."

CHAPTER 10

WE BETTER LEARN HOW TO MAKE BETTER PRODUCTS

How Callaway Competes in the Global Economy

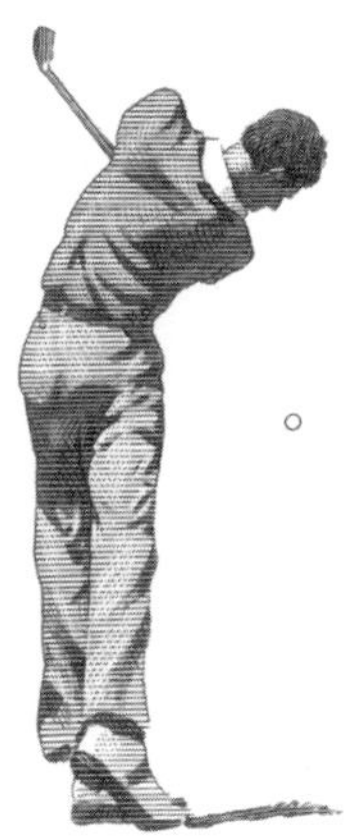

The Slump of '98

In the summer of 1997, a once-in-a century El Niño storm emerged across the Pacific, blanketing California in record rainfall and causing a whole bunch of problems all over the world. It turned out that "when it rains it pours" wasn't just a cliché but a prophecy, because this El Niño was immediately followed by an economic crisis in East Asia and Japan, which accounted for 10 percent of our total sales, and threw the global market into chaos.

Every golf company suffered setbacks during the "Asian Flu" of 1998, and some like Lynx even filed for bankruptcy. Sales were slow in Callaway's three major markets – the U.S., Japan, and Southeast Asia. Meanwhile, two new wannabes, Adams and Orlimar, took a bite out of Callaway's market share by offering lower-quality metal woods at meaningfully lower prices. In response, we cut our wholesale prices, something I hated doing.

Before the panic in the golf club market, Callaway Golf Company had already ventured far afield into business opportunities beyond golf clubs, and was spreading itself quite thin. Two years earlier, I had handed over day-to-day operations of the company to Don Dye, taken semi-retirement, and focused my energy on our golf ball manufacturing program, on which I bet the farm with a $150 million capital risk, and which so far had produced a whopping total of zero balls.

I had also just signed a long-term lease at Harry Macklowe's 540 Madison Avenue at 55th Street for a street-level, 18,000-square-foot, three-story-high Callaway Golf Experience. I was back on my home turf, where I'd spent 30 years of my life. This was to be the first high-tech-interactive-swing-analysis-meets-bespoke-fitting-experience in the heart of midtown Manhattan. Golfers from around the block and around the world would come to Callaway's flagship retail destination, where they could enter an augmented-reality version of a championship golf course like Augusta National, hit real golf balls into an immersive video projection, and have their golf swing instantly analyzed by computers to determine their ideal set of Callaway equipment. Customers could then view the on-demand manufacturing of their clubs, which they could carry home with them or have shipped for next-day delivery. This was my sequel to The Mill at Burlington House a generation earlier, and a golf version of being fitted by a bespoke tailor.

By July, several members of the board and key chief operating managers had lost confidence in the leadership of my hand-picked successor, Don Dye. After much discussion with the board, top managers, and even members of my family, I came to realize that the man I'd left in charge of my company – my business partner, best friend, protégé, and until recently my personal lawyer and the executor of my estate – was a terrible executive who nobody liked (if I've had any shortcomings in my life, it's choosing wives and successors). I reluctantly supported the board's unanimous decision to fire Don and take his place.

Two days after I fired Don, I went to his mother's birthday party at Disneyland. Don was obsessed with Disney, and had even tried hiring Disney Imagineers to work for Callaway. I hoped I might smooth over our personal relationship, but Don was not happy to see me – though he kept a brave face. Some weeks later, Don sent me an email accusing me of stabbing him in the back, when I was the only one at the company who had supported him. We had been friends for 20 years and founded this great company together, but now this is what our relationship had been reduced to: fighting over email.

I returned to the chief executive's chair in October, but our stock price and revenue continued to slide. Callaway needed to reduce costs, which meant permanently shelving my dream project, the New York Golf Club experience. We'd cut costs on one previous occasion, during my Golf Wars with Cobra in 1995. Back then, I insisted that the thing we weren't going to do was cut labor. Instead, we saved money by being smarter and more efficient. We were more clever about how we bought our supplies and our golf club components, and we used our power to purchase more at once for a cheaper per-component price. But these remedies weren't enough in 1998, and in November I made the decision to lay off 700 employees (25 percent of our total workforce), much of it from our manufacturing sector.

People have analyzed what the hell went wrong in American manufacturing during the second half of the 20th century, and came to a lot of conclusions that were just plain dumb. A lot of people on Wall Street blamed this lousy era on unions. Labor, in particular organized labor, had long been the scapegoat of incompetent, greedy, and incompetently greedy businessmen, when the real culprit has been bad management.

Callaway's 700 workers were the victims of bad management, and I don't exclude myself from responsibility. Don Dye was the man I'd bet on and so, in a real sense, his shortcomings were mine. My ex-employees, and the rest of the hundreds of thousands of Americans who lost their manufacturing jobs in 1998, were also the victims of two larger management problems: the failure of our country's leaders – in both business and government – to adapt to the forces of international trade (a situation I'd anticipated and tried to prevent for 50 years); and the fact that American companies no longer made the best products.

The Rise of Japan, Inc.

One of the advantages of being old is you've seen a lot of things happen. In 1945, it was easy for us to make the best products, because nobody else in the world was making anything.

I saw Japan and Germany in ashes after World War II. The U.S. trounced them in the war, but we decided to bind up the wounds of our former enemies and put them back on their feet. The Japanese and, to a lesser extent, the Germans have been winning the trade wars ever since.

I believe our reasons were ideological – we needed Japan as our ally in the Pacific to resist the rising specter of Communism – and driven by guilt over what we'd done to their country during the war. In the beginning, it was okay for us to feel guilty, as opposed to feeling vindictive and going in and butchering the conquered enemy, the way most victorious nations have done throughout history. For a number of years, our guilt produced a good result; it was both humane and morally necessary. But the problem was that the guilt outlasted its usefulness.

Billions of dollars left our pockets and flowed into the Japanese economy. Between the end of the war and 1970, the United States spent about $150 billion rebuilding Japan's industries. When the United States gave Japan a lifeline, their government, under the direct supervision of General MacArthur, got together and focused their investments on automobiles, consumer electronics, and textiles. Next, they handpicked the companies they wanted to succeed and rigged their economy and trade policies to make sure they did. Their government imposed strict limits on foreign imports, fixed prices to keep the cost of their products below America's, and fostered monopolies.

Their whole nation was one giant company, and it was the most magnificent monopoly that's ever existed in modern commerce. We called this system of centralized industrialization Japan, Inc. Some people inaccurately credited that phrase to me, because I was one of the first people to call attention to this problem in the late 1950s when I joined the U.S.-Japan Trade Council, but I believe it was futurist Herman Kahn who coined the term.

Everything Japan did, we did the opposite. While they made the best televisions, the best cars, and the best clothes, we stopped investing in research and development, which used to be our bread and butter. There's an old saying: "The Allies won World War II with Russian blood, British intelligence, and American steel." I would've amended that phrase to "American steel and woolens." The ingenuity of our products and the power of our manufacturing gave us a competitive advantage over our enemies. I had learned this firsthand in the army as a soldier, and I wanted to continue to play a part as a private citizen. That's why I went to work for Roger Milliken. He'd built the most advanced R&D institute in the entire textile industry, which we used to make many innovative and great products.

Textiles were the first American victims of Japan's economic attacks, placing me on the frontlines of the trade war. Throughout the 1960s, they took over the American textile market bite by bite. Every textile company dealt with this crisis in its own way. Burlington's response was to go monopolistic, crooked, and, after I was fired, expansionist internationally as a last resort.

Meanwhile, the Japanese didn't seem to mind living in Japan, Inc. They were willing to suffer and pay five times as much for textiles as they should. All that sacrificial public-private money went into undercutting the competition and subsidizing an all-out attack on any market they wanted to conquer, such as ours.

When I represented the textile industry on the U.S.-Japan Trade Council, I sat across the table from gentlemen like Akio Morita, the co-founder of Sony. We were trade adversaries, but I admired Morita-san enormously as one of the key product innovators and historic figures of post-war Japan, who helped resurrect the country after its nuclear and economic devastation. Morita essentially created the global consumer electronics industry (with the collusion of the Japanese Ministry of Investment, Trade & Industry), and had a huge influence on Silicon Valley, Detroit, and Hollywood (Sony bought Columbia Pictures in 1989, from Coca-Cola no less).

There is no doubt in my mind that Japan played a rigged game. But I can't entirely blame them; their government only did what it believed was in the best interests of its people. I fault America's politicians, along with the press, corporate leaders, and other opinion makers, who were all asleep on this issue. But whether or not they chose to acknowledge it, we were already in a trade war with Japan, and in as much danger as we would've been in any other kind of war. The textile industry was not an isolated incident, but the beginning of a global trend that is only getting worse and worse.

By the early 1970s, Burlington was working with GM, supplying all their seat cushions for Chevrolets, Pontiacs, Oldsmobiles, and the rest. We had lived through Japan's incursion into our markets long enough to know what was about to happen to the American automotive industry, and we raised the alarm with GM's CEO, James M. Roche. It didn't take a Nostradamus to predict that the Japanese car market might capture at least 30 percent of the California automobile market and then flood the rest of the U.S. market within the next 10 years. Detroit was in a state of denial, and despite our warnings to various automotive executives, they ignored us. The head of GM went to the mat for free trade, along with everybody else.

Trade barriers were an unpopular idea back then, as they still are now, but I believed that a reasonable and enlightened form of economic nationalism was necessary to stop the country from going broke. Nobody wanted to take extreme measures, but I knew we were in a crisis that threatened our national security and future prosperity.

On the other hand, protectionism can be dangerous because people are greedy. If companies are shielded from foreign competition, they are tempted to charge too much for their products, and the consumer suffers as a result. Wage and price controls are one remedy. They don't need to be absolute, as they were in World War II, but we can adopt reasonable price and wage protections.

When I sat on the Japan-U.S Trade Council, I was the only voice advocating for any kind of trade protections. Unfortunately, the real problem was that our side of the Trade Council was full of CEOs who cared more about their narrow corporate self-interest than the shared strategic goals of American business. The chairman of the Council was Najeeb Halaby, the head of Pan American Airways, which eventually went bankrupt – not from Japanese competition, but because of their excessive reliance on expensive Arab oil. Don Kendall of Pepsi only worried about Coke. Walter Wriston of National City Bank, later Citicorp, was busy lending money to the Third World so he could win a different competition: making the most profit by putting the greatest number of developing nations into the most debt.

My Appeal to Congress

In 1971, America officially flipped from having a trade surplus to a trade deficit. We've yet to flip it back. That same year, leaders from the American textile industry attempted to negotiate directly with the Japanese Textile Federation, hoping to convince them to unilaterally limit future exports of certain Japanese goods into America while allowing more American imports into their market, something the Nixon administration had been unable to accomplish in the past two years. I was an active member of those trade negotiations, during which I had heated disputes with my friend Shinzo Ohya, president of Teijin Limited and Japan's ex-minister of commerce.

Teijin was a classic case of de-worsification and exposed the double-edged samurai sword of Japan, Inc. – a textile company with roots in rayon fiber that grew into a massive but unwieldy conglomerate, and nearly went bankrupt because of it. I also became lifelong friends with his wife Masako Ohya, also known as Madame O, an utterly eccentric billionairess who ran Teijin after her husband's death. She was a pop singer, patron of the arts, and a true golf nut, who owned six golf courses. She played exclusively with Callaway clubs, always dressed head to toe in pink baby-doll dresses and extravagant bonnets. In the 1960s, the Ohyas had sent me a five-foot-tall ancient Japanese stone lantern that weighed several tons – a priceless gift that became the centerpiece of the Japanese water garden I designed and had installed at my New Canaan estate. It was a magnificent gift that could be seen either as a great expression of friendship and personal admiration, or an eternal obligation that I had incurred by accepting it – or both. As with Akio Morita of Sony, we were businessmen who had grown up as enemies in wartime but then became both personal friends and professional adversaries.

I tried to negotiate with Ohya-san, but in the end I couldn't accept the Japan Textile Federation's proposal for a simple reason: it wasn't fair. Japan's solution fell far short of a workable agreement to deal with the import/export problems.

We had able and skilled professionals negotiating with Japan, but we didn't have a chance of securing a better deal without the support of Congress, who enacted trade legislation and set the tone for the country. I made this case in my "Point of View" column entitled "U.S. Trade Deal" for *The New York Times* on March 7, 1971. I argued, "The United States is fast losing its position as front runner in the international trade race in spite of the fact that we were almost at the finish line and were practically the only ones in the race 25 years ago." The Japanese were taking large segments of the U.S. market for high-technology product categories like automobiles, airplanes, and televisions, "the very ones in which American ingenuity allowed us to prosper until recent years." Our technological superiority had made us such a dominant force in international trade for so long that when the rest of the world finally caught up, our elected officials were too arrogant to take action.

In May of '71, *Time Magazine* asked me to participate in an all-day symposium with nine of the top men in American business, including Thorton F. Bradshaw of Atlantic Richfield Company, Walter Wriston, and Don Kendall, Chairman of Pepsi. We debated the merits of free trade versus protectionism, and I made the case that Congress needed to enact new trade legislation that would protect the interests of the American people and the economy in a reasonable way. I argued, "With the political clout of the laws having been passed in this country, we might have a pretty good opportunity to get the members of GATT [General Agreement on Tariffs and Trades] to adopt some rules that would represent fair trade."

That same month I appeared before the U.S. Congressional Subcommittee on International Trade, in the hope of waking up our elected representatives. I told them that our government had become a slave to its ideology of free trade, because we believed our system needed to be the opposite of whatever communism was. Here's a bit from my official statement before the Subcommittee: "The Congress needs to develop enforceable Government to Government arrangements, keyed to global coverage, with suitable category delineation of specific textile products. Now all of this should be done in the context of a fair and reasonable base period and an equitable sharing in the increased demand in the domestic market between domestic production and imports. Anything short will not work."

Several senators accused me of being an alarmist, arguing that we actually did have a favorable balance of trade. These denialists trotted out fake good news statistics that claimed our trade revenue from banking made up for our trade losses in goods. They even talked about how Japan was not going be a problem because their wage rates were getting so high that pretty soon they'd no longer even have a textile industry. Baloney!

Congress was digging its own grave by telling itself a story that wasn't true, so I told them what was really going to happen: Japan would build textile mills in Korea, Taiwan, and all over the Far East, import those goods back into their own country, and increase their exports to America and the rest of the world.

Congress did go on to pass the Trade of Act of 1971, but this bill was not strong or decisive enough to have a meaningful impact.

In fact, it was such a half-hearted measure, and I felt these matters were so important for America's future, that I briefly toyed with entering politics.

For the past 30 years, I have watched our government try various ways to fix the trade problem, and none of them have amounted to a hill of beans. Nixon's shocks and price controls later in 1971 seemed promising, but didn't reverse the deficit. In the 1980s, Reagan avoided trade protections by foisting the myth on America that we didn't need a big central government. He told Americans, "I'm coming in to get the government off your back," and then he immediately forced the government *on* their backs by increasing defense spending and creating deficits. In the past decade, I have fundraised for Bill Clinton, who is a friend and golf buddy, but when he signed NAFTA in 1992 (a deal negotiated by his predecessor), it only made the situation worse.

As far as I can tell, nobody of any political persuasion has the foggiest idea of how to handle our trade deficit. Everybody is obsessed with a "free market." But free for whom? Not for American business. Not for the American worker.

American business owners have been put in a bad spot, no doubt about it, but their solution has only exacerbated the situation: they've stopped making the best products. Like the golf club business, the American textile industry today is run by fundamentally incompetent people. This was not the case when I joined Burlington Industries in the late 1950s. We made better textiles than anyone in the world, and we outsmarted our competition. But as cheaper Japanese products invaded our market in the 1960s and 1970s, Burlington didn't try to compete with Japan by making better products. Instead they divested from research and development, cut labor costs, and focused on diversifying and expanding through capital gains. It didn't work.

In 1987, Burlington narrowly avoided a hostile takeover attempt from Asher B. Edelman and Canada's Dominion Textile Inc. They only survived by agreeing to a $2.04 billion leveraged buyout from Morgan Stanley – a brutal deal that crippled the once great company. When Burlington had closed The Mill in 1980, they claimed it was too old-fashioned. I wonder what seemed outdated – the technology, or the fact that it portrayed a thriving American textile industry?

Lots of companies from a variety of industries followed the Burlington model. Today I look around and see the de-worsifications of the 1960s and 1970s, and the takeovers of the 1980s, becoming largely undone. The owners of these companies couldn't look beyond their short-term profits to foresee the consequences of making lousy products.

Products over Profit

Here's what American business has to focus on for the next half-century: we have to make better products. And if we do, we will regain our position of leadership in the world and we will bring jobs back to this country. I know this is true because during the 1990s, in an era when manufacturing was mostly in retreat, Callaway has created the most desired products and the most recognizable brand in its industry in the world.

On any given Friday, there are professionals using the Big Bertha driver in 26 different professional tour events in 26 different countries. We sell 40 percent of our clubs abroad in 100 countries on six continents. The Japanese don't desire Honma, Mizuno, or Miura clubs like they do Callaway golf clubs. They're buying Callaway's because there is no better club on the market.

The international markets won't open to American products unless we offer something so terrific that the Japanese, the Chinese, the Germans, or whoever else can't live without them, and furthermore we've got to make them in America. Callaway makes its clubs in Carlsbad because we create a better product, we have more control, and we like employing Americans.

Callaway Golf was my solution to the problems I've witnessed in American business for the past 60 years. And what we've done can be replicated in any industry, if we make the effort, maintain our focus, get the right talent, and don't prioritize our short-term profits over products. Let me be clear: it ain't easy. I've shed blood, sweat, and tears to become the best at merchandising and manufacturing in one single field. Maybe Callaway Golf Company lost its focus in the years leading up to the crisis of 1998, but this challenge forced me to return my company to our core principles of innovation and quality. Fortunately, Callaway was already in the process of making its biggest oversized driver yet, the ERC II.

"Don't let the problems kill the promise."

CHAPTER 11

CHANGING THE GAME

Elitism, Endorsements, and Tiger Mania

The Two Games

The past decade has been a golden era for the game of golf. I have witnessed and maybe played an itty-bitty part in its evolution from being primarily an elitist pastime of the rich and powerful to a global mass sport enjoyed by tens of millions of people. There are now 40 million golfers around the world, buying more clubs and playing on more golf courses than at any other time in history. When Callaway released Big Bertha, we changed the game by making it easier for more people than ever to enjoy the experience of making a golf shot. It wasn't that our clubs lowered handicaps or increased distance off the tee, they just made it more likely that golfers would hit shots that made them go, "Oh boy, that's a great shot!" It's really that simple.

We made the game of golf a little more pleasurable, and that alone radically changed the golf club business; we injected energy and innovation into what had long been a hidebound, sleepy industry. But it's not enough to change the game once. At Burlington, my success depended upon anticipating and staying ahead of evolving fashion trends, and at Callaway it was the same. To stay ahead of our competitors, we push the limits of technology over and over again to make more forgiving and more rewarding golf clubs, particularly drivers, and release a new line every year, just like cars and computers.

But the USGA, the governing body for golf in the United States, stopped us from making bigger and better clubs in early 1998, when they updated their guidelines on clubhead size and the "trampoline effect," the springiness that allows a club to generate more distance off the tee. Overnight, they put severe limits on the kinds of technological advancements we could make. I had a meeting with some of the rule-making heads on the USGA's executive committee. They told me and my whole staff they thought all these bigger and more advanced drivers were causing the ball to fly too far off the tee. According to them, Big Berthas were threatening the game by making it too easy for too many people, and they planned to ban our latest club, called the Biggest Big Bertha, from professional tours.

We convinced the USGA to listen to the American golfers, who said with one voice, "You're not going to take Big Bertha from us." The USGA wisely raised their limits to accommodate the Biggest Big Bertha, but there was now little chance that any further innovations would still conform to their guidelines. My team talked about it and decided that the average golfer should at least be given the choice to play with the best possible driver that technology would allow. We decided to move ahead and develop a next-generation driver to be called the ERC II, an acronym for Ely Reeves Callaway, Jr.

I knew this non-conforming driver would inevitably lead to accusations that anybody who used it was a cheater, but I didn't care. I knew the rules were stupid, and in order to change the game again, I would have to challenge the powers that be.

My feud with the USGA continued for the next two years. The ERC II was still months away from going to market in early 2000 when Arnold Palmer flew his Citation X down to Carlsbad and landed at the tiny airport next door to our plant. He spent a whole day trying out a prototype of the ERC II at the Ely Callaway Test Center. Callaway had no endorsement deal with The King, but he was interested in the development of golf clubs, and told me that testing the ERC II was one of the great experiences of his life. Even at 70 years old, having been as devoted to golf as anybody on the planet, he had learned something: "I had no idea that modern technology could help *me* enjoy the game more."

Steve McCracken, Arnie, and I stopped for lunch at Aviara Golf Club in Carlsbad, just a few miles from company headquarters. Arnie of course ordered an Arnold Palmer as his beverage, and the waiter responded, "Oh you mean a Callaway?" Unfortunately, the restaurant had rechristened it "The Callaway" because I had lunch there almost every day. Arnie was none too happy about that, and Steve, as the mastermind of the negotiations, was worried that this accidental rebranding might kill the deal. Nevertheless, Arnie signed a 10-year endorsement contract with us.

He shot a commercial for us promoting the ERC II and received a lot of angry fan letters and unfair criticism in *Sports Illustrated* and the golf press because of it. When we warned him that the ERC II was going to be non-conforming, Arnold simply asked, "Well, why shouldn't these help everybody? Why should ordinary people be deprived of it?"

What Arnold and I understood – and what the USGA evidently did not – is that there are really two games of golf. Bobby Jones came up with this idea a long time ago, and I've kept his lesson close to my heart. There is the game of championship golf, which Arnold Palmer, Tiger Woods, Annika Sörenstam, and other top pros play. This game is a wonderful thing to be involved in (although I'm glad I don't have to make a living that way), but it's a different game entirely than what the rest of us play. We play the game for fun, exercise, camaraderie, love, competition, and lifestyle.

I don't know for sure why the USGA adopted their attitude, but I've got a pretty good idea. Golf started out in Scotland many years ago, and developed around the world and in the United States slowly and carefully as an elitist game. It developed fundamentally in private clubs in the United States, with people who had the money to join private clubs and the time to play the game and become skilled at it.

There's an elitist attitude that can develop from being really good at the game. I know because I had it myself. I won four or five club championships as a kid, and I thought I was pretty hot stuff. Because I worked at the game and became skillful, I didn't even wanna play with a hacker. The USGA was the same. They worked hard to become good at a tough game, and they wanted to keep it tough (I did some research and learned that the average handicap of the 16-person Rules Committee was slightly under five).

The trouble was that the people they were ignoring account for 97 percent of the golfers in the world. The USGA Rules Committee had convinced themselves that it was logical, reasonable, and fair to decree that there is only one game, and there must be only one set of rules governing everybody – pro, amateur, men, women, young, or old. It seemed to me that somebody somewhere was feeling threatened and was outta touch.

At Callaway, these aren't our values, because they're a good way *not* to grow the game. We're not saying the ERC II or any other club that doesn't adhere to the USGA rules should be allowed to play in tournaments. That's okay! I would say 92 percent of golfers don't wanna play in tournaments, they just want to go out and have fun. We don't think it's cheating or harmful or bad to give them a choice that will allow them to play the game a little better for a little longer. Fortunately, the Royal and Ancient Golf Club of St Andrews, which set the rules for most of the golf world outside the United States, agreed with me.

As a result, the ERC II sold very well internationally. We didn't sell one ERC II in America last year, but American golfers got their hands on it anyway – buying it second- and third-hand at absolutely silly-high prices. The people had spoken.

Endorsements and Influence-Makers

There is another way in which the golf business has radically changed in the past decade: athlete and celebrity endorsements. The phenomenon itself is nothing new – I tried to license Bobby Jones's name and likeness for a line of men's suits at Burlington back in the mid-1960s – but today it is a whole different ball game. The market for golf pro endorsements exploded in 1991 when Cobra, our old nemesis, made Greg Norman the face of its company. The Great White Shark was one of the most popular players on tour and a shrewd businessman. He invested $1.8 million of his own money into the company, acquiring a 12 percent share, which by 1997 was worth $40 million. Norman expanded his business ambitions by starting his own golf tour to compete with the PGA, though it was short-lived.

The partnership between Cobra and Norman set the tone for the rest of the industry. Now locking up a star player could cost several million a year, and that wasn't counting stock options and other bonuses. Any of Callaway's top pros, like Paul Azinger, Colin Montgomerie, or John Daly, got an extra $1.5 million if they won a major tournament, which was more than the cash prize paid by the tournament itself. For a minor tournament, the going rate was $150,000. Every victory had its price, and it was paid by the golf club manufacturers.

Signing the best pros is as competitive a business as creating the best clubs. We had a Callaway representative, such as senior vice president of sports marketing Mike Galeski, looking for talent on each of the five big pro tours: Ladies, Men's, Senior, the European, and Nike for the younger players. When Callaway broke through, most of the star players of the day were already locked up in expensive contracts with one manufacturer or another, and to get tomorrow's star players, we had to scout the minor leagues like a baseball manager.

Several years ago, I spotted a big young talent on the practice tee at the Aviara Country Club north of San Diego. It was Annika Sörenstam. I immediately fell in love with Annika's swing. Jim Dent, another Callaway pro, agreed with me. After about 10 minutes of watching the graceful way she moved the clubhead through the ball, I walked over and introduced myself to this shy, little-known golfer. Soon, we had a contract.

The 25-year-old Annika lived up to her promise and then some by coming out of nowhere to win the 1995 Women's U.S. Open after her opponent flubbed a putt on the final hole. The next day, the front page of *The New York Times* displayed a picture of her holding the trophy, with the Callaway logo on her hat and shirt. The *Times* wouldn't sell you an ad in the middle of the front page for any amount of money, so this was priceless advertising. We don't know how many golf clubs Annika sold that day, but we got 15,000 orders for Callaway hats.

Callaway's biggest advertising opportunities for the men's and women's games were the major championships. Almost five million people watched the final round of the 1995 PGA Championship on television, when Callaway athlete Colin Montgomerie hit 17 of 18 greens and birdied the final three holes to break the major tournament record for the lowest score in a single round. But the problem with the endorsement business is the announcers don't say, "Montgomerie just hit a perfect 300-yard drive with a Great Big Bertha." Instead, they say, "He hit a perfect drive." The only way the audience could tell if a player had anything to do with Callaway was if he had the Callaway logo on his bag, or if he wore a Callaway hat. But

Colin Montgomerie wouldn't wear a hat. He just flat refused!

We had had the same problem with Patty Sheehan, but she made up for it by having the company name embroidered across her tee shirt a few inches below the neck. I thought maybe there was a place on Montgomerie's big billboard of a body he could stick a "Callaway" to help the company, and help himself when the stock went up. But upon further investigation, we discovered that all the surface rights to the Scot Montgomerie below the neck were already owned by Pringle, the Scottish luxury sweater maker, and they had no interest in sharing their territory with us. So that left us with limited possibilities: a Callaway headband, perhaps? Or Callaway sunglasses? Or painting his forehead with sunscreen so his sunburn would spell "Callaway?" In *Raiders of the Lost Ark,* Indiana Jones's student had "I love you" tattooed on her eyelids. Maybe Colin could get "Callaway" tattooed on his forearms? We discussed all these options, but Colin's solution was to just get rid of Pringle. As well he should have. Montgomerie played Callaway clubs to five straight European Order of Merits and a number 2 world ranking. Name one sweater that can boast comparable benefits.

Fortunately for us, Annika Sörenstam believed in the virtue of hats. The last time she came to see us to renew her contract, she brought along her agent, Mark McCormack. One of the most powerful men in all of sports, Mark founded International Management Group (IMG) in 1960, and we have been friends for nearly that long, going all the way back to my time at Burlington (he pitched his early client, Jean Shrimpton, the most famous fashion model in the world, to me as a spokesperson). He first built IMG around the Big Three of golf: first Arnold Palmer, then Gary Player and Jack Nicklaus shortly thereafter.

Mark and I were both good golfers in our youth and played together throughout the years, including a foursome at the 1968 Bing Crosby National Pro Am at Pebble Beach, with Arnold Palmer as his ringer. Like mine, Mark's business grew from his passion for the game of golf, as well as a maverick's love of doing things diffrunt and bettuh.

For the first time, Mark unlocked the economic potential of leveraging an athlete's star power for marketing and business opportunities, and in doing so revolutionized sports, fashion, and entertainment. The year Arnold signed with Mark, Arnold was making $50,000 in annual income. Within three years, Arnold was making $500,000 a year. McCormack worked with everyone from Joe Montana to supermodel Tyra Banks to the Pope. He even invented a popular world golf ranking system.

We had a little surprise in store for Annika the day she signed her contract. We put her in the backseat of a golf cart full of flowers, alongside her fiancé, whom we had brought in for the occasion. I was in the front seat, driving the cart, with Johnny Miller, another Callaway pro, at my side. Annika wondered what this was all about, and I told her we were taking a tour of the new buildings. After we passed the second or third building and I could see she was completely bored, I turned the cart into an alley where a thousand Callaway employees were clapping, cheering, and waving placards. It was our own Annika Sörenstam victory parade. She broke into tears, and so did our accountant after we signed the new contract.

Callaway was as unconventional with our pro endorsements as we were with every other aspect of our business. John Daly embodied the everyman we wanted to bring into the game. The size of his frame was matched only by the size of his drives, which were powered by his self-taught swing wherein he drew the clubhead further back than any other golfer, then brought it down through the ball with startling ferocity. Nobody could know where a Daly drive would land – the fairway, the rough, the moon – but when it did, you could bet that ball would be further from the tee box than anyone else's. Daly even came up with the tagline of our campaign: "Hit it straight, John!"

I admired his underdog reputation, unpretentious attitude, and "grip it and rip it" style, qualities that made him one of the most beloved golfers on the tour. When he became available in 1997, we signed him to a five year contract worth $2 million. That year Daly became the first man to average 300 yards per drive for an entire season. This was the dream of Big Bertha coming full circle.

I wanted to include spokespeople who countered the elitist, country club attitude many traditionally associated with golf. But it was also important to me that every man and woman we paid to promote our clubs embody the values of Callaway Golf – demonstrably superior and pleasingly different. Over the years, we've had a deep stable of influence makers promoting our brand; everyone from Smokey Robinson to Sugar Ray Leonard to Tommy Smothers to Celine Dion to jazz saxophonist Kenny G (an excellent golfer) have appeared in our ads.

I remember we shot one commercial with rock star Alice Cooper, who was known more for his shock rock and pet snake than skill with a 9 iron (which was actually very good!). I'd met Alice at a party, and figured he'd be the last person anybody would ever expect to see in a golf club commercial – which made me want to put him in one right away. Alice was in fact a golf nut. He used to play 36 holes a day and even credited the game for helping him get past his alcoholism. "I traded one addiction for another," he once said.

Alice showed up the day of the shoot and was stunned to find a live boa constrictor on set. My idea was that Alice would put the snake on the green, take his new Tuttle II putter, and hit the ball off the snake and into the hole. Alice told me it would take 12 hours to get that shot. He made it on the third take. In my opinion, funny advertising generally doesn't sell the goods, because people remember the ad and not the product. But everybody had a blast making that commercial, and I kept Alice on my roster for years after. I suppose it was worth breaking my own rule, even if consumers remembered the snake and not Tuttle II.

Callaway was so prestigious in those days that oftentimes the endorsements came to us for free. Word got back to me that Microsoft Chairman Bill Gates was a very enthusiastic new golfer, and had been playing with our Big Bertha for a while. I invited him to our Performance Center in Carlsbad to have his swing analyzed, but in truth, I had ulterior motives. Bill and I had lunch together, and I suggested it might be good for him to tell golfers that even a billionaire computer genius struggled with the unconquerable game. I asked him to shoot a commercial for us. Bill liked the idea right away. What better way for this master of the software universe to show he was only human after all than playing golf on TV?

In the commercial, Bill stood behind a desk with a Big Bertha and spoke directly to the camera: "I started to play golf about five years ago. It was humbling. I really like it, but it's so frustrating. My dad and my sisters have played for a long time, so I asked them for some advice. They said to take some lessons and get a Big Bertha. I think I'm getting better." The screen faded to black, revealing the Callaway Golf logo and our tagline, "How Golf Should Feel."

Bill appeared one more time: "I love a big idea."

Twenty-five million golfers saw Gates struggling with the game just as much as they did, and suddenly they could relate to this celebrity businessman. Golf is a game that levels everybody – almost.

In 1998, Donald Trump reached out to me, leaving a message with my executive assistant, Diana Duvall, asking me to return his call about being featured in our celebrity advertising campaign, following big names like Alice Cooper and Bill Gates. He also spoke frequently with Larry Dorman, our Senior VP of Global Press and PR, with the idea of naming a Callaway club after him. Trump's name had been well-known in New York since the 1960s, and I'd heard he was diving into the golf course business—a challenging industry that requires real vision. Appreciating his enthusiasm, I sent over a set of Big Berthas, hoping he'd enjoy the clubs as he worked on bringing his ideas to life.

"The Biggest Mistake You'll Ever Make"

In most sports, a pro athlete who endorses the equipment has an obligation to use it on the field. When Michael Jordan got paid millions a year to endorse Nike, you didn't see him running around the basketball court wearing Reeboks. This is not the case in golf. Johnny Miller played with Callaway clubs, but other golf pros didn't necessarily play with the clubs they were paid to represent. To confirm this, we set up a surveillance operation and sent undercover agents to every major tournament in 1993. Their mission was to check what clubs were carried around in those bags. They took incriminating photographs.

When we snapped a photograph of Freddie Couples at the 1994 Masters, you didn't have to have 20/20 vision to see that Couples was swinging a Big Bertha driver. He swung the Big Bertha all through that Masters Tournament, while the ads on TV showed him playing with clubs made by Lynx, the company that paid Couples a fat endorsement contract of several million a year. Couples wore a Lynx visor and carried a Lynx bag, so most people made the assumption that every time he hit off the tee, he was hitting with the Lynx Boom Boom Driver (Couples's nickname). But that day at the Masters, Boom Boom wasn't hitting those booming drives with a Boom Boom, he was hitting them with a Big Bertha, and nobody but a few golf nuts knew it.

Our undercover agents got the inside story of how this happened. Couples's buddy, Ernie Els, had been using the Big Bertha for 18 months, in spite of the fact that Els also had a big endorsement contract with Lynx. The two of them were playing a practice round together. Couples said, "I've been hearing about this damn Big Bertha for so long, I want to try it," so Els loaned him the Bertha, and Couples played with it the rest of the day. He must have liked the results, because he asked our company rep to send him a selection of Big Berthas with different shafts and different lofts, and we shipped them to Augusta overnight. Couples went into the tournament with his favorite Big Bertha snuck into his Lynx bag. He played with it all four rounds, but he didn't win the Masters. He was beaten out by Ben Crenshaw, who also used a Big Bertha. Crenshaw happily publicized that fact because we paid him to advertise our clubs.

Couples and Els were hardly the only golfers with freelance clubs in their bags. By the middle of the '90s, 47 percent of all pros on the PGA Tour carried a Big Bertha driver, and Callaway had far less than 47 percent of pros on our endorsement roster. Half the women in the 1995 Women's U.S. Open used a version of the Big Bertha, even though some of them endorsed other products. Vicki Goetze was paid by Yonex, but there she was, teeing off with a Callaway driver.

There are 14 clubs in a golf bag, and you couldn't expect a pro who represents a manufacturer to use all 14 of that manufacturer's clubs. Every golfer wanted the freedom to carry a favorite old putter, or special wedge, or whatever, and he ought to get the opportunity, especially if it made him shoot a lower score and win a big tournament. But whoever represented Callaway had to use at least 10 Callaway clubs. That's the "Rule of Ten" written into all our contracts with pros. Some of our competitors didn't have such a rule. They allowed their pros to endorse their product and then play with none of their clubs.

Of course, every rule has exceptions. I was in the gallery of Pumpkin Ridge Golf Club in Portland, Oregon, on August 25, 1996, where I watched a then 20-year-old Tiger Woods, wearing his famous bright red shirt, stride up to the 18th green and two putt for par, completing a thrilling comeback that earned the Stanford freshman his third straight U.S. amateur championship. Hundreds of golf fans surrounded Tiger that day, but one in particular caught my eye: his new agent, Mark McCormack.

The day after Tiger's triumph at Pumpkin Ridge, I caught wind that Mark had already negotiated Tiger to a record-setting five-year, $40 million endorsement deal with Nike. The company's chairman, Phil Knight, had built Nike's success on the back of a superior running shoe, and when he signed Michael Jordan, Nike exploded into a globally recognized lifestyle brand with billions of dollars in revenue. With Tiger Woods, they were hoping lightning would strike twice.

Callaway could not match Nike's figure, and we didn't want to. I told Knight that I never believed that a great pro's name in and of itself meant success for a company. The one advantage we had was that for all Nike's wealth, they did not yet have a golf club division, and Tiger needed a driver. I asked my son Nicholas to weigh in on the matter. He shot back, "If you lose Tiger, it will be the biggest business mistake you'll ever make." I didn't like that answer one bit.

I sat down and wrote a letter to Phil Knight and Mark McCormack, congratulating them on the deal and offering one of my own. I proposed that Mr. Woods come down to Carlsbad and make a serious evaluation of our Big Berthas. If he became convinced that a Callaway driver was the best club to enhance his skills, and if he were willing to consistently use that driver in competition and endorse it exclusively, we would waive our Rule of Ten. Callaway would also agree to pay Nike or Woods the annual sum of $1.5 to $3 million, plus bonuses, for the three years following his first and continued use of any Callaway driver he might choose. We would not require him to endorse or carry any other Callaway club. I made the observation that since many of Nike's players were already using Callaway drivers, short of outright buying our company, this might be the best arrangement for all.

A Callaway/Tiger/Nike partnership would've been transformative. Not since watching Bobby Jones in my childhood had I seen anyone who epitomized the game of golf and pointed the way to its future like Tiger. Signing him would have been the triumphant capstone to everything I had achieved with Callaway Golf, and set the course for the company for the next generation.

Neither Nike nor IMG responded to my offer. Instead, we learned in the press that we had been outbid by American Brands, the conglomerate that owns Titleist and, yes, that's right, Cobra. A few months later, when Tiger won the 1997 Masters – his first – he accomplished it with a King Cobra, the driver of my nemesis.

Instead, I put all my chips on the product. Three years later, in February of 2000, we finally released our long-awaited golf ball, which I named "Rule 35." There were 34 official rules in golf, and our ball referred to my personal 35th: "Enjoy the Game." Rule 35 was a whole new ball game, containing a thin urethane cover, ionomer boundary layer, and solid polybutadiene core (as opposed to the much more common wound liquid core). We developed the ball utilizing the same aerodynamic computer program Boeing and GE use to develop airplanes, evaluating over 300 dimple patterns and 1,000 combinations of covers, boundary layers, and cores. The final product came in two types: Firmfeel and Softfeel. There were complex scientific differences between the two, but the only distinction that really mattered was an individual golfer's preference for one feel over another.

Callaway's global brand recognition wasn't enough on its own to ensure success for the ball launch. It took four years and nearly $200 million to create a product that I believed was more pleasing and more rewarding than the competition. Rule

35 offered "complete performance," combining distance, control, spin, and durability all at once. Arnold Palmer liked the ball so much, he started playing with it on the Senior Tour before he'd even signed his endorsement deal with us.

However, that same year, Nike released a new ball called Tour Accuracy with a solid rubber core, created by mechanical engineer Hideyuki "Rock" Ishii of Bridgestone. Tiger Woods worked closely with Nike to develop the ball, and upgraded from the wound core Titleist ball that he'd used his whole career (and that led the golf ball market with 32 percent of all sales). Tiger won three consecutive majors that summer, in the most dazzling and dominant run of championship play I or anybody else had ever seen. Tour Accuracy snagged a portion of the market share we were hoping to capture, and Rule 35's sales came in at half of the $70 million we had expected. Tiger just won his fourth consecutive major last month at the Masters, and almost the entire professional field has switched to solid core balls.

But here's an added twist: last year, when Tiger won the U.S. Open at Pebble Beach by 15 strokes, Nike didn't have the manufacturing infrastructure in place to supply the massive surge in demand. Unlike Big Bertha a decade earlier, Nike hadn't believed in the superiority of their product enough to take such a huge risk – they weren't willing to bet the farm like I did. Last October, Titleist debuted a solid core ball of their own, which they'd been secretly working on for years, and Tour Accuracy suddenly became yesterday's news. That's how quickly innovation can become old hat.

In my opinion, going into the golf equipment business will be a real problem for Nike. They formed Nike Golf for just that purpose in 1998 and are very bullish on the market opportunity, and I've had meetings with Phil where one outcome might be Nike buying Callaway. But I have my doubts.

Nike is the greatest sports apparel brand in the world, and Phil Knight is a marketing genius, but that doesn't mean they're gonna be able to succeed in hard goods. Tiger Woods himself might not be able to save a company from the perils of de-worsification.

Nevertheless, my losses in what *The New York Times* dubbed the Golf Ball Wars of last year have forced me to do some soul-searching: what if I had matched Phil's record-setting 1996 $40 million apparel deal with a $40 million Callaway club equipment deal? What if I had decided to bet the farm on this great golfer instead of on a ball? What might it have meant for the future of our company and the future of the sport? Because there's never been anyone in the game of golf like Tiger, maybe even including Bobby Jones. In 1996, the year Mark signed Tiger to IMG, *Golf Digest* listed Tiger as the third most powerful person in golf, behind only the PGA tour commissioner and the USGA executive director (Mark was fourth, I was eighth).

The television broadcast of the final round at Pebble Beach scored an 8.8 share, the highest since 1975. Tiger had long since locked up the championship, but the world watched Tiger all the same, because the way he played golf was demonstrably superior and pleasingly different.

The sport of golf and the golf equipment industry continue to change. Phil bet on the person. I bet on the product. In order for Callaway Golf to stay ahead of our competitors, maybe I need to change too. Good night! I've spent a lifetime reinventing myself. Why stop now?

"We made the game of golf a little more pleasurable, and that alone radically changed the golf club business."

"Everything in life is a matter of attitude."

CHAPTER 12

ENJOYING THE GAME

Final Thoughts on Golf, Business, and Life

The Emotional Lifestyle Brand

Perhaps the biggest misconception that's dogged me throughout my career is also the thing people have praised me for the most: that I am a sales and marketing man. I really shouldn't complain because it's meant as a great compliment, but what I really am is a creative merchant. I define a merchant as someone who oversees and orchestrates everything, from the idea to the manufacturing, distribution, marketing, sales, and advertising.

To be successful in any business, you have to create a new and better product or service and then understand how to articulate the benefits of that product to the consumer or buyer in an intelligent, persuasive way. Business success usually calls for creative merchandising. That is an ability to create something for somebody that they want, but that they don't know they want until it is brought to their attention and demonstrated.

I built the Callaway brand from my lifelong obsession with the game of golf. The Callaway name is now admired by millions of golfers around the world for making the highest-quality products that evoke strong feelings of attachment, that people are proud to own, and that enhance their lives. I believe we are one of the few athletic equipment companies (and certainly the only golf equipment company) to transcend our industry and become not just something people own, but something that they are. In short, Callaway is now a lifestyle brand.

In my mind, there are seven principles required to create a lifestyle brand like Callaway, Apple, Nike, Coca-Cola, or Bentley. Because you've been such a lovely audience and listened to my stories for 250-plus pages, I'm gonna put 'em all in one place and give 'em to you in a few pages. If you're an entrepreneur – man or woman, young or old, actual or aspiring – feel free to rip this page out of the book and keep it in your pocket, where I've always kept little quotes and sayings that inspire me.

QUALITY. Callaway makes the best golf clubs, plain and simple. We use the best materials and the latest technology, and spend more time, money, and effort developing golf clubs than anybody else in the history of the world. There's no such thing as being dissatisfied with your Callaway clubs (but if you are, we'll replace them!). Quality also means surrounding yourself with the best people, and I've been fortunate to have some pretty smart men and women working with me at

Callaway Golf. Quality also requires relentless focus and avoiding the trap of de-worsification. Before you get started as an entrepreneur, make an honest assessment of yourself and your competition. Unless you think you've got a reasonable chance to be the best, you should not even start, because it is so hard to be the best.

CREATIVITY. This can mean many things: a never-before-seen product that is beautiful and different, a memorable name, an instantly recognizable logo. All of this creativity should flow from a clear vision that is executed consistently throughout the company. Since Callaway began, we have spoken with a single voice. I set an example, and I am the face of the brand, but I encourage everyone in the company to apply their passion, knowledge, talent, personal taste, and life experience in a creative way.

IMPROVEMENT. Like I've said, there's never been a product in the history of humanity that couldn't be improved in some significant and surprising way. Constant innovation keeps customers coming back to you because they know that even if they've got your newest product, it's a pretty good bet that the next one is going to be even better. At Callaway, we've never gotten self-satisfied. We make the best and then ask ourselves, "How can it be better?" The highest form of innovation fundamentally changes your industry in some radically new way. This is hard to do on purpose. When we started developing Big Bertha, I didn't tell Dick Helmstetter, "Now, Dick, I want you to make a driver that will change the game of golf and the golf club industry forever." That would've been insane! But if you continually push the limits of your product, eventually you might change your industry.

EMOTION. A product must inspire a specific feeling or strong reaction in the customer. As it applies to golf, my lifelong experience with it has led me to understand that the fundamental reason people play the game is to experience a feeling: the overwhelming sensation of a well-struck shot. The result is a feeling I call "satisfaction" or "more pleasing," but it can just as easily be excitement, love, or fun. In fact, my lifelong friend and lawyer Jimmy Wilson once called me The Merchant of Fun. I distilled our brand identity that comes from that feeling down to a single phrase, which appears at the end of nearly all of our TV commercials: "Callaway: How Golf Should Feel."

INTEGRITY. This principle is the easiest to forget and is perhaps the most important of values. There's plenty of entrepreneurs that make good products that inspire affection in the customer, but who don't give a damn about *how* they achieved their success. They act greedily, lie, cheat, cut corners, choose profits over people, and don't have one iota of integrity. This is a self-defeating strategy (look at what happened to Burlington!). People have accused me of being a cockeyed optimist, but good ethics is good business, and always will be. I am convinced that we won our battles against the USGA and Cobra because of the golfing public's faith and trust in the integrity of the Callaway name. Their goodwill helped us overcome accusations that we were cheaters.

ENHANCEMENT. Our clubs help people feel better about themselves by allowing them to enjoy the game more than they thought was possible. Golf is the most difficult game on Earth, so anything that improves people's experience of the game has a pretty good chance of success. A great brand is empowering and life-enhancing; it elevates a person's image of themselves and the aspirations they might have for their life, and therefore confers a greater sense of self-worth. It can even help fulfill a fantasy of being a movie star, a superstar athlete, or a sex symbol.

COMMUNITY. Finally, every lifestyle brand creates a community of people who share their love for the product and the way of life that it helps them to lead. A sense of belonging to a community forges bonds of loyalty – between people and ideally with the company itself.

Hit 'til You're Happy

I've tried to retire four times in my life. After I got fired from Burlington, I thought I might live off my severance, but the siren song of California and the grapevines had a different plan for me. The second attempt came in 1981, when I sold the Vineyard & Winery to Hiram Walker and was ready to devote myself to unlimited rounds of golf with as many mulligans as I wanted – a style of play I call "hit 'til you're happy." A chance encounter with a Hickory Stick would disabuse me of that notion. The third time came in 1996, when at the ripe young age of 77 years old I stepped down as CEO but remained chairman – still the head honcho but not quite so involved in the day-to-day operations. I unretired two years later to right the ship during our slump of '98.

The more fundamental problem was that I really hated being retired. I hated not waking up each morning with a task to do or a problem to solve, and I hated taking vacations – my whole life, I hardly ever bothered with them. I liked staying busy. Actually, I find that being retired is tiring and that doing nothing makes me restless.

For years, the specter of my retirement loomed large. Shareholders and potential shareholders would ask me when I thought I might retire, and I would tell them, "If you're thinking of buying Callaway stock, you should buy it under the assumption that I will drop dead the day after you buy it." I was being glib, but I knew I couldn't be CEO forever.

We're supposed to move from one state of progression to another in our lives, aren't we? We know a person will grow old and lose their outer beauty – if they were lucky enough to have it to begin with – but most of the time we can't accept that it will happen to us. We convince ourselves we can beat time. But you can't if you're human. You simply cannot conquer time. Like the George Harrison song says, "All things must pass."

Back when Callaway went public, we put in the prospectus that I was going to sell most of my stock during the first 12 months. I was 73 or 74 at the time, and even then I had enough sense to know that it's more fun to do something with your money when you're alive than when you're dead. It's just that simple. I was getting to the point where I wanted to have my estate settled, and could then continue to give money away and spend it.

I believe that it's better to give than to receive. Maybe I had a different idea about the timing than other people. I think it's so much better to enjoy giving while you're alive than when you're dead. I put just about every dollar I ever made from Burlington into the vineyard, and every dollar I made from the vineyard into the golf club company, and I've given quite a bit away besides. I built a Physics Center at Emory, a hospital in LaGrange, Georgia, and for decades I contributed to the United Negro College Fund, among other causes I believed in. Most people leave their money behind after they die and never get any benefit out of it when they're alive.

We can't be pigs and try to keep all the money for ourselves. "Don't be greedy" – that's another simple lesson courtesy of my folks. Greed is the great problem our whole industrial society had in the '70s and '80s. It didn't work out, did it? We've got to learn to be more generous with money – to give it away to people who need it, and the people who work for us. In general, we've gotta learn to recognize and appreciate human talent – select it, take a gamble on the person, then give them free rein and a lot of rewards.

Last Lessons from the Master

Around my 75th birthday, I found myself starting to do some replay of my life. I thought about things that have happened to me: things I'd done; things I was proud of or not too proud of; things that were so long ago they probably don't have any bearing over who I am today, except for the fact that they occupied a lot of real estate in my mind and by doing so shaped my attitudes toward the world and toward myself. As I've said, people have a tendency to rewrite history – not to solve the problem but to justify the outcome.

My loved ones told me I was becoming wistful. Maybe that's why my son, Nicholas, recommended that I write a book. A lot of my contemporaries, celebrity CEOs like Sam Walton and Jack Welch, and Donald Trump, were writing books around that time, offering both business advice and biography. I guess some people thought I might have a story to tell too.

This was in 1994, I think, and over the next five years I worked with no less than four different biographers. None of them worked out, but not all for bad reasons. In fact, I liked the last writer, Larry Dorman, so much that I convinced him to quit his job as *The New York Times* golf correspondent and work for Callaway Golf as a public relations executive. I began to carry a tape recorder around with me wherever I went. I thought a lot about my childhood – my past, my parents, and Bobby Jones.

Bobby was the great force in my life and the greatest man I've ever known. I think my company was an expression and fulfillment – on a business and personal level – of Bobby's spirit. It's only now that I can look back and see how by creating Callaway Golf, I could keep alive the spirit and values of my hero, mentor, and friend. This included rediscovering, restoring, and re-releasing Bobby Jones's famous *How I Play Golf* instructional films, the ones that had inspired me more than 50 years before.

People wonder what made him such a great golfer. He had the most beautiful swing anybody had ever seen, that's for sure, but there was something else about Bobby Jones, something deeper and more elusive. As I've said from the beginning, golf is as much a mental war within oneself as it is a physical test. In order to become the greatest, Jones first had to win that mental battle. He had to master himself.

Nobody could doubt the mental acuity of Bobby Jones. He graduated from Georgia Tech with a degree in engineering before abandoning that career altogether to pursue a master's degree in English from Harvard. He graduated from Emory Law School, passed the bar after only three semesters, and practiced law as his profession after retiring from golf. He cultivated his mind as well as his game and invented golf clubs. And of course, he co-founded Augusta National Golf Club with Cliff Roberts in 1932, home since 1934 to the annual Masters Tournament.

But Bobby was no saint. Back in the mid-1920s, before Bobby Jones was the Bobby Jones the history books remember, he got so angry with his lousy play that he struck his custom-made club against a tree, and broke it clean in half. This was a real moment of truth for Bobby, the kind every person faces: how do we respond to failure? How do we overcome our problems before they kill the promise of our lives? If you're Bobby Jones, you learn to change your attitude.

Everything in life is a matter of attitude. The great thing about life is that in three seconds, it's possible for you to change your attitude about everything. I don't say it's easy, but it's possible, because we all live in a mental world. A person can change their world by changing their attitude toward whatever is happening to them. That's the greatest lesson of Bobby Jones.

We've got to strive toward something better, whether it's a product or inside ourselves. We've got to be kinder, more caring, and more loving toward others. Do that, and you can conquer anything.

This attitude applies especially to marriage, the one area where I have failed more than in any other aspect of my life – and I'm not proud of it. I acknowledge my failings, and I wish I had the ability to succeed in this arena, but it doesn't make me despair or give up. Call me a hopeless romantic, but I still believe in the possibility of true love.

Looking back, I believe I was unfair to all of my romantic partners – no question. In hindsight, it's a wonder any of them stayed with me as long as they did. I once told a reporter, "If you really want to know about me, ask me about my company. I am my company." The truth is that for most of my life, business came first and family came second.

Nothing tests a person's attitude more than the end of his life. Bobby Jones was diagnosed with syringomyelia in 1948, a disease in the spinal cord that causes debilitating pain and eventually paralysis. The disease took away Bobby's beautiful swing, then the use of his legs, confining him to a wheelchair for the last years of his life. But although syringomyelia robbed Bobby of his physical talents, it couldn't rob him of his positive outlook. The world handed him challenges, and he met them with the grace and humility he demonstrated on the golf course until the day he passed away in 1971. You can't beat time, but you can retain your inner beauty and kindness. Bobby showed me that no matter how bad off we might be physically, we can master our attitudes toward ourselves, toward other people, and toward the world.

The Last Product I'd Like to Improve

I have written my own version of the Lord's Prayer. When I was still a young man, I started thinking, what's wrong with most people's prayers? I thought about my own prayers and decided they were too selfish. In other words, they ask for things that they want personally – achievements, good luck, the daughter is going to win the beauty contest or something like that. That's not the purpose of prayer, and it doesn't work.

So I took the Lord's Prayer and I tore it apart, because I think it is selfish. It starts out by telling the Lord what to do: "Give us this day our daily bread." Well, the Lord is not going to be called upon to give you the bread. He's given you life and the opportunity to get bread, maybe. "Forgive us our trespasses" is okay. That's very human. "Lead us not into temptation." Well, that's an insult to the Lord. The Lord doesn't lead anybody into temptation, we do it ourselves. They are calling on the Lord to do something you ought to do yourself.

A lot of people in the world use the Lord's Prayer, which makes it the perfect product to improve. That's what I do: take a known product, the best or most popular one I can think of, and figure out how to make it better. That's the way I created Big Bertha, and if a person is really serious about the spiritual, you can do the same thing. I'm not trying to compare the two, I'm just saying a lot of the Lord's Prayer to me is just words. "For thine is the kingdom, the power, and the glory forever and ever, amen." So what? The Creator doesn't need to be told that.

It's presumptuous to think you've got the best prayer, but I happen to think my version of the Lord's Prayer is pretty good: "Send me to heaven, that's all I ask." That's my only request of the Creator. I don't fear death at all. I don't want to die in pain, but I don't fear what comes after. I think it's probably a pretty good bet that it's going to be a new awakening or a new something nobody can conceive of. The human brain, in my opinion, at this stage of development isn't designed to understand yet what Creation is and what life is.

On the other hand, I think it's silly for people who don't believe in a Creator to claim that it's all chaos and that life is some big accident. It's no accident. There is an order and a design to the universe, and each individual is a piece of the Creator, we just can't see it from our perspective here on Earth.

Maybe at the end of the road for humankind, there will be an ability to see and understand, but not now.

I don't fear death, because it's going to be fun to have it revealed. What happens when we die? I think everybody will get all the answers to all the questions forever.

"And One More Thing . . . "

But I'm not worried about the end just yet. Why should I be, when I just bought a $2 million share of heaven? Now before you accuse me of heresy, I'm not talking about the heaven that sits behind the pearly gates, I'm talking about that heaven-designed golf course called Pebble Beach, to paraphrase my friend Johnny Miller.

In 1999, Arnold Palmer formed a consortium to purchase Pebble Beach from Sumitomo Bank (the same Sumitomo who left Callaway Hickory Stick at the altar) and Taiheiyo Golf Glub for $832 million. Arnie's partners included Clint Eastwood, the former mayor of Carmel, a devoted golfer who also did a bit of acting on the side; Dick Ferris, former CEO of United Air Lines and chairman of the Policy Board of the PGA; and former Major League Baseball Commissioner Peter Ueberroth, among others.

The new ownership of Pebble Beach was divided into itty-bitty shares of $2 million each, and I was invited to buy one of those shares. The only problem was that I've always felt that golf course ownership was a lousy business.

Nevertheless, I've had a long love affair with the magnificent courses on the Monterey Peninsula, going back to playing in the 1968 Crosby Clambake with Arnie and Mark McCormack. In fact, it was that week in January 1968 playing golf at "the greatest meeting of land and water in the world" when I succumbed to the siren song of California and decided to buy land and grow grapes in Temecula.

And Pebble Beach has been hugely important to Callaway Golf Company. My friend Paul Spengler, EVP of Operations and a former amateur champion, selected Callaway golf clubs to be the exclusive rental sets offered at Pebble Beach. We opened our first mobile Callaway Test Center outside of Carlsbad at Spyglass Hill and for the last half decade have sponsored the Callaway Golf Pebble Beach Invitational. So I ignored my own better business sense and happily deworsified.

As you can see, I have no plans for slowing down. I am too busy enjoying the game. Our sales have rebounded; I've guided Callaway Golf through the most difficult three-year stretch of its existence; I am confident that our golf ball business will succeed in the long term; the ERC II is on the market; and there are new innovations coming down the pike. For example, a few months ago Steve McCracken and one of our directors, Rick Rosenfield, took a trip to Watford, England, to see about a high-tech new golf practice and leisure facility called Topgolf. It sounded like a new version of the Callaway Golf Experience on Madison Avenue that I envisioned a few years ago, which would have been a consumer version of the Callaway Performance Center in Carlsbad which we opened in 1995. Both had their roots in The Mill at Burlington House. Both Steve and I were very intrigued about buying this fledgling company, but when it came to talk turkey, who should suddenly appear – my old friend and golf buddy Mark McCormack of IMG! Just like with Tiger Woods, Mark's price was too high, but I think Topgolf will be another example of how to grow the game.

Speaking of new ideas, like Steve Jobs, I want to share with you "one more thing." A few months ago, around when I attended the Masters, I received phone calls from Jack Nicklaus and Gary Player on the same day, expressing their support for my embattled friend, Arnold Palmer, and my outlawed club, the ERC II. Take that, USGA!

Since then, I have been pondering a vision for a remarkable, interesting, and unusual concept: a brand new division or company that will put Callaway Golf, Arnold Palmer, Jack Nicklaus, and Gary Player in business together. The seeds of this idea were planted 40 years ago by none other than Mark McCormack, when he started the International Management Group with the Big Three.

My collaboration with the Big Three will begin with designing, producing, manufacturing, promoting, and selling full lines of golf clubs for each player under the umbrella of our new venture. Planned and executed properly, each Big Three line will include special design features to please each golfing legend. In my opinion, this concept is sound and doable, personally and emotionally rewarding for all involved, and will probably be one of the best profit potential businesses in golf's future. I've just written a draft of a letter to Arnold, Jack, and Gary outlining my plan. The time for action and rewards is now!

Despite my recent diagnosis, and even if things don't go as well as expected with my health, the basic idea I am presenting is more than doable and likely to succeed under the conditions I see for our company in the future. And I feel pretty sure this could not have been done in the past.

I am excited for the new year, the new decade, the new century, and the new millennium. I am 81 years old but feel I have the energy and the attitude to lead Callaway Golf for the next 10 years, or the next hundred. I still have the same drive to compete that ignited in me when my father gave me my first golf club when I was 11 years old in 1930.

Nevertheless, Callaway Golf deserves a healthy and qualified full-time CEO right now. Our company presently faces many opportunities which should be studied and, if appropriate, seized. For instance, my executive team has just informed me that they met with Phil Knight and Nike, who have expressed interest in buying us – right now. Despite this ghoul play, if the price is right, and therefore good for our shareholders, and if we carefully and intelligently take advantage of all of these possibilities, our future has never looked brighter. For these reasons, I have decided not to delay my retirement any longer, and have appointed Ron Drapeau as our new CEO. I will remain chairman.

As I look back on my life that has encompassed most of the 20th century, and think about all that has happened to me and all that I have done, I have an overwhelming sense of gratitude. And so, as promised in Chapter 1, I am going to reveal my own epitaph, which I will have engraved on my memorial tombstone at Shadowlawn Cemetery in my hometown of LaGrange, Georgia:

"He considered himself very fortunate in all aspects of his life."

Back in December, the board of directors had announced that I would remain the CEO and chairman indefinitely.

Funny word, "indefinitely." It can mean either 10 years – or two minutes . . .

"Rule 35: Enjoy the Game"

POSTSCRIPT

Ely Reeves Callaway, Jr., was diagnosed with pancreatic cancer in early April 2001; he died on July 5, 2001, at the age of 82. He never sent his letter to the Big Three.

His ashes were scattered at Callaway Gardens, which was founded by his cousin, Cason J. Callaway. Vernon Jordan delivered the eulogy.

A memorial tombstone in Shadowlawn Cemetery in LaGrange, Georgia is inscribed with his own epitaph: "He considered himself very fortunate in all aspects of his life."

AFTERWORD

By Andrew Moorhead

The Unconquerable Game would be incomplete without the story of how the book was made. The project began nearly 30 years ago, in 1995, when several of Ely's contemporaries in business, most notably Warren Buffett and Sam Walton, released their own memoirs. Nicholas told his father that his life story might also make a compelling and popular book. Never one to back down from the opportunity to compete or tell a story, Ely loved the idea. So did Bill Shinker at Broadway Books, a division of Random House, who gave Ely a large advance (though as Ely would point out, not nearly as big as Sam Walton's).

Ely went through four different writers over a span of six years: John Rothchild, a freelance writer specializing in finance; Bud Shrake, who co-authored the best-selling golf books by Harvey Penick; John Huey, who had to quit the project when he became editorial director of more than a hundred Time Inc. magazines; and finally, Larry Dorman, whom Ely convinced to leave his post as the head golf writer for *The New York Times* to become head of PR & Communications for Callaway Golf.

Each of these writers conducted extensive interviews with Ely and ghost-wrote early drafts of certain chapters. To aid in the writing process, Ely brought a tape recorder with him wherever he went and recorded his business meetings, dinners, and speaking engagements. Diana Duvall, Ely's executive assistant in the 1990s, was invaluable to the book project. But despite everyone's best efforts, no manuscript was ever completed. When Ely passed away, the unfinished book materials were added to his already sprawling archive, which sat in storage for the next 20 years.

In the spring of 2022, Nicholas decided to complete his father's book, which is where I entered the story. Nicholas hired me to be his archival assistant. At first, my job was simply to review, organize, digitize, and take detailed notes on the more than hundred hours of audiotapes in Ely's archive, which of course turned out to not be so simple. When I opened the suitcase Nicholas had dropped off at my apartment, I discovered dozens of unlabeled audio files in a plethora of formats, from 1.5 mil reel-to-reel tapes to DATs. The production manager, Ivan Wong, and I scoured nearly every audio store in New York City to find the right media players.

Some of the files had deteriorated beyond repair, but most were well preserved, and I was finally introduced to the world of Ely Callaway. Like everyone who ever knew him, I was enchanted right away by his rapscallion charm, intellect, and sense of humor. I listened to Ely give speeches to Callaway's shareholders, hold strategy meetings with chief executive teams, and share private dinners with his most intimate friends. Nicholas described seeing the twinkle in his father's eyes, but I think Ely might be the first person to have a twinkle so bright you could hear it. To put it simply, he is probably the most charismatic man I've ever encountered.

I got to know Ely Callaway quite intimately that summer — the man and the showman — and soon became Nicholas's editorial assistant, then his co-editor. Together, Nicholas and I pored through Ely's archive: tens of thousands of personal and professional documents, detailed daily agendas going all the way back to the 1950s, 75 years' worth of newspaper articles on various subjects that Ely had clipped himself, over a thousand pages of interview transcripts and early drafts of manuscripts, and of course the audio files that started it all.

We worked tirelessly to assemble this intricate puzzle, pulling and arranging stories and quotes from a wealth of primary sources, supported by research and conversations with people who knew and worked with Ely. Some stories came complete and intact from one document or audiotape, while other stories had to be reconstructed from many sources. We then compiled these stories into 12 thematic chapters, guided by the original outlines of Dorman and Rothchild.

One day by pure accident or fate, Nicholas discovered the keystone of our puzzle: a previously unknown, unopened manila envelope that read, "Private Paper To Be Opened Only in Case of Mr. Callaway's Death." Inside was Ely's entire account and record of the Madison matter described in chapter 4, in a dossier he gave to Covington Hardee and Bob Lynn in 1973. He never told the true story of why he left Burlington to any of the previous writers, only vaguely referring to it on one tape. Nobody in Ely's life, even his children, knew this story even existed until now. This was about as close to a real-life "Rosebud" moment as it gets.

The new discoveries didn't stop with the Madison matter; each new box and envelope revealed another hidden tale — the wellspring seemingly inexhaustible. If you're reading this, the book has been published, and I'm still not sure we reached the bottom. I know for certain there are enough Ely stories not included in *The Unconquerable Game* to fill another volume. And I know that I will be forever grateful for getting to spend the last couple of years with Ely Callaway, and for the trust Nicholas showed by allowing me to help tell his father's story and complete his legacy.

More than 30 years after Ely began work on the book, and two years after I joined the project, Nicholas and I completed the long and winding road to publication of *The Unconquerable Game,* the summation of Ely's prodigious life and work, told in Ely's distinct and remarkable voice.

ACKNOWLEDGMENTS

The Editors would like to acknowledge the following individuals and institutions for their contributions to the book:

- The Callaway family: Issey Callaway; Lisa Callaway; Mark Callaway; Nikeyu Callaway, Design and Digital Marketing Director at Callaway Arts & Entertainment
- The Ely Reeves Callaway III family: Augusta Boone Callaway, Dale Vosburgh Callaway, Peter Reeves Callaway; Sebastian Callaway, Sue Zeziger Callaway, Walker Callaway
- The original co-writers of the book: Larry Dorman; John Huey; John Rothchild; Bud Shrake
- At Callaway Arts & Entertainment: Jason Brown, Imaging and Production; Janice Fisher, Copyeditor and Proofreader; Toshiya Masuda, Art Director and Designer; Thomas Palmer, Imaging and Prepress; Manuela Roosevelt, Vice President, Associate Publisher, and Editorial Director; Cosett Torres, Personal Assistant; Ivan Wong, Production Manager
- At Topgolf Callaway Brands Corp: Chip Brewer, CEO; Nick McInally, Vice President of Global Marketing; Glenn Hickey, Executive Vice President
- Additional assistance: David Beal; Anthony Dreyer; Michael Lomax; Isolde and Joel Motley; Rhea Nair Callaway; John Polkis; Terry Rowles; Paul Spengler; Troup County Archive, La Grange, Georgia; Stephanie Wei; Barbara Yates

We'd also like to thank Karen Stokes, Executive Secretary to Ely at Burlington Industries, 1963–1973; Tom Geismar, co-founder of Chermayeff & Geismar & Haviv; and these former associates of Ely at Callaway Golf who provided invaluable stories:

- Larry Dorman, Senior Vice President, Global Press and PR, 1997–2007, and former golf writer, *The New York Times,* 1993–1997, 2007–2011
- Ron Drapeau, various positions including Chairman and CEO, 1996–2004
- Diana Duvall, Executive Assistant to Ely Callaway, 1994–2001; Director of New Zealand Operations for Julian Robertson/Tiger Management; Vice President of Operations, Greyson; Vice President of Real Estate Sales, Cabot Management Company; Chief of The Callaway Family Office.
- Jason Finley, Global Director, Brand and Product Management
- Mike Galeski, various positions including Senior Vice President Sports Marketing, 1993–2006
- Steve McCracken, Senior Executive Vice President and Chief Legal Officer, 1994–2012

ABOUT THE EDITORS

Thea Traff, 2024

NICHOLAS CALLAWAY is the Founder & CEO of Callaway Arts & Entertainment, a cross-platform media company that works with renowned artists to bring their work to a global audience. The company creates print, digital, and audio books; computer-animated television series; mobile and tablet applications; design-driven lifestyle brands, and immersive exhibitions. Recent titles include *Bob Dylan: Mixing Up the Medicine; The Beatles: Get Back; The Sistine Chapel* trilogy; *Mark Rothko at Pace;* and *Leonardo by Leonardo.*

Nicholas Callaway is the son of Ely Callaway, who taught him to play golf starting at the age of five. His father also gave him a camera at the age of seven, and he hasn't put down his clubs or his camera since.

He received his BA in Classics and Visual Studies from Harvard University in 1975 while studying photography with Minor White in the Visible Language Workshop at the Massachusetts Institute of Technology.

Nicholas Callaway had his first museum exhibition in 1974 at The Addison Gallery of American Art, Andover, Massachusetts, of photographs made before and after his first visit to Georgia O'Keeffe at her home in Ghost Ranch, New Mexico. Years later, Callaway became O'Keeffe's publisher with *One Hundred Flowers, The New York Years,* and *In the West.*

He founded Callaway Editions in New York at the age of 26, after four years in Paris, where he studied art and served as the first director of the pioneering photography gallery Galerie Zabriskie.

He has two children, Nikeyu and Issey, and lives in East Hampton, New York with his wife Rhea Nair Callaway.

Thea Traff, 2024

ANDREW MOORHEAD is a playwright, book editor, historical researcher, social satirist, and science communicator from Piedmont, California, now based in New York City.

His work for theater includes *This Purple F***ing Pot* (The Tank), *Bravo* (Azusa Pacific University; Ball State University; Winner: NMI's Search For New Musicals; live concert album available on Spotify), *The Colonialists* (play/ground theatre; NYU), *Loaded Questions* (The Sherry Theater), and *Nothing Happens and Nobody Knows What They're Talking About* (Berkeley Repertory Theater).

Through the creative agency Hello SciCom, Andrew has written and produced science comedy for *Nautilus Magazine*, Paris Fashion Week, the United Nations, Honda Research Institute, and Hanson Robotics. He has worked as a political speechwriter and board game writer.

He received his BFA from Chapman University and his MFA from New York University. Once upon a time, he performed bird calls on *The Late Show with David Letterman.*

While working on this book, Andrew thought often of his dad and Grandpa Bob, who took him golfing as a little kid, and his brother Zach who, despite Andrew's seven-year head start, is an infinitely better golfer.

INDEX

Ely, 1932
Jeanne, 1938
Ely, 1942
Ely & Jeanne, 1942
Jeanne, 1936
Jeanne, 1948
Jeanne, 1944
Ely, 1944
Lisa, Nicholas, & Jeanne, 1958
Ely, 1948
Jeanne & Ely, 1955
Jeanne & Ely, 1958
Reeves, 1950
Nicholas, 1955
Reeves, 1954
Lisa & Nicholas, 1958
Nicholas & Lisa, 1957
Ely, 1962
Jeanne, 1957
Jeanne & Ely, 1957
Ely, 1959
Ely, 1958
Ely, 1963
Nicholas & Lisa, 1962
Ely, 1963
Jane, 1963
Jane, 1963
Ely, 1962
Reeves, Nicholas, & Lisa, 1969
Ely & Lisa, 1973
Ely & Nicholas, 1977
Nicholas & Reeves, 1977
Reeves, Nicholas, Ely, & Lisa, 1979

John Moramarco & Ely, 1973
Nancy, 1974
Vineyard, 1968
Ely & Callaway Vineyard staff, 1974
Ely, 1994
Nicholas, 1994
Ely & staff, 1976
Ely & Reeves, 1976
Dale Callaway, 1976
Ely & Nicholas, 1983
Ely, early 1980s
Reeves, 1973
Reeves & Ely, 1998
Cindy, Reeves, & Ely, 1994
Callaway family, 1992
Ernst Wöhr, Reeves, & Ely, 1996
Reeves, Nicholas, & Ely, 1994
Reeves, 1992
Ely & Sue Callaway, 1998
Ely & Reeves, 1990
Ely & John Moramarco, 1998
Ely & Cindy, 1992
Issey & Ely, 1998
Ely, Issey, Nicholas, & Nikeyu, 1996
Nikeyu & Ely, 1998
Pete, Reeves, Ely, Nikeyu, & Yukine, 1993
Pete & Ely, 1996
Issey, 1998
Nikeyu & Issey, 1998
Reeves & Nicholas, 2022
Pete & Reeves, 2022
Ely, 1994
Cindy & Ely, 1994
Ely & Diana Duvall, 1999
Ely, 1994

This book has been published on March 25, 2025 by

CALLAWAY

CALLAWAY ARTS & ENTERTAINMENT
76 Georgica Road, East Hampton, New York 11937

Nicholas Callaway, *CEO & Publisher*
Manuela Roosevelt, *Associate Publisher and Editorial Director*
Toshiya Masuda, *Art Director* · Ivan Wong, *Production Manager*
Jason Brown, *Graphic Design & Production* · Janice Fisher, *Copyeditor & Proofreader*
Nikeyu Callaway, *Creative Director*

First Edition
1 3 5 7 9 10 8 6 4 2

Library of Congress Control Number: 2024932298

ISBN 978-1-7372051-4-2

VISIT WWW.CALLAWAY.COM

Printed in Canada

Callaway GOLF

CALLAWAY GOLF COMPANY

ELY CALLAWAY

Marriage is Like Your Job —
It's Much Better if
You Like Your Boss.

Revenge is Sweet — To the Sour

We Learn from Experience —
That We Never Learn from Exper.

It is Better To Have Loafed
and Lost
Than Never To Have Loafed
at all

I have been a Success:
For 78 Years I Have Eaten
and Have avoided Being Eaten

If You Do a Favor — forget it.
If You Receive One — Remember it.

2285 Rutherford Road Carlsbad, CA

Telephone: (619) 931-1771 • FAX (619) 929-8120

Final "Ely-isms," handwritten by Ely Callaway, Rancho Valencia, California, June 2001

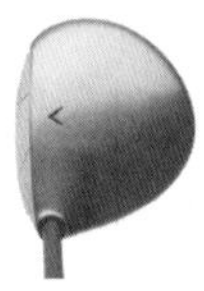

A NOTE ON THE TYPE

This book was set in Requiem and Gotham Gothic, designed by Jonathan Hoefler.

The typeface takes inspiration from a set of inscriptional capitals found in Ludovico Vicentino degli Arrighi's 1523 writing manual, *Il Modo de Temperare le Penne,* and its italics are based on the chancery calligraphy, or *cancelleresca corsiva* of the period.

The "Ely-isms" and subtitles were set in Centaur Foundry, Jerry Kelly's digital rendering of the original Centaur, which was designed by Bruce Rogers, one of the most important American book designers of the twentieth century. This type was born of the late nineteenth-century quest to create a modern revival of Nicolas Jenson's humanist roman of 1470, long considered to be both the origin and the apogee of the Venetian roman.

The dingbat is rendered from the original Big Bertha clubhead.